《金砖国家国别与合作研究》 总主编：董洪川
副总主编：刘玉梅

BRICS Studies

# 金砖国家
# 国别与合作研究

第三辑

刘梦茹·主 编　段孟洁·副主编

**B**razil
**R**ussia
**I**ndia
**C**hina
**S**outh Africa

时事出版社
北京

### 图书在版编目（CIP）数据

金砖国家国别与合作研究. 第三辑 / 刘梦茹主编. --
北京：时事出版社，2025.7. -- ISBN 978-7-5195
-0675-9

Ⅰ．D812

中国国家版本馆 CIP 数据核字第 2025LC9698 号

出 版 发 行：时事出版社
地　　　　址：北京市海淀区彰化路 138 号西荣阁 B 座 G2 层
邮　　　　编：100097
发 行 热 线：（010）88869831　88869832
传　　　　真：（010）88869875
电 子 邮 箱：shishichubanshe@sina.com
印　　　　刷：北京良义印刷科技有限公司

开本：787×1092　1/16　印张：19.25　字数：300 千字
2025 年 7 月第 1 版　2025 年 7 月第 1 次印刷
定价：170.00 元
（如有印装质量问题，请与本社发行部联系调换）

# 《金砖国家国别与合作研究》编委会

**总 主 编**：董洪川
**副总主编**：刘玉梅

**编委会委员**：（按姓氏拼音为序）
　　　　　　　谌华侨　刘梦茹　龙兴春　孟利君　段孟洁
　　　　　　　蒲公英　严功军　游　涵　张　庆　朱天祥

**学术顾问**：（按姓氏拼音为序）
蔡春林　　（广东工业大学）
陈　才　　（西南科技大学）
程　晶　　（湖北大学）
崔　铮　　（辽宁大学）
邓瑞平　　（西南大学）
江时学　　（上海大学）
蓝庆新　　（对外经贸大学）
林跃勤　　（中国社会科学院）
卢　静　　（外交学院）
王　磊　　（北京师范大学）
徐　薇　　（浙江师范大学）
徐秀军　　（中国社会科学院）
杨　娜　　（南开大学）
张淑兰　　（山东大学）

# 卷 首 语

四川外国语大学金砖国家研究院成立于2013年5月，是重庆市人民政府外事办公室与四川外国语大学协商共建的应用研究型机构。如今，金砖国家研究院既是中联部金砖国家智库合作中方理事会的理事单位（四川外国语大学为副理事长单位），又是教育部国别和区域研究备案中心，同时还是重庆"走出去"战略与金砖国家研究省级2011协同创新中心的牵头单位。在学校提出创建高水平应用研究型外国语大学目标的新背景下，金砖国家研究院将继续努力在应用研究和社会服务方面作出相应的贡献。

经过多年的实践和探索，研究院已正式将人文交流确定为川外金砖国家研究的主攻方向。这不仅有利于发挥学校外国语言文学学科的传统优势，而且有助于外语学科与其他人文社会学科的融合发展。目前，研究院借助学校英语、俄语、葡萄牙语、印地语、中文等专业优势，逐步展开对金砖五国国别人文状况和金砖国家人文交流的深度研究。为了能让同仁们分享我们的研究成果，同时也为该领域的专家学者提供一个专门的发表园地，研究院决定编辑出版《金砖国家国别与合作研究》系列成果。

《金砖国家国别与合作研究》原则上每年出版一辑，每辑由一至两名主编署名，侧重发表国内外专家学者对金砖国家国别与合作研究的最新成果，特别是以金砖国家国别人文状况和金砖国家人文交流为重点，力求打造国内外金砖国家研究尤其是人文交流研究的重要平台。

《金砖国家国别与合作研究》突出三个特点：1.国内第一个以金砖国家人文交流为研究重心的系列成果；2.以中英文双语出版，以便更好地在国内外金砖国家研究领域扩大学术影响；3.既立足于人文交流，又不局限于人文交流，特别鼓励从人文交流的视角对金砖国家的全方位合作，如政治安全对话与经贸财金合作进行分析和解读，以期产出更多跨学科、跨专业的交叉研究成果。

《金砖国家国别与合作研究》设有三个栏目：1.《理论探讨》主要就人文、人文交流及人文与政治、经济的互动关系进行学理分析，为金砖国家人文交流构建核心概念，搭建分析框架；2.《应用研究》主要就金砖国家国别人文状况和人文交流合作中存在的现实问题进行解读，并针对性地提出应对和解决的方案与建议；3.《学术书评》主要就国内外学者近期发表的学术论文或智库报告进行述评，并就此提出新的观点与看法，激发专家学者的进一步讨论。

我们热忱欢迎国内外专家学者不吝赐稿，共同推动跨学科背景下的金砖国家研究更上一个新台阶。

董洪川
四川外国语大学校长、博士生导师
四川外国语大学金砖国家研究院院长
《金砖国家国别与合作研究》总主编
2021年3月5日

# 目　录

金砖国家跨区域主义分析 …………………………………… 蒲公英 / 001

巴西"金砖观"的演变与中巴金砖合作研究 ……… 谢乐天　刘梦茹 / 019

印度印地语主流报刊媒体及其报道研究 …………………… 段孟洁 / 036

俄罗斯贫困治理的现状、举措及前景 ……………… 王梓凡　游　涵 / 046

新时代中国与金砖国家深化人文交流的路径思考 ………… 游雨频 / 062

金砖国家命运共同体的构建：基于危机管理
　　理论的视角 ……………………… 张　庆　陈　果　孙昊洋 / 079

金砖国家地方合作的发展现状与未来趋势 ………………… 郑佳宝 / 094

《世界贸易组织中的金砖五国：巴西、俄罗斯、印度、
　　中国和南非的贸易比较》书评 ……… 裴尹琦　谢小丽　周心语 / 107

# CONTENTS

The Analysis of BRICS Transregionalism ········· Pu Gongying / 124

The Evolution of Brazil's BRICS View and the Study of
    China – Brazil BRICS Cooperation ······ Xie Letian   Liu Mengru / 149

A Study on the Mainstream Indian Newspapers and Media and
    Their China Related Reports ············· Duan Mengjie / 175

The Status Quo, Measures and Prospects of Poverty Governance in
    Russia ··············· Wang Zifan   You Han / 188

Thoughts on the Approaches of Deepening People – to – People Exchanges
    Between China and BRICS in the New Era ············· You Yupin / 209

The Building of a Community of Shared Future for BRICS:
    Based on the Perspective of Crisis Management
    Theory ············· Zhang Qing   Chen Guo   Sun Haoyang / 236

Development Status and Future Trend of Local Cooperation in
    BRICS Countries ············· Zheng Jiabao / 255

Os BRICS NA OMC: Políticas Comerciais Comparadas de Brasil, Rússia, Índia, China e África do Sul:
Book Review …………… Pei Yinqi　Xie Xiaoli　Zhou Xinyu / 275

# 金砖国家跨区域主义分析

蒲公英[*]

**摘　要**：在新冠疫情和"逆全球化"的冲击下，金砖国家面临着外部因素和内部发展的双重挑战，但同时也迎来了深入参与全球治理和区域治理的良好机遇。金砖国家是一个由来自世界不同区域的新兴市场国家组成的跨区域集团，跨区域主义理论能够为金砖国家思考自身发展提供一个新的角度。金砖国家打破了传统地理区域和文明属性的框架，构建了一个开放、多元、包容的跨区域对话与合作空间。金砖国家作为一个跨区域主义机制，与世界互联互通的愿景相辅相成，同时也是构建人类命运共同体的重要抓手。金砖国家跨区域主义的发展实践需要由强大的国家力量来引领，我国应努力将金砖国家打造成新兴市场国家和发展中国家进行全方位互利合作的跨区域平台，使之成为区域治理和全球治理的典范。

**关键词**：金砖国家；跨区域主义；区域治理；全球治理

---

[*] 蒲公英，四川外国语大学俄语学院副教授。

## 一、金砖国家发展面临的挑战与机遇

金砖国家作为具有全球影响力的跨区域集团和世界新兴经济体力量的代表，一直坚持并倡导多边主义，致力于在全球治理中发挥积极作用。金砖国家的务实合作始于2008年全球金融危机之后，面对全球性危机带来的挑战与机遇，金砖国家展示出了蓬勃的生命力。自2009年金砖国家领导人会晤在俄罗斯叶卡捷琳堡峰会召开以来，金砖国家合作机制不断完善，合作领域不断扩展，逐步在金融、经贸、人文交流、国际和地区问题治理等领域开展合作与交流，走过了自身发展的"第一个金色十年"。然而随着2020年初新冠疫情的暴发，又一个全球性危机席卷世界，金砖国家要如何应对新冠疫情带来的巨大挑战，又该如何把握全球性疫情危机背后的历史性机遇延续"第二个金色十年"？

新冠疫情的全球性暴发直接导致了全球人员和经贸往来受阻，病毒的快速跨境跨洲传播在作为全球化体现的同时，也为"逆全球化"和"反全球化"提供了温床，给全球化进程带来了巨大的冲击。实际上，自全球化开始之时，"反全球化"的力量就应运而生，由点及面的全球性危机往往也会引发"逆全球化"。2008年全球金融危机后的"逆全球化"现象持续至今，加之自特朗普出任美国总统以来，美国通过一系列单边主义和保护主义行为成为世界最主要的"反全球化"力量，在当前新冠疫情的背景下，世界正在受到"逆全球化"和"反全球化"的叠加冲击。不论是金砖国家整体，还是金砖国家个体正在受到严峻的定力考验，金砖国家关于全球化和多边主义的根基性共识面临着可能被分化的风险。与此同时，金砖国家未来发展也面临着来自成员国、成员国之间以及自身机制的多重挑战。在新冠疫情背景下，金砖国家成员国经济发展面临着更加巨大的压力，部分成员国之间存在的经济利益冲突和政治互信赤字问题时有凸显，金砖国家在国际问题处理中的不和谐之音时有发出，金砖国家多边合作机制面临的失衡风险正在日益加大，合作成效也在面临质疑。在后疫情时代，金砖国家作为分享了经济全球化红利的新兴市场国家集团，吸须通过自身的创新发展，强化凝聚内部共识，进一步发掘合作潜力。

诚然，新冠疫情冲击了全球化进程，但我们更应看到，全球化是不可逆的世界大势，由于科技发展和网络空间的建立，新冠疫情无法阻断全球信息和数据的交互传输，反而开始让人们意识到，全球性的非传统安全威胁对于国家经济和个人生活有着巨大的负面影响。新冠疫情的到来，没有一个国家或地区能够独善其身解决问题，当前的全球性危机正在倒逼人类社会的反思与变革。各类全球性问题的凸显对全球治理体系以及跨国、跨区域协调机制都提出了更高的要求。在此背景下，随着综合实力和国际影响力的不断增大，金砖国家集团也正在背负更多的国际责任和来自新兴市场国家、发展中国家的国际期待。金砖国家已经从国际金融危机的被动应对者成为对国际新秩序的积极塑造者，其对当前国际经济政治秩序的思考，对国际行为主体间新型对话与合作模式的实践探索都显得愈发重要。当下全球治理体系框架脆弱、效用乏力的问题暴露无遗，加之单边主义和保护主义的叠加影响，在全球和区域治理中正在出现发达国家"回撤"后的权力真空，这对于金砖国家来说也是难得的历史机遇。

伴随着全球化进程，区域主义蓬勃发展，逐渐出现了新区域主义、区域间主义和跨区域主义等概念，不同层次的机制合作愈加频繁。金砖国家作为一个跨区域集团，面对当前的机遇和挑战，是否可以从新的维度思考自身的发展问题？金砖国家的跨区域优势是否被充分施展和利用？在此，跨区域主义或许能够为金砖国家思考发展提供更为广阔的视域空间，帮助金砖国家探寻可行的发展思路与路径。

## 二、跨区域主义理论再思考

跨区域主义（transregionalism[①]）是伴随着全球化和区域化发展出现的国际关系中客观存在的现象。当前学界对于跨区域主义概念并没有统一的界定，对跨区域主义的研究通常是和区域间主义（interregionalism）交织在一起的，关于如何定义跨区域主义仍然存在着争论。

---

[①] 有国内学者也将该词译为跨地区主义。

## (一) 跨区域主义的界定

冷战后，伴随着区域主义和区域一体化的发展，区域逐渐成为新型国际关系层次，区域间主义随之兴起。在诸多学者对于区域间主义的研究中，跨区域主义被视为区域间主义的形式之一。以海纳·汉吉为代表，其将区域间主义定义为世界区域间制度化的关系，并分为五种类型：两个区域组织或集团间的关系（如欧盟—东盟对话），区域组织或论坛与区域一体化集团的关系（如亚欧会议—欧盟对话），来自不同地区国家集团间的关系（如东亚拉美论坛），区域组织或集团与其他区域单个国家的关系（如欧盟—美国关系），来自世界不同区域的国家间的关系（如亚太经合组织）。[1] 在汉吉看来，只有两个区域组织或集团间的关系是纯区域间主义（pure interregionalism），区域组织或集团与其他区域单个国家的关系是准区域间主义（quasi-interregionalism），来自世界不同区域的两个以上国家间的关系为跨区域主义，是大区域间主义（mega-regionalism）的一种。[2] 郑先武在进一步考虑到区域间行为主体和制度化程度多样性的基础上，将区域间主义划分为三大类：某一区域的区域组织、集团或一组国家与另一区域的单个国家之间的半区域间主义，两个不同区域的区域组织、集团或一组国家之间的双区域间主义，来自两个以上区域的一组国家、区域组织、集团或非国家等多个行为体构成跨区域主义。[3] 在分析区域间和跨区域关系时，刘宗义认为虽然地理上或战略意义上的区域仍然起着重要作用，但这二者主要是建立在功能型区域思想上的，非地理区域性因素是推动区域间建立互动关系的主要动力，区域间主义形式可以被分为双边区域

---

[1] Heiner Hänggi and Ralf Roloff and Jürgen Rüland, "Interregionalism and Interational Relations," Oxon: Routledge, 2006, p. 40.

[2] Heiner Hänggi, "Interregionalism as a Multifaceted Phenomenon: In Search of a Typology," Heiner Hänggi and Ralf Roloff and Jürgen Rüland, "Interregionalism and International Relations: A stepping Stone to Global Governance?" New York, London: Routledge, 2005, pp. 31 – 62.

[3] 郑先武：《国际关系研究新层次：区域间主义理论与实证》，《世界经济与政治》2008 年第 8 期，第 63 页。

间主义、跨区域主义和混合的区域间主义。①陈志敏认为，区域间关系是区域之间的或者跨区域的关系，北大西洋公约组织和亚太经合组织属于跨区域关系。②肖斌则以东亚为例，将东亚区域间主义归为地区集团对地区集团，双边和跨区域制度安排以及混合形式三类。③

然而，也有许多学者主张对区域间主义和跨区域主义予以区分。克里斯多弗·邓特将区域间主义定义为两个独立区域间关系，而跨区域主义是指在区域和区域内部的行为体之间建立的共同空间。④杰根·鲁兰也认为有必要将区域组织之间的互动划分为区域间主义和跨区域主义两种形式，区域间主义诞生于两个区域组织间以软制度化为基础的对话互动进程之中，是双边的区域间主义，如东盟—欧盟对话，而跨区域主义则是不同区域组织或国家之间的制度化合作进程，如亚欧会议。⑤贺平指出，区域间主义研究因较少从全球视角透视区域间合作，本质上仍属于区域主义的研究范畴，并认为跨区域主义是继区域间主义之后的新一轮发展，同时将跨区域主义定义为两个或两个以上区域的国家或国家集团之间开展合作的深度一体化进程，如跨太平洋战略经济伙伴关系协定等。⑥

俄罗斯学者近年来对于跨区域主义的研究也十分值得关注，其更多的是从全球层面思考区域间的空间问题，对跨区域主义的研究通常与"大区域化"（макрорегионализация）概念联系在一起。在俄罗斯学者看来，"大区域化"是对国家区域空间的聚合，是在更大的区域层面实现的一体

---

① 刘宗义：《地区间主义的发展及对我国的意义》，《世界经济与政治论坛》2008年第4期，第43—45页。

② 陈志敏、杨小丹：《地区间主义与全球秩序：北约、亚太经合组织和亚欧会议》，《复旦国际关系评论》2006年第1期，第8页。

③ 肖斌、张晓慧：《东亚区域间主义：理论与现实》，《当代亚太》2010年第6期，第36—38页。

④ Christopher Dent, "From Inter - regionalism to Trans - regionalism? Future Challenges of ASEM," Asia Europe Journal, No. 1, 2003, p. 224.

⑤ Jürgen Rüland, "The EU as an Inter - and Transregional Actor: Lessons for Global Governance from Europe's Relations with Asia," 2002, p. 3.

⑥ 贺平：《跨区域主义：基于意愿联盟的规制融合》，《复旦国际关系评论》2014年第2期，第268—269页。

化①，如欧盟和美洲自由贸易区。科索拉波夫指出，空间是一种在地理区域之上的概念，跨区域主义必须有空间概念作为支撑。② 沃斯克列先斯基认为，跨区域主义既是区域的"大区域化"，也是"大区域"之间的关系。③ 根据库兹涅佐夫的观点，跨区域主义是在新区域主义框架下的全球化形式，区域集团和国家通过跨区域合作打破地理边界的藩篱，为维护自身利益建立新的经济、政治和社会空间。④ 耶夫列莫娃进一步阐释，跨区域主义的逻辑不同于国家加入区域组织或签订区域间协定的逻辑，如果说区域和区域间集团的建立是为了发展政治、经济和安全合作，那么跨区域集团建立的目标则是使成员国有机会参与全球治理进程，跨区域主义合作的基础是政治因素，其特点是寻求妥协，保证立场一致，从而在国际事务，包括在全球政治、贸易和金融体制改革谈判中建立统一战线。⑤ 可见，在跨区域主义研究中，俄罗斯学者更擅长空间建构，但其对跨区域空间建构的设想往往是具有间隔和封闭性质的，包含着保护主义和对抗的潜意识。

不论是在区域间主义范畴，还是从跨区域空间的视角，以上学者们对跨区域主义理论的探讨，都为我们理解和解释国际关系提供了一种介于区域和全球维度之间的跨区域视域。在国际行为主体日益多元的今天，各类国际行为主体之间的互动方式也在增多，跨区域主义是对国际合作日益密切和多样化的理论回应。国际关系的多维空间仍然处在发展变化之中，跨区域主义的理论研究也仍然需要进化发展。在笔者看来，跨区域主义是来自世界不同区域的两个以上国际行为主体开展的制度化对话与合作。印度

---

① К. А. Ефремова, "От регионализма к трансрегионализму: Теоретическое осмысление новой реальности," Сравнительная политик, Vol. 8, No. 2, 2007, p. 65.

② Н. А. Косолапов, "Пространственно – организационный подход к анализу международных реалий," Международные процессы, Vol. 5, No. 3, 2007, p. 59.

③ А. Д. Воскресенский, "Мировое комплексное регионоведение," Магистр: ИНФРА – М, 2014, p. 18.

④ Д. А. Кузнецов, "Феномен трансрегионализма: Проблемы терминологии и концептуализации," Сравнительная политика, 2016, Vol. 23, No. 2, p. 24.

⑤ К. А. Ефремова, "От регионализма к трансрегионализму: Теоретическое осмысление новой реальности," Сравнительная политик, Vol. 8, No. 2, 2017, pp. 68 – 70.

学者拉杰斯利曾将跨区域主义的历史分为两个阶段：第一个阶段从1963年欧洲经济共同体与18个非洲国家签订了《雅温得协定》开始划分，该阶段跨区域主义特点是围绕欧洲经济共同体建立了区域间联盟；第二阶段则开始于20世纪90年代，在全球化、区域化和贸易自由化进程加速的背景下，该阶段跨区域主义的出现主要和经济合作、能源、生态、非传统安全等领域问题紧密相关。[1] 而实际上，在1963年之前，跨区域主义就已存在于国际社会，在冷战背景下出现了一系列以安全、能源事务协调为目的的跨区域联盟，如北大西洋公约组织、东南亚条约组织、中部公约组织和石油输出国组织，而在进入21世纪后国际社会的跨区域主义实践愈发频繁和多样化，出现了中等强国合作体、金砖国家、共建"一带一路"倡议、东盟"10+3"、《区域全面经济伙伴关系协定》、《跨太平洋伙伴关系协定》等一系列跨区域的制度化进程。

### （二）跨区域主义的内在逻辑

根据本文对跨区域主义的定义以及以上跨区域主义实践的共性，在此还有必要对跨区域主义做出以下阐释：

跨区域主义的底层逻辑是区域主义。区域的划分是受地理、地缘政治和地缘经济多重影响的结果，在经济全球化深入发展的今天，所谓"区域"日益体现出一种"主观空间"的意味，甚至变身为一种"想象的共同体"[2]，正如查德·萨科瓦教授所言，欧亚大陆并不是被发现的，而是被创造出来的一种叙事。[3] 跨区域主义是围绕被建构出的区域的国际行为衍生而来的，同时跨区域主义也在构建新的区域空间。一方面，跨区域主义更强调行为主体与他者之间的制度化进程是"跨出"自身所在的区域范围的，并且这种"跨出"是具有主体性的；另一方面，跨地区主义会倾向于

---

[1] Rajasree K. R. , "The Evolution of Transregional Cooperation: A Case Study of Indian Ocean Rim Association for Regional Cooperation," Online International Interdisciplinary Research Journal, Vol. 5, No. 5, 2015, pp. 289-291.

[2] 贺平：《跨区域主义：基于意愿联盟的规制融合》，《复旦国际关系评论》2014年第2期，第266页。

[3] ［英］理查德·萨克瓦、丁端：《欧亚一体化的挑战》，《俄罗斯研究》2014年第2期，第15页。

跳出原有的区域合作状态，而以重新洗牌的方式创建跨越传统地理区域的新的区域架构①，强化新的身份认同，同时也影响着与之相关的区域治理。如在亚太经合组织中，对于分别位于亚洲、大洋洲、北美洲和南美洲的成员国来说，亚太经合组织在全球经济治理、多边贸易体制、非传统安全、人文交流等领域的制度化对话与合作都"跨出"了各个成员国所在传统地理区域范围，同时，亚太经合组织的存在也强化了"亚太"概念，影响着亚太区域的经济治理。

多边主义与开放性是跨区域主义的搭建逻辑。以郑先武为代表的部分学者在对跨区域主义进行定义时，明确地指出跨区域主义的参与主体数量是"两个以上"，但也有部分学者将跨区域主义的参与主体描述为"来自世界不同区域的国家或区域组织"，在后者的定义中其实还存在另一种情况，即如果两个来自不同区域的国家进行制度化合作，这其实是属于国家间双边合作的大范畴的，我们不能因为是从跨区域视角进行解释，就为其戴上跨区域的帽子。因此，我们有必要在厘清跨区域主义概念时将这一种情况剔除，将跨区域主义的参与主体数量明确限定在"两个以上"，这就为跨区域主义赋予了多边主义的构建逻辑。如果更进一步解读，"两个以上"的参与主体同时也是跨区域主义开放性的体现，因为我们无法对参与主体的数量设定上限，这就意味着跨区域主义的参与主体可以发生动态增减，如《跨太平洋伙伴关系协定》最初是由新西兰、新加坡、智利和文莱4国发起，后美国、澳大利亚、越南、日本、墨西哥等共12国相继加入了该协定，2017年美国又退出了《跨太平洋伙伴关系协定》。可见，跨区域主义的开放性是加入和退出的双向开放。

制度化是跨区域主义的运行逻辑。在已有的研究中，跨区域主义既有被宽泛地定义为是一种"关系"，也有被明确定义为"制度化合作进程"

---

① 朱天祥：《地区间主义研究：成就与缺失》，《当代亚太》2010年第6期，第27页。

"制度化对话与合作"① 等。可以看出，对跨区域主义内部而言，其建立的目的和初衷绝不是为了对抗，而是为了对话、协调与合作。不同的跨区域主义制度化的高低程度是不一样的，但其共通之处是一定都会得到参与主体共同的认可。跨区域主义制度化的形式可以是对话、论坛、会议，可以达成备忘录、声明、宣言和协议协定。由于跨区域主义的天然属性，其较区域主义来说具有更大的合作难度，因此在一般情况下，低制度化是跨区域主义的初始运行逻辑，同时也不排除低制度化向高制度化转变的可能。低制度化的跨区域主义通常更易在低政治领域实现，部分跨区域集团也会在高政治领域开展制度化合作，如七国集团和北大西洋公约组织。需要说明的是，跨区域主义是一体化的形式之一，但并不是在所有的跨区域主义中都存在一体化进程。如在跨越多个区域的共建"一带一路"倡议中，中国与区域国家的跨区域合作绝不是以一体化为目标，而是要促进共同发展，实现共同繁荣与合作共赢。截至 2019 年 11 月底，中国已与 167 个国家和国际组织签署了 199 份共建"一带一路"合作文件，与 8 个国家建立了贸易畅通工作组，与 22 个国家建立了电子商务合作机制，与 14 个国家建立了服务贸易合作机制②，这些都是跨区域主义制度化运行的体现。

跨区域主义还具有全球化的升维逻辑。跨区域主义的出现和发展不是由某一个国家决定的，跨区域主义伴随全球化和区域化的发展而来，其出现和发展具有一定的客观性。对于区域主义来说，区域的边界是其发展的界限，而跨区域主义不受到区域边界的限制，在某种程度上，跨区域主义是全球性的。跨区域主义使参与主体可以通过自己更能接受的程度和方式参与全球化，国家和区域的经济活动、经验模式，甚至是立场构想都有可能通过跨区域合作传导进入其他区域，从而有可能上升到全球层面。在跨

---

① 俄罗斯学者玛利亚·列别杰娃认为，跨区域主义是指来自世界不同区域的国家和区域组织间的制度化合作进程。朱天祥对地区间主义的定义是"来自世界不同地区或次地区的民族国家和地区组织，依赖其原有且独立的地区架构或致力于在新的总体地区架构之下所展开的制度化对话与合作"。参见 М. М. Лебедева, Д. А. Кузнецов, "Трансрегионализм – новый феномен мировой политики. Полис," Политические исследования, No. 5, 2019, p. 73；朱天祥：《地区间主义研究：成就与缺失》，《当代亚太》2010 年第 6 期，第 12 页。

② 《商务部：2019 年"一带一路"工作取得六方面积极成效》，中国产业经济信息网，2020 年 1 月 30 日，http：//www.cinic.org.cn/xw/bwdt/715978.html? from = singlemessage。

区域空间出现的国际行为体制度化合作看似在"割裂"全球化，实际上则是为全球化提供了一种新的路径，通过在跨区域空间的互动，全球的"互联互通"将更加多维而紧密。

跨区域主义与区域治理和全球治理之间也存在着逻辑关联。在跨区域主义中，国际行为主体"跨出"自己所在区域进行多边制度化合作，这种在跨区域空间的国际合作可以被视为一种积极的全球化行为，具有一定的全球意义。国际合作在国家、区域和全球层面开展，而跨区域空间是一个能够将此三个层面的国际合作进行串联的维度。已有的跨区域主义实践呈现出制度化合作极大的多样性，贸易协定、机制化会议、对话论坛是较为传统的跨区域主义合作方式，随着跨区域合作的逐步增多，更多国家开始在跨区域主义合作方式上做出创新与尝试，共建"一带一路"倡议就是其中典型的案例——中国通过项目合作的低制度化方式逐步扩大自身的跨区域合作范围，同时推动建立金融实体机构，为跨区域合作开展提供可靠支撑，中俄两国也在积极开展丝绸之路经济带与欧亚经济联盟的对接，实现跨区域合作机制与区域一体化组织的合作创新。跨区域主义合作模式的本质是国际合作模式，伴随跨区域主义的开放式发展，这些合作模式就有可能演变为有效的区域治理和全球治理模式。长久以来，全球治理面临的一个难题即很难在不同国家和区域间达成协调共识，而在跨区域主义中，来自不同区域的国际行为主体能够通过集体认同的合作模式，就不同领域的不同问题达成某些共识。跨区域主义的合作模式对区域治理和全球治理具有参考价值，跨区域主义的合作成效则能够成为推动全球治理发展的新动力。

跨区域主义可以被视为一种特定的国际行为主体之间开展制度化合作的新的框架模式，随着跨区域主义的发展，在同一片区域范围内，可能交织存在有多重跨区域主义进程，在全球范围内，则必然共存交错纵横，甚至是相互竞争的跨区域主义集团。跨区域主义之间，以及跨区域主义与区域主义之间如果不能形成良性的互动体系，那就会在区域和全球层面出现"意大利面条碗"效应。

## 三、金砖国家跨区域主义分析

金砖国家在作为多边对话合作机制的同时，其"跨区域"的特性不应被忽视。"金砖国家"这个名词的诞生，最早源于2001年美国高盛公司首席经济师奥尼尔对巴西、俄罗斯、印度和中国作为未来全球增长最快的新兴经济体的"金砖四国"（BRIC）称谓。在"金砖四国"被提出8年之后，在全球金融危机的浪潮冲击之下，4个来自不同世界不同大洲的国家领导人于2009年6月在叶卡捷琳堡举行首次正式会晤，标志着"金砖四国"多边对话合作机制成立。会晤期间发表的《"金砖四国"领导人俄罗斯叶卡捷琳堡会晤联合声明》指出，"'金砖四国'对话与合作不仅符合新兴市场国家和发展中国家的共同利益，而且有利于建设一个持久和平、共同繁荣的和谐世界"。2010年12月，经"金砖四国"一致协商，位于非洲的南非正式加入，自此"金砖四国"正式成为金砖国家（BRICS）。十多年间，来自拉丁美洲、欧洲、亚洲和非洲的金砖五国确定了轮值主席国制度，建立了多层次的对话机制，每年定期举行领导人会晤和部长级会议，在经贸、金融、农业、人文交流各领域开展形式多样的合作对话。金砖国家是由来自世界不同区域的5个国家构成的典型的跨区域主义集团，金砖国家跨区域主义符合跨区域主义的共性，也具有自身的特性。

### （一）金砖国家构建了新兴市场国家与发展中国家的跨区域互动空间

美国学者约瑟夫·奈曾指出，21世纪的国际政治正在经历着两大权力转移，其中之一就是权力在不同国家间转移[1]，金砖国家作为新兴国家的代表性集团，兴起于世界格局深刻调整变革之际，引起国际社会高度关注。金砖国家是不同区域的新兴市场国家代表，同时在经济体量、工业化和科技水平等方面也都位居发展中国家前列。金砖国家跨区域主义不仅是新兴市场国家的合作典范，也在创新引领着南南合作。南南合作是广大发展中国家基于共同的历史遭遇和独立后面临共同的任务而展开的经济、技

---

[1] [美]约瑟夫·奈著，王吉美译：《权力大未来》，中信出版社2012年版，第22页。

术、贸易等多领域的互助性合作，是发展中国家独立自主、自力更生谋求发展的重要途径。① 历经国际金融危机等重大挑战的考验，金砖国家探索出了一条新兴市场国家和发展中国家团结合作、互利共赢的新路子。② 对于金砖五国来说，金砖国家的跨区域对话与合作打破了传统地理区域和文明属性的框架，金砖国家基于新兴市场国家的共同身份，构建了跨区域互动空间，通过在跨区域空间的互动，金砖国家的相互了解、经贸合作和政治沟通不断加深。与此同时，金砖国家跨区域主义具有开放性，当前金砖国家跨区域主义仍处于发展阶段，金砖国家建立的跨区域空间能够吸引和容纳更多的新兴市场国家和发展中国家加入跨区域对话与合作。

金砖国家跨区域主义以区域主义为底层逻辑，集合了四大洲主要的新兴市场国家，伴随着金砖国家制度化合作的发展，金砖国家也在跨区域空间内与更多的新兴市场国家和发展中国家开展对话合作，金砖国家在跨区域空间的合作效应也正在传导进入不同国家各自所在的区域。新兴市场国家和发展中国家是世界政治经济体系的重要组成部分，金砖国家为新兴市场国家和发展中国家团结合作、积极融入国际体系构建了空间通道。当金砖国家跨区域主义合作达到一定程度时，该跨区域空间的合作效应还将外溢至全球层面。因此，金砖国家构建的新兴市场国家和发展中国家跨区域互动空间既具有区域意义，也具有全球意义。需要指出的是，金砖国家跨区域主义并不追求让渡部分主权的一体化发展，其构建的是一个开放、多元、包容的跨区域对话与合作空间，其发展将有利于新兴市场国家和发展中国家利益共同体、责任共同体和命运共同体的构建。

**（二）"金砖+"是金砖国家跨区域主义开放发展的制度化创新**

在 2017 年金砖厦门峰会上，"金砖+"第一次正式出现在金砖国家的正式宣言中。习近平总书记在金砖国家工商论坛开幕式上指出，金砖国家奉行开放包容的合作理念，高度重视同其他新兴市场国家和发展中国家合

---

① 孙靓莹、邱昌情：《"一带一路"建设背景下的南南合作：路径与前景》，《广西社会科学》2016 年第 2 期，第 135 页。
② 《习近平在金砖国家领导人厦门会晤记者会上的讲话》，中国政府网，2017 年 9 月 5 日，http://www.gov.cn/xinwen/2017-09/05/content_5222821.htm。

作，建立起行之有效的对话机制，要扩大金砖合作的辐射和受益范围，推动"金砖+"合作模式，打造开放多元的发展伙伴网络，让更多新兴市场国家和发展中国家参与到团结合作、互利共赢的事业中来。[①] 从跨区域主义视角来看，"金砖+"是金砖国家作为整体与不同区域的其他国际行为主体进行对话与合作的制度安排。金砖国家构建了新兴市场国家与发展中国家的跨区域互动空间，"金砖+"则是新兴市场国家与发展中国家进入该空间的通道机制。

"金砖+"的出现是金砖国家跨区域主义的特性所要求的。在南非加入，"金砖四国"成为"金砖国家"之后的2011年三亚峰会上，金砖国家跨区域主义发展的定位逐渐被明确——从之前的致力于"推动国际金融机构改革"扩大到"着眼于为人类社会发展以及建设一个更加平等和公正的世界作出重要贡献"，"在相互尊重、集体决策的基础上，加强全球经济治理，推动国际关系民主化，提高新兴国家和发展中国家在国际事务中的发言权"[②]，从而为金砖国家扩大对话与合作范围提供了基础支撑。在2013年金砖国家德班峰会上，南非作为轮值主席国，第一次践行了金砖国家跨区域主义的开放性发展，在金砖国家合作框架下举办了金砖国家领导人同非洲国家领导人对话会，邀请了包括塞内加尔、乍得、安哥拉、科特迪瓦、贝宁、刚果共和国、莫桑比克、乌干达、赤道几内亚、几内亚、埃及总统，埃塞俄比亚总理和非洲联盟委员会主席在内的非洲国家和组织领导人参会。巴西在2014年的福塔莱萨峰会中也邀请了11个拉美国家与金砖国家进行了对话。2015年的金砖国家乌法峰会则首次与上海合作组织峰会同时同地举行，金砖国家同欧亚经济联盟成员国、上海合作组织成员国及观察员国家就提高人民福祉的主题，共商新兴市场国家和发展中国家团结合作。在2016年金砖国家果阿峰会框架下，金砖国家领导人同南亚区域的环孟加拉湾多领域经济技术合作组织成员国领导人召开了对话会。2017年，中国作为轮值主席国，正式提出"金砖+"，邀请了来自不同区域的

---

[①] 《习近平在金砖国家工商论坛开幕式上的讲话（全文）》，新华网，2017年9月3日，http：//www.xinhuanet.com/politics/2017-09/03/c_1121596338.htm。
[②] 《金砖国家领导人第三次会晤〈三亚宣言〉（全文）》，中国新闻网，2011年4月14日，http：//www.chinanews.com/gn/2011/04-14/2973144.shtml。

埃及、几内亚、墨西哥、塔吉克斯坦和泰国参加了金砖国家峰会。通过"金砖+"，2018年的约翰内斯堡峰会除邀请了非洲国家和地区的领导人外，还邀请了阿根廷、牙买加、土耳其、印度尼西亚和埃及共同商讨包容增长和共同繁荣等话题。2019年金砖国家巴西利亚峰会期间并未启用"金砖+"，但可以确定的是2020年俄罗斯已计划再一次同时举办金砖国家与上海合作组织峰会。值得一提的是，俄罗斯在轮值主席国期间制定的2020年金砖国家发展优先方向中提出要"通过'金砖+'与拓展模式（outreach）实现与伙伴国家的互动"①。俄罗斯外交官员和学者认为，较"金砖+"而言，拓展模式是指吸引轮值主席国所在区域的邻国参与金砖国家互动，最早在2013年南非德班峰会中就已出现②，其实俄罗斯提出的拓展模式本质上还是一种强调地理区域原则的"金砖+"。

可以看出，"金砖+"已经成为金砖国家跨区域主义的一种开放性制度安排。现有的"金砖+"实践秉持的既有地理区域原则，也有发展中国家身份原则，"金砖+"的对象有国家，也有区域组织。尽管有学者将2019年巴西利亚峰会"金砖+"的一次中止视为"金砖+"困境③，但我们更需要看到，在金砖国家已就"同其他新兴市场国家和发展中国家合作"达成高度共识的前提下，不论未来此方面合作以何种形式开展，其本质上皆是对"金砖+"的实践，即让更多的新兴市场国家和发展中国家进入金砖国家构建的跨区域空间进行对话与合作。伴随着金砖国家跨区域主义的发展，金砖五国正在从不同角度理解和思考"金砖+"问题，"金砖+"的内涵建设仍然是开放性的，仍有待于被进一步完善与发展。

### （三）平衡、治理与认同构建是金砖国家跨区域主义的主要功能

杰根·鲁兰将跨区域主义的功能划分为力量制衡、搭便车、制度建

---

① "Приоритеты председательства Российской Федерации в БРИКС," https://brics-russia2020.ru/russia_in_brics/20191226/1362/Prioritety-predsedatelstva-Rossiyskoy-Federatsii-v-BRIKS.html.

② "В МИД допустили возможность проведения саммита БРИКС в расширенном формате," РИА Новости, Ноября 11, 2019, https://ria.ru/20191111/1560805535.html.

③ 谢乐天：《巴西利亚峰会看"金砖+"困境及解决设想》，海国图智研究院，2020年7月23日，https://www.essra.org.cn/view-1000-896.aspx.

构、合理化、议程设定、认同建构和稳定发展七个方面。① 金砖国家是由国家为主体构成的跨区域集团，对于金砖国家跨区域主义来说，金砖国家构建的跨区域空间并不是封闭的空间，其需要金砖五国合力，通过与区域和全球层面的互动产生作用，金砖国家跨区域主义功能在国家、区域和全球层次均有体现，可以主要被概括在平衡、治理和认同构建三个方面。

金砖国家跨区域主义的平衡功能首先是外部制衡。金砖国家跨区域主义促进了五个国家的制度化合作，形成了新的新兴市场国家集团。金砖国家希望在全球结构中通过发展跨区域关系，打破区域界限对于发展的限制，聚合新兴市场国家和发展中国家的各类资源，追求与发达国家之间的力量平衡，从而在国际体系中处于更加有利的地位。金砖国家跨区域主义的平衡功能也同样适用于内部。金砖五国通过平等对话与各类追求互利共赢的合作机制，不断强化彼此之间各领域联系，协调内部利益，达成发展共识，在为五个国家参与全球事务、巩固国际地位、提升竞争力提供通道与机会的同时，也实现跨区域集团内部的权力平衡与稳定发展。

金砖国家跨区域主义的治理功能体现在参与区域治理和全球治理。金砖国家具有代表新兴市场国家和发展中国家在联合国、世界贸易组织（以下简称"世贸组织"）、国际货币基金组织、二十国集团等重要全球治理平台发声的重要作用。金砖国家跨区域主义的制度化合作形式多样，覆盖区域广，涉及众多国际合作领域，其中金砖国家新开发银行是金砖国家切实参与区域与全球治理的重要抓手。新开发银行是金砖国家跨区域合作的第一个实体机构，由五个国家共同出资1000亿美元作为初始资本，总部设立在上海，于2015年正式投入运营。5年来，新开发银行在能源开发、交通建设、河流治理、环境保护、公共卫生等领域为金砖五国及机构公司提供了大量贷款，如向巴西提供10亿美元用于抗击新冠疫情。② 2017年8月，金砖国家新开发银行非洲区域中心成立，该机构的命名彰显了金砖国家为非洲提供可持续发展基础设施建设资金，帮助非洲治理区域问题的承诺与

---

① Jürgen Rüland, "The EU as an Inter - and Transregional Actor: Lessons for Global Governance from Europe's Relations with Asia," 2002, p. 7.

② "Approved - projects," New Development Bank, https://www.ndb.int/projects/list - of - all - projects/approved - projects/page/1/.

决心。金砖国家新开发银行开放、平等、共赢的合作理念将在区域和全球层面产生示范效应,为全球金融秩序调整提供可鉴模式,同时新开发银行也是对当前区域和全球金融治理体系的必要补充。随着金砖国家跨区域主义优势的不断发挥,其在国际金融、贸易、能源、环境保护、公共卫生等领域的作为将继续作用于区域与全球治理进程。

金砖国家跨区域主义的功能还在于进行"金砖国家"的认同构建。金砖国家不是一个天然的地理概念,"金砖国家"的集体身份需要在跨区域主义合作中不断被灌注内涵,金砖五国对集体身份的认同需要不断被巩固提升。对于来自不同区域的金砖五国来说,其巨大的差异性不言而喻,通过跨区域主义合作,作为新兴市场国家的金砖五国才能发挥聚合作用。跨区域合作有助于加深金砖国家之间的相互了解,在求同存异的基础上达成对待国际和地区问题的共识,在国际舞台集体发声,从而激发和促进集体凝聚力。随着金砖国家跨区域主义的深入发展,金砖五国在历年峰会中不断重申多边主义的重要性,共同致力于建设更加公平、公正、平等、民主和有代表性的国际政治经济秩序,培育出了"互尊互谅、平等相待、团结互助、开放包容、互惠互利"的金砖精神①,金砖国家的认同不断加深。

金砖国家的"第二个金色十年"已经开启,为了实现"提高新兴国家和发展中国家在国际事务中的发言权,建设一个更加平等和公正的世界"的美好愿景,金砖国家跨区域主义构建的互动空间能够联通国家、区域和全球多个层面,具有与生俱来的优势。我们应当看到,金砖国家的跨区域主义国际合作是战略性合作,其涉及国家作为新兴市场国家一员的长远发展与繁荣的根本利益,不是"就事论事"的一般性合作。虽然金砖国家内部尚存在一些短期内无法弥合的分歧与矛盾,但这并不会影响金砖国家跨区域主义的大方向,金砖国家构建的新兴市场国家和发展中国家跨区域合作空间具有一般性合作空间所不具备的超稳定性。通过分析金砖国家跨区域主义的功能能够发现,外部制衡与内部平衡也是金砖国家发展的目标之一,区域治理和全球治理是金砖国家发展的具体路径,认同构建则是金砖

---

① 《金砖国家领导人厦门宣言(全文)》,新华网,2017 年 9 月 4 日,http://www.xinhuanet.com/world/2017-09/04/c_1121603652.htm。

国家发展的基础核心，同时，金砖国家跨区域主义的功能是三位一体的整体，通过治理和实现平衡，金砖国家的认同构建也会不断被强化，从而出现金砖国家跨区域主义的良性发展。从跨区域主义视角看来，金砖国家的制度发展和认同建构均已初具成效，可以预见，能否实现好自身的治理功能将成为影响金砖国家下一阶段发展的关键。

## 四、结语

习近平总书记在2019年出席中法全球治理论坛闭幕式时向世界提出了破解全球治理"四大赤字"的中国方案——"坚持公正合理，破解治理赤字""坚持互商互谅，破解信任赤字""坚持同舟共济，破解和平赤字""坚持互利共赢，破解发展赤字"。与此同时，随着区域大国的崛起和区域竞争的加剧，区域治理的重要性以及区域治理和全球治理的关系都开始受到更多关注。中国是一个有责任有担当的世界大国，始终有能力也有意愿在全球治理和区域治理中发挥积极作用。金砖精神符合中国破解全球治理"四大赤字"的方案，金砖国家既是中国推动全球治理体系改革的重要平台，也能够为中国参与区域治理提供更加多元的渠道。我国作为一个亚洲大国，可以充分开发利用金砖国家跨区域主义制度的基础和优势，以推动金砖国家在欧亚地区的跨区域发展为路径，努力将金砖国家塑造为区域治理和全球治理的典范。金砖国家跨区域主义发展的区域路径不仅有助于不同区域内部实现联通，还能够促成实现区域间的联通，与共建"一带一路"倡议促进世界互联互通的愿景相辅相成。

人类命运共同体是中国特色大国外交理论体系的重要组成部分，是中国为构建新型国际秩序观贡献的宝贵智慧。人类命运共同体超越了地理区域、文明归属和政治制度的界限，其中也蕴含着跨区域主义逻辑。人类命运共同体的构建需要从双边、区域、跨区域等多层次、多维度逐步推进，金砖国家作为一个跨区域主义机制可以成为构建人类命运共同体的重要抓手。在"第一个金色十年"发展后，金砖国家实际已经形成了利益共同体，在当前新冠疫情和"逆全球化"的冲击下，构建金砖国家责任共同体的时机已经到来。金砖国家为新兴市场国家和发展中国家构建了一个平等、开放、互利的跨区域空间，在金砖国家利益、责任共同体的基础上，未来在金砖国家构建的跨区域空间互动中将有机会形成新兴市场国家和发展中国家命运共同体。在此过程中，金砖国家跨区域主义的发展实践需要由强大的国家力量来引领，我国应明确思路，努力将金砖国家打造成新兴市场国家和发展中国家进行全方位互利合作的跨区域平台，成就金砖国家的"第二个金色十年"。

# 巴西"金砖观"的演变与中巴金砖合作研究

谢乐天\*　刘梦茹\*\*

**摘　要**：作为金砖"创始四国"之一的巴西，其金砖身份定位经历了从追求大国地位到重视经济效益再到淡化金砖身份以及现今重新调整重视金砖政策的发展演变。这种变化与不同时期内巴西政府所表现出的金砖利益诉求有关。在巴西新一届政府上台的大背景下，同为金砖国家重要成员的中国应当发挥其独到优势，从金砖合作"三根支柱"出发，着眼于加强安理会改革合作、扩大经贸往来、建立高级别人文交流机制，通过双边合作带动金砖多边合作，助力巴西强化金砖身份认知并推动金砖机制不断向前发展。

**关键词**：巴西；巴西外交；金砖国家；中巴关系

金砖机制兴起很大程度上是源于俄罗斯和巴西的积极奔走。虽然经过十余年发展，金砖国家合作机制已经成为新兴市场国家和发展中国家参与

---

\* 谢乐天，复旦大学国际关系与公共事务学院国家安全学在读博士。
\*\* 刘梦茹，四川外国语大学西方语言文化学院葡萄牙语专业教师、葡萄牙科英布拉大学博士研究生、四川外国语大学金砖国家研究院研究员。

全球治理的一股不可忽视的重要力量。随着金砖机制的不断成熟，为保证新兴市场国家能够在全球治理中发挥更大作用，新一轮的扩员是需要且必要的，能够让更多志同道合的对话伙伴加入金砖机制。巴西对于金砖机制的最初认可来源于自身扩大国际影响力的利益诉求，同时可以发现，巴西在不同时期对于金砖合作的领域倾向性上有一定的共性与差异，甚至表现出了对于金砖合作的冷淡与反感。那么，这种共性与差异的深层原因是什么？中巴合作又如何能够在金砖机制中正确定位？这些是本文将要讨论的问题。

## 一、巴西政府"金砖观"的演变

### （一）卢拉时期巴西"金砖观"

1. 对金砖机制的总体定位

卢拉执政期间，巴西积极参与金砖国家各项活动并于2010年作为轮值主席国主办了第二届"金砖四国"领导人峰会。卢拉政府认为，南南合作是巴西对外政策优先考虑的重点与核心。鉴于此，加强与以金砖国家为代表的新兴发展中大国关系是巴西外交的战略重点之一。[1]

基于此种考量，卢拉政府对金砖国家合作机制的认知与看法总体上看是较为积极的。在金砖机制下，巴西与发展中大国的联系使得巴西有望实现政治大国目标，提升其国际地位。具体表现在，一方面，在巴西主办2010年金砖峰会期间，巴西极力推进金砖国家合作机制化、定期化。相较于第一次峰会《"金砖四国"领导人俄罗斯叶卡捷琳堡会晤联合声明》而言，第二次峰会《"金砖四国"领导人第二次正式会晤联合声明》的篇幅更长、涉及领域更多、涵盖范围更广，[2] 且初步确定了金砖国家政治安全和经贸财金"双轨并行"的下一步合作模式。此外，在合作机制扩大方

---

[1] 吴志华：《巴西潜心塑造大国形象》，《人民日报》2010年12月29日。
[2] 《"金砖四国"领导人俄罗斯叶卡捷琳堡会晤联合声明》，《人民日报》2009年6月17日；"2nd BRIC Summit of Heads of State and Government: Joint Statement," BRICS Information Centre, April 15, 2010, http://www.brics.utoronto.ca/docs/100415 - leaders.html。

面,卢拉政府也认为金砖国家应当提升在新兴市场国家和发展中国家中的代表性。例如,2010 年峰会不仅在 2010 年《"金砖四国"领导人第二次正式会晤联合声明》中明确了未来一段时间内金砖国家将要在哪些领域开展合作,[①] 且时任南非总统祖马也同期到访巴西并与"金砖四国"展开双边会谈,讨论南非加入金砖国家的相关事项。在金砖国家成员国的共同努力下,南非于 2011 年正式加入金砖国家。[②]

2. 对巴西金砖诉求的认知

2003 年卢拉上台之后曾明确指出,巴西应尝试改变以往只注重美欧发达国家的传统外交路线,采取更加大胆、更为明智的对外政策,即巴西将努力寻求在北方国家与南方国家之间保持平衡。[③] 为此,卢拉积极推动巴西国内经济恢复的同时推行全方位外交,不仅保持与传统伙伴的关系,还优先发展与南非、中国和印度的伙伴关系。[④] 这种积极作为在很大程度上为日后金砖机制的建立埋下了伏笔。卢拉政府之所以选择拥抱金砖,是因为金砖机制符合巴西大国外交与加强国际影响力的利益诉求。在这一机制下,巴西能够有效提升巴西的政治大国地位并实现外交转型与突破。因此,卢拉政府的金砖诉求核心在于"五个国家远比单个国家在国际舞台上能够获得更大影响力"。[⑤]

除此之外,2008 年世界金融危机的爆发,使得奉行出口导向型经济政策的巴西受到了极大冲击。为应对这一危机,巴西政府有必要采取一定的主动政策,寻求扩大国际市场,对冲危机风险。这时,二十国集团机制和金砖国家合作机制的适时出现为巴西对外贸易破局提供了契机。在出席 2009 年"金砖四国"领导人首次会晤期间,卢拉强调,国际金融危机使国

---

① See "2nd BRIC Summit of Heads of State and Government: Joint Statement," BRICS Information Centre, April 15, 2010, http://www.brics.utoronto.ca/docs/100415-leaders.html.

② "Minister Nkoana-Mashabane on SA Full Membership of BRICS," Department of International Relations and Cooperation of Republic of South Africa, December 23, 2010, http://www.dirco.gov.za/docs/2010/brics1224.html.

③ 周志伟:《巴西参与金砖合作的战略考量及效果分析》,《拉丁美洲研究》2017 年第 4 期,第 111 页。

④ 成志杰:《金砖国家合作机制源起》,《国际研究参考》2017 年第 6 期,第 6 页。

⑤ 贺双荣:《巴西与金砖国家合作机制:战略考量、成果评估及可能的政策调整》,《当代世界》2017 年第 8 期,第 26 页。

际社会意识到新兴经济体的重要性，新兴经济体加强合作将极大地影响国际关系，金砖四国合作具有巨大发展空间，要扩大双边贸易，增加在金融等领域的协调和合作，致力于建设一个更加美好的世界。①

卢拉政府认为，金砖合作实际上是巴西通往政治大国的必经之路，为此，卢拉政府竭尽所能地推进金砖合作并乐于见到金砖影响力的日渐扩大。

### （二）罗塞芙时期巴西"金砖观"

1. 对金砖机制的总体定位

作为卢拉的继任者，罗塞芙的外交政策基本延续了卢拉时期积极进取的"多元化自主"风格，依旧积极推动"金砖扩员"之后站在历史新起点的金砖国家合作机制，且于2014年承办了金砖国家领导人福塔莱萨峰会。

在主持福塔莱萨峰会期间，罗塞芙提出，金砖国家应当放眼未来、团结自强，着手建立紧密、牢固的伙伴关系，改善全球治理，促进世界多极化和国际关系民主化。② 显然，在罗塞芙政府看来，金砖国家应当继续扮演好国际秩序坚定维护者和改革践行者的角色。鉴于此，巴西政府力推金砖国家加强在全球经济治理方面的改革进程，最终推动金砖国家迎来了成立下属分支机构的重要里程碑。③ 以美国为代表的发达国家对改革的态度开始由积极转向拖延，并谋求重新掌握在这一过程中的主导地位④。与此同时，面对2010年国际货币基金组织改革方案饱受争议的严峻形势时，巴西同其他金砖国家成员国一道积极推动金融安全领域的合作，最终形成了金砖国家新开发银行法定资本、各国出资比例、投票份额及建立初始资金规模为1000亿美元的应急储备安排协议等重要共识，以期帮助金砖国家及

---

① 马述强、韩显阳：《"金砖四国"领导人会晤在叶卡捷琳堡举行》，《光明日报》2009年6月17日。

② 《习近平出席金砖国家领导人第六次会晤并发表重要讲话》，《世界知识》2014年第15期，第6页。

③ "End of the Brazilian BRICS Chairpersonship," Ministério das Relações Exteriores, March. 31, 2015, https://www.gov.br/mre/en/contact-us/press-area/press-releases/closing-of-the-brazilian-presidency-of-the-brics.

④ 张嘉明：《国际货币基金组织改革与金砖国家应急储备安排》，《理论探讨》2014年第6期，第101页。

其他新兴市场和发展中国家解决基础设施缺口、满足可持续发展需求、防范系统性金融风险，并对现有的国际机制形成补充。①

总的来说，罗塞芙政府将金砖合作视为增强自身经济实力，推动巴西出口导向型经济取得更大成就并有效增强巴西自身抗系统性金融风险能力，从容应对经济危机的重要渠道。

2. 对巴西金砖诉求的认知

由于巴西经济自我生长能力较弱，其经济结构敏感脆弱②，这也使得巴西经济发展存在较大风险。而在罗塞芙时期，受制于美国和欧元区经济低迷、国际大宗商品价格波动等因素，加之巴西国内原本就严峻复杂的经济形势③，这一风险被无限放大，进而导致巴西经济发展受挫。秉持实用主义的罗塞芙政府在外交层面根据实际情况对其进行适当调整。其核心原因在于经济是影响巴西外交的重要因素。同时，巴西"入常"实现地区领袖和世界大国等目标并未发生根本性改变。④ 这种实用主义的调整便是前文所述之当面对发达国家拒绝在全球经济治理改革议题上做出让步时，巴西选择"主动求变"，积极谋求在任期内实现金砖突破。

罗塞芙政府认为，巴西参加金砖国家合作机制并推动机制各项工作的顺利开展仍然是基于巴西自身利益不受损害这一基本考虑。在新开发银行和应急储备安排问题上，巴西政府的切身利益便是并不满足于获得二十国集团成员以参与全球经济治理事务的身份，而是进一步扩大在其中的投票权和发言权。对此，罗塞芙将其形容为"这是时代的标志，要求对国际货币基金组织进行改革"。⑤ 与之类似，在联合国层面，巴西政府依然认为通

---

① "The 6th BRICS Summit: Fortaleza Declaration," BRICS Information Centre, July 15, 2014, http://www.brics.utoronto.ca/docs/140715 - leaders.html.

② 王云平、盛朝迅：《不同经济体制造业复苏背景、路径与对策措施》，《中国经贸导刊》2011年第23期，第28页。

③ 刘永辉、周昀主编：《中国—其他金砖国家贸易指数报告2017》，中国经济出版社2019年版，第81页。

④ 吴国平：《从卢拉到罗塞芙：巴西外交的特点与政策调整》，《中国国际战略评论》2011年，第245页。

⑤ Andrew F. Cooper and Asif B. Farooq, "Testing the Club Dynamics of the BRICS: The New Development Bank from Conception to Establishment," International Organisations Research Journal, Vol. 10, No. 2, 2015, p. 9.

过金砖国家合作能够为本国扩大政治影响力，对谋求政治大国地位有所裨益。2014年乌克兰危机爆发后，尽管面临国内反对势力的巨大压力，罗塞芙政府仍然认定金砖国家在乌克兰问题上的一致立场符合巴西本国利益。因此，同年3月，巴西连同其他金砖国家在联合国大会批评克里米亚公投的决议案中投下弃权票以表明自身态度。①

### （三）特梅尔时期巴西"金砖观"

1. 对金砖机制的总体定位

经过激烈的国内政治斗争，特梅尔接替罗塞芙就任代总统，不久后正式转为总统继续完成罗塞芙的总统任期。特梅尔在政治光谱上属于右翼，且鉴于内政与外交之间的紧密联系，巴西政治变动是否会导致重视金砖机制与南南合作的外交政策发生转变或有所倾斜，成为了备受关注的问题。

面对国际社会上出现的有关"金砖褪色"的质疑，特梅尔政府从实际行动上给出了答案。具体来说，特梅尔就任之初便赴二十国集团杭州峰会，向外界表明巴西新政府仍将推动全球多边合作的立场。不仅如此，次年特梅尔出席金砖国家厦门峰会时还正面回击"金砖褪色论"，强调金砖合作是在强化而不是在衰弱，而且"金砖+"理念的提出也意味着金砖机制在国际上得到肯定。② 此外，特梅尔政府的外交部部长塞拉在就职仪式上也公开表示，新政府的外交政策将致力于把同亚洲国家尤其是中国的新伙伴关系置于优先地位。③ 显然，这也从侧面表现出特梅尔政府一如既往地对金砖合作持支持态度。

总的来说，特梅尔政府并未像外界所预想的那样，对金砖机制的合作态度发生转向，依旧坚定不移地支持金砖国家在全球治理议题上发挥更大作用。2018年11月30日，金砖国家领导人于二十国集团峰会期间举行非正式会晤时，特梅尔还特意强调他邀请了新任总统博索纳罗出席峰会，但博索纳罗因身体原因未能成行。这一举动也更加证明了特梅尔政府对于金

---

① 杨凌：《金砖国家机制下巴西与俄罗斯关系新发展》，《拉丁美洲研究》2015年第3期，第22页。
② 陈效卫：《金砖机制不断完善——访巴西总统特梅尔》，《人民日报》2017年9月3日。
③ 王飞：《后罗塞芙时代的中巴经济合作》，《世界知识》2016年第20期，第59页。

砖机制的积极态度，并竭尽所能地想要给 2019 年接棒金砖国家轮值主席国的巴西留下一笔丰厚的"金砖财富"。

2. 对巴西金砖诉求的认知

特梅尔在对待新兴经济体和发展中国家合作问题上采取同先前劳工党政府较为类似的政策，原因在于在罗塞芙执政后期受到了国际金融危机的影响，导致巴西经济增速明显放缓。这种经济层面的衰退表现出了明显的扩散性，但政府却未能及时转变经济结构和发展模式，从而导致人民生活水平不断下降，激起民愤，这最终成为罗塞芙被弹劾下台的主要原因之一。[①] 更为重要的是，巴西国内的"左右党争"也导致巴西所处国际环境受到冲击。在弹劾案盖棺论定后，以委内瑞拉、玻利维亚、厄瓜多尔为代表的拉美多个左翼政府都相继"召回大使"以示抗议。在严重的内外交困情况下，特梅尔政府不得不低调务实。

特梅尔政府选择的解决方案之一是利用多边场合争取更多国家对其执政事实的认可。[②] 基于这一政治考虑，增加巴西在金砖国家合作机制中的存在感是取得其他国家外交支持的一个重要途径。在金砖机制下，经贸财经的双边与多边合作为巴西加快经济复苏带来了可能，不仅如此，也为巴西与其他发展中国家扩大经贸合作提供了机会，从而扩大商品出口、促进巴西本国经济复苏、维护社会稳定，最终达到利用金砖合作来稳定国内经济社会秩序的目的。

### （四）博索纳罗时期巴西"金砖观"

1. 对金砖机制的总体定位

左右政治分野是巴西政治发展中不可回避的固有顽疾。[③] 2018 年极右翼博索纳罗的强势崛起使巴西的内政外交几乎出现 180 度大转圜。鉴于博

---

① 徐世澄：《巴西总统罗塞芙被国会弹劾的过程和前因后果》，《中国人大》2016 年第 14 期，第 54 页。
② 周志伟：《总统弹劾后的巴西政治生态及外交走势》，《当代世界》2016 年第 10 期，第 69 页。
③ 方旭飞：《巴西左右政党的分野、变迁和前景》，《拉丁美洲研究》2020 年第 5 期，第 49 页。

索纳罗曾发表过诸多反多边主义的言论,这意味着巴西新政府对金砖合作的态度不甚积极。①

在金砖合作层面,虽然博索纳罗依旧主持了金砖国家巴西利亚峰会,但却并未举办"金砖+"对话会,这在很大程度上弱化了各成员国的金砖热情。此外,2020年金砖国家应对新冠疫情特别外长会期间,在关于"疫情政治化、污名化"的立场上,巴西表现出与其他成员国明显不一致的态度。

随着巴西国内疫情形势的愈发严峻,经济复苏、疫苗合作研发与接种等方面的迫切需求,博索纳罗此前的不友好态度也发生了一些改变。除了经贸财金领域之外,也逐渐重视卫生健康与医疗领域上同其他金砖成员国的合作。2020年金砖国家峰会期间,博索纳罗明确抨击"疫情政治化",强调克服疫情不利影响需要包括金砖国家在内的全世界所有伙伴共同努力。而且他还认为,金砖合作不会因被迫转为线上而被疫情击垮,相反地,金砖成员国之间的合作会变得更加紧密。② 2022年2月,博索纳罗更是顶住美国压力③,在乌克兰局势升级之际访问莫斯科,同普京讨论在联合国安理会、金砖国家和二十国集团等多边平台上开展合作等议题。④

总体而言,博索纳罗对于金砖合作的态度由消极转为积极,这不仅意味着金砖国家之间的合作在改善巴西目前存在的民生经济问题上起到了明显积极的作用,而且彰显了金砖国家合作机制韧性十足。

2. 对巴西金砖诉求的认知

国家外交政策转向通常由领导人更迭触发且多发生于新领导人执政初

---

① See "No Reason for 'Tropical Trump' to Disrupt Relations with China: China Daily Editorial," China Daily, October 29, 2018, https://www.chinadaily.com.cn/a/201810/29/WS5bd702e9a310eff303285424.html.

② "Discurso do Presidente da República, Jair Bolsonaro, na Cerimônia de Cúpula de Líderes do BRICS," Fundação Alexandre de Gusmão, Novembro. 9, 2021, https://www.gov.br/funag/pt-br/centrais-de-conteudo/politica-externa-brasileira/discurso-do-presidente-da-republica-jair-bolsonaro-na-cerimonia-de-cupula-de-lideres-do-brics.

③ See in Jonny Tickle, "US Trying to Prevent Brazilian President Visiting Russia," Russia Today, February 1, 2022, https://www.rt.com/russia/547909-us-pressuring-brazils-bolsonaro/.

④ 《俄外长:俄罗斯支持巴西成为联合国安理会常任理事国》,俄罗斯卫星通讯社,2022年2月16日,https://sputniknews.cn/20220216/1039326593.html。

期。① 以反建制（anti-establishment）和不可预测（unpredictability）执政风格著称的特朗普上台之后，一系列的"黑天鹅"事件接踵而至。② 以特朗普的成功为代表，在受全球化负面影响较深的国家和地区，其政治极化现象同样也日益凸显，保守主义、民粹主义和"反全球化"思潮此起彼伏。③ 具体到2018年的巴西大选，极右翼政治素人博索纳罗在竞选时便有着"热带特朗普"之称，在其执政初期甚至重新考虑了巴西外交优先事项、目标和目的，并毫不掩饰地将主要目标放在巴美关系的进一步推进上，而先前巴西历任政府所强调的团结南方政策则被无情抛弃。④

尽管如此，巴美关系并未因博索纳罗的一腔热忱而取得重大突破。面对国内疫情的日益严峻，巴西对外贸易受到前所未有的冲击，国内社会秩序也出现不稳定因素。在部分左翼政党和一大批社会运动组织下，不仅在首都巴西利亚，而且在圣保罗、里约热内卢等州府，以及全国200多个城市爆发了大规模游行，抗议政府应对新冠疫情不力，要求弹劾总统博索纳罗。⑤ 鉴于此，博索纳罗原先所确定的大幅度向美国及其极右翼盟友靠近、对南南合作及全球治理不感兴趣、以意识形态亲疏处理与地区国家的关系、无意领导地区一体化的外交布局存在重重危机。⑥ 他不得不重新重视其他金砖国家的外交努力，开始重新思考政府的金砖战略选择，希望通过适当推动金砖合作的外交政策缓解这一紧张局势。所以说，博索纳罗的外交政策及其对金砖国家合作的态度出现巨幅摇摆的核心原因在于对其自身政治利益的考虑，表现出鲜明的利己属性。

---

① 查雯、李响：《外交政策突变原因探究》，《国际政治科学》2022年第3期，第76页。
② Bentley, Michelle and Maxine David, "Unpredictability as Doctrine: Reconceptualising Foreign Policy Strategy in the Trump Era," Cambridge Review of International Affairs, Vol. 34, No. 3, 2021, pp. 383–406.
③ Broz J. Lawrence, et al, "Populism in Place: The Economic Geography of the Globalization Backlash," International Organization, Vol. 75, No. 2, 2021, p. 465.
④ Dmitry Razumovsky, "BRICS – How Will the Organisation Get a 'Second Wind'?" Valdai Discussion Club, July 14, 2022, https://valdaiclub.com/a/highlights/brics-how-will-the-organisation-get-a-second-wind-/?sphrase_id=139361.
⑤ 孙岩峰：《博索纳罗政府遭遇最大执政困境》，《世界知识》2021年第13期，第48页。
⑥ 王慧芝：《巴西外交政策右转的原因及前景》，《和平与发展》2021年第2期，第99页。

## 二、金砖机制内中巴合作的进展与未来

### （一）政治安全支柱下的中巴安理会事务合作

早在2009年的"金砖四国"领导人首次会晤期间就达成了"支持联合国在应对全球性威胁和挑战方面发挥中心作用"[①]的共识，而加强金砖国家在联合国框架下安理会层面的合作是深入政治安全领域合作的重要一环。

当前，国际社会存在着四国同盟、非盟、加勒比共同体、L69和"咖啡俱乐部"等推动安理会改革的组织，但它们在推动安理会改革进程上的作用表现得并不明显。一方面，它们彼此之间甚至是成员内部存在着严峻的竞争关系，很容易被各个击破，分而治之；另一方面，安理会五常在支持哪些国家"入常"这一问题上难以达成统一意见，这也在相当程度上加大了改革集团开展工作的难度。此外，增加其成员数量虽然是一种可行之举，但会导致安理会常任理事国在全球大国能力中所占的份额大幅减少，这将直接挑战联合国最为核心的"雅尔塔共识"。[②] 因此，安理会改革议题的进程较为缓慢。

尽管如此，为展现金砖国家合作的"全球视野"以及坚持在联合国框架下参与全球治理的意愿，金砖国家合作也必然会涉及安理会改革议题。不过，改革问题关乎各国核心利益的得失，这使得金砖五国在这一议题上很难取得实质上的突破。中俄同印度、巴西、南非存在鲜明的利益分割线，难免会损害金砖国家开展全方位合作的意愿与决心。[③] 这也是迄今为止未有任何一份金砖宣言明确地就巴西、印度、南非的"入常"问题做出

---

[①] 《"金砖四国"领导人俄罗斯叶卡捷琳堡会晤联合声明》，《人民日报》2009年6月17日。

[②] Matthew D. Stephen, "Legitimacy Deficits of International Organizations Design Drift and Decoupling at the UN Security Council," Cambridge Review of International Affairs, 2018, Vol. 31, No. 1, p. 115.

[③] 朱天祥编著：《金砖国家与全球治理》，时事出版社2019年版，第185页。

一致承诺的原因所在。① 除此之外，虽然中俄两国都支持安理会改革，但两国在具体支持哪些国家这一问题上就明显存在表述差异，这也是金砖国家在安理会改革议题上分歧不断的一个缩影。这一差异与分歧也使得金砖国家在联合国安理会改革这一议题上只能"空喊口号"。

现阶段，中巴开展安理会改革相关合作的最好方法便是以"常任理事国＋非常任理事国"的模式开展合作。这种合作办法在金砖国家合作起步之初的2011年就已得到验证。

2011年金砖五国恰恰均为安理会成员。纵观2011年安理会共举行235次会议，② 共通过66份决议。③ 其中有两份有关中东局势的决议草案（S/2011/24）和（S/2011/612）④，分别因美国和中俄两国的"一票否决"而未能通过。此外，该年度安理会通过的有关利比亚局势的第1973号决议和有关非洲和平与安全的第2023号决议分别以10票赞成、0票反对、5票弃权和13票赞成、0票反对、2票弃权的投票情况得到通过。⑤ 由于这四份决议与安理会内部各成员国的利益纠纷密切相关，在此选取S/2011/612决议草案为例做出如下分析。

2011年10月4日讨论中东局势的联合国安理会第六六二七次会议于下午6时召开。在会议表决过程中，中俄投下了反对票致使决议草案无法通过，同时，印巴南三国也投了弃权票，且表决之后，金砖五国均申请了发言。⑥ 其中，中国代表李保东指出，中国同不少安理会成员国一样，认为在当前形势下，制裁或威胁无助于叙利亚问题的解决，反而可能导致局

---

① 朱天祥、谢乐天：《金砖国家政治安全合作的内涵与挑战》，《拉丁美洲研究》2020年第6期，第41页。
② 《2011年联合国安全理事会会议记录》，联合国安全理事会，https://www.un.org/securitycouncil/zh/content/meetings-records-2011。
③ 《2011年安理会通过的决议》，联合国安全理事会，https://www.un.org/securitycouncil/zh/content/resolutions-adopted-security-council-2011。
④ 《安全理事会常任理事国在公开会议上所投的否决票》，联合国安全理事会，https://www.un.org/securitycouncil/zh/content/veto-90-present。
⑤ 《2011年联合国安全理事会会议记录》，联合国安全理事会，https://www.un.org/securitycouncil/zh/content/meetings-records-2011。
⑥ 参见联合国安理会，https://undocs.org/zh/S/PV.6484。

势进一步复杂化。① 巴西代表维奥蒂夫人则强调叙利亚摆脱危机的唯一出路是进行有意义和包容性对话并实施有效的政治改革。为此，巴西将继续为和平解决叙利亚危机提供力所能及的帮助。② 更为重要的是，俄罗斯代表丘尔金还尤其对金砖国家在此份决议草案投票问题上所保持的高度一致的立场表示了肯定。③ 金砖国家的一致立场有效遏制了西方国家借西亚北非政局动荡搞垮叙利亚政府的图谋，为维护中东局势的总体稳定起到了积极作用。

2022年巴西再度当选安理会非常任理事国，在安理会改革问题难以得到实质性推进的情况下，中巴乃至更大范围内的金砖国家甚至是整个南方世界都可以通过"常任理事国+非常任理事国"的模式开展合作，尽可能多地在安理会会议上发出发展中国家的声音，代表其根本利益与诉求。

### （二）经贸财金支柱下的中巴经贸合作

巴西是中国在拉丁美洲地区的最大贸易伙伴。自2009年起，中国便连续保持巴西最大贸易伙伴地位。④ 2022年一季度，中国对巴西出口总额约190亿美元，占巴西进口总额的23%；中国自巴西进口总额约197亿美元，占巴西出口总额的29%。⑤ 2022年5月，中巴高层协调与合作委员会召开第六次会议，就包括促进两国农产品贸易发展、低碳和清洁技术投资等领域合作事项达成一致意见，同意在数字经济等领域积极开展一系列实质性的合作。⑥

大宗商品是中巴经贸往来的压舱石。中国商务部公开数据显示，巴西向中国出口的最主要商品是以铁矿石为代表的矿产品和以大豆为代表的植

---

① 参见联合国安理会，https：//undocs. org/zh/S/PV. 6484。
② 参见联合国安理会，https：//undocs. org/zh/S/PV. 6484。
③ 参见联合国安理会，https：//undocs. org/zh/S/PV. 6484。
④ 参见《中国同拉丁美洲进出口总额（万美元）》，国家统计局，https：//data. stats. gov. cn/easyquery. htm? cn = C01。
⑤ 李宁：《中国巴西经贸合作新机遇现》，中国商务新闻网，2022年6月8日，https：//www. comnews. cn/content/2022 - 06/08/content_10031. html。
⑥ 《中巴（西）高委会第六次会议成果清单》，中国商务部，2022年5月24日，http：//www. mofcom. gov. cn/article/syxwfb/202205/20220503313636. shtml。

物产品。以2019年为例，上述两类产品共占巴西向中国出口主要商品的79.7%。①

鉴于巴西主要是初级产品出口国并且这种出口商品结构完美契合了中国经济发展中进口原材料的需求，所以中巴贸易存在着明显的互补关系。②但地缘政治的不确定性、两极分化导致的全球经济失衡、协调合作机制的减少，使得中巴贸易往来的未来充满了不确定性。与此同时，巴西贸易结构过度依赖初级产品出口，既不可持续又不能为巴西带来更大的国际收益。③这样"资源诅咒"的结构性压力也使得历任巴西政府均面临着如何调整进出口贸易结构的难题。

中巴经贸往来具体表现为双方高附加值产品贸易匮乏，使得经贸合作难以得到实质性提升。例如，在2017年1月至11月期间，高附加值的商品仅占巴西向中国出口总额的3.76%，但在同期巴西向美国出口的商品中，工业化加工产品占出口额的比例则高达56%，达到137.1亿美元。巴西航空工业公司生产的飞机作为其中第二大类别产品，占对美出口总额的8.1%。④更有甚者，2018年巴西航空工业公司就已经同美国波音公司展开合作，成立合资企业，开发KC-390军用运输机。⑤在此基础上，2022年9月巴西航空工业公司还与美国L3哈里斯公司（L3Harris）共同宣布将为KC-390运输机加装硬管加油设备和现代化通信设备，使其成为多用途的运输/加油机并尝试出售给美国空军。⑥

---

① 参见《2019年巴西货物贸易及中巴双边贸易概况》，中国商务部，https：//countryreport. mofcom. gov. cn/record/view110209. asp？news_id =67262。
② 诺华侨：《中国、巴西发展战略框架下的双边贸易关系研究》，华中师范大学博士学位论文2012年。
③ 沈艳枝、刘厚俊：《资源依赖型经济体的可持续发展研究：以巴西为例》，《现代管理科学》2013年第8期，第7页。
④ 《中国是巴西最大的大宗商品出口目的地》，《南美侨报》网，2017年12月13日，http：//epms. br - cn. com/static/content/news/qs_news/2017 - 12 - 13/887318451058638849. html。
⑤ Valerie Insinna, "Boeing, Embraer Agree to KC-390 Joint Venture," Defense News, December 17, 2018, https：//www. defensenews. com/air/2018/12/17/boeing - embraer - agree - to - kc - 390 - joint - venture/。
⑥ Stephen Losey, "L3Harris, Embraer Team up on KC-390 Tanker, Eye US Air Force sales," Defense News, September 19, 2018, https：//www. defensenews. com/air/2022/09/19/l3harris - embraer - team - up - on - kc - 390 - tanker - eye - us - air - force - sales/。

巴美高附加值产品贸易的密切往来表明，巴西并不能仅仅被视作原材料出口国，在今后中巴经贸合作上应当思考新的路径、找到新的突破口，进一步巩固与深化中巴贸易伙伴关系。

在航空领域，巴西航空工业公司是全球130座级及以下商用喷气飞机市场的领先者，其产品广泛出口世界各国。包括南方航空、东方航空在内的中国内地数家重要的航空运营商旗下都拥有巴西航空工业公司支线客机。当前，中国商飞正在同俄罗斯联合航空制造集团公司开展联合研制C929大型远程宽体客机相关工作。这种布局高精尖制造业领域的合作在一定程度上加强了中俄两国工业创新能力。未来，应当关注中国是否能同巴西开展像中俄一样的航空合作，联合研制支线客机或开展"飞机外交"，追加客机订单以促进中巴经贸合作。

同样，在航天领域，从1988年开始，中巴就开始联合研制中巴地球资源系列卫星。截至2019年，双方已合作研制6颗卫星，并在南非、新加坡等地升级改造卫星数据接收站以扩大卫星应用能力。此外，2014年中巴还共同建立中国—巴西空间天气联合实验室，旨在依托中巴地理位置的天然优势，进行低纬地区近地空间环境的探测与研究。这一领域的既有合作甚至反哺了金砖层面的多边航天合作。2015年，中国国家航天局发起金砖国家遥感卫星星座合作倡议。2021年，五国正式签署了《关于金砖国家遥感卫星星座合作的协定》，明确将依托包括中巴地球资源卫星在内的已有卫星开展合作。显然，中巴既有航天合作如何有效融入金砖国家航天合作并增强金砖国家航天合作整体竞争力，也应被视为中巴未来尖端前沿领域合作的重要突破口。

除此之外，中国早已发出邀请希望巴方尽快加入共建"一带一路"倡议①，但巴西至今仍未与中国签署共建"一带一路"合作文件。虽然如此，同为拉美地区有着重要影响力且正在申请加入金砖国家的阿根廷在这一方面却走在了巴西的前面。2022年阿根廷总统费尔南德斯访华期间，双方达成了《关于深化中阿全面战略伙伴关系的联合声明》《关于共同推进丝绸

---

① 《驻巴西大使杨万明接受巴西〈圣保罗页报〉专访实录》，中国外交部，2022年3月6日，http：//br.china‐embassy.gov.cn/dsxx/dshd/202203/t20220306_10648380.htm。

之路经济带和21世纪海上丝绸之路建设的谅解备忘录》等一系列成果文件,标志着双方将共同制定有利于可持续发展和包容性经济合作的框架,以促进两国经济关系深化、革新与多元化和增强区域联通。① 在其他拉美国家已同中国签署共建"一带一路"合作规划的基础上,并结合中巴合作的实际发展需要,2024年11月,中巴两国签署《中华人民共和国政府和巴西联邦共和国政府关于共建"一带一路"倡议同"加速增长计划""巴西新工业计划""生态转型计划""南美一体化路线计划"对接的合作规划》。该文件的签署能够起到表率作用,推动其他金砖国家和"金砖+"伙伴尽早同中方签署共建"一带一路"合作规划。

### (三) 人文交流支柱下的中巴双边人文交流

自1974年中国与巴西建交以来,两国从建交之初的"谨慎外交"发展成多领域广泛合作的战略伙伴关系。特别是进入21世纪以来,两国在政治、经贸、文化等方面的合作进入高速发展的新时期。② 2009年5月,时任巴西总统卢拉对华进行国事访问,此次访华期间双方共同制定了《中华人民共和国政府与巴西联邦共和国政府2010至2014年共同行动计划》并于2010年正式实施,这一成果性文件的最终出台标志着中巴关系正朝着夯实战略伙伴关系的政治基础、拓宽和深化各领域双边关系、促进在两国共同关心的领域交流经验等多方向综合发展。③ 此外,2012年双方签署两国政府《十年合作规划》。2013年两国决定建立中巴工商论坛并确定两国外长年度会晤机制,基本实现了高层交流框架搭建。2014年7月,习近平主席在第六次金砖国家领导人峰会后对巴西进行了国事访问,双方发表了《关于进一步深化中巴全面战略伙伴关系的联合声明》,涵盖了文化、教育、体育、旅游等领域的人文交流合作。这不仅是对先前中巴共同行动计

---

① 《中华人民共和国和阿根廷共和国关于深化中阿全面战略伙伴关系的联合声明(全文)》,《人民日报》2022年2月6日。
② 周志伟:《中巴关系:历史回顾与展望——纪念中国巴西建交35周年》,《当代世界》2009年第8期,第55页。
③ 参见《中华人民共和国政府与巴西联邦共和国政府2010年至2014年共同行动计划》,中国外交部,2010年4月22日,https://www.mfa.gov.cn/web/zyxw/201004/t20100422_307566.shtml。

划的延续，更意味着中巴高层有着加强人文交流并使其实现质的飞跃的共识。

从已有人文交流成果来看，中巴两国在音乐、戏剧、杂技、造型艺术、广播、电影、电视、图书、出版等领域开展了一系列交流活动。近年来，中国在巴西成功举办中国文化节、文物展览、艺术作品展、商业巡演等大型文化活动。2013年，两国分别在对方国家互办"文化月"活动。中国教育部在巴西利亚大学和圣保罗大学建有汉语教学点，中国教育部中外语言交流合作中心在巴西建有11所孔子学院和6所孔子学堂，中国学相关研究中心超过40家，中国问题研究机构数量居拉美国家之首。中国传媒大学和巴西圣保罗亚洲文化中心分别设有葡萄牙语水平考试和汉语水平考试考点。中国社会科学院拉美研究所和北京大学分别设有巴西研究中心和巴西文化中心。中央电视台和中国国际广播电台分别在巴西建有拉美中心站和拉美地区总站。[1] 虽然这些人文交流合作基本涵盖了人文交流的主要领域，但这些人文交流成果呈现散点化特征，彼此独立缺乏协调连贯。

需要注意的是，虽然早在1993年中国就与巴西建立战略伙伴关系并以此为开端开启中国与巴西战略伙伴关系的全新篇章[2]，但令人遗憾的是，由于两国地理位置较远且官方语言不通，双方民众彼此了解甚少，存在极大的交流瓶颈，[3] 以至于两国之间的人文交流开展艰难，进而影响到中巴高级别人文交流机制的创建。为此，寻找合适的方法来纾解困局尤为重要。

2019年习近平主席在出席金砖国家领导人巴西利亚峰会时曾明确指出："金砖国家为世界文明交流提供了最佳实践。"[4] 就当前金砖国家人文

---

[1] 参见《中国同巴西的关系》，中国外交部，https：//www.mfa.gov.cn/web/gjhdq_676201/gj_676203/nmz_680924/1206_680974/sbgx_680978/；《2022巴西中国学研究调查报告发布》，澎湃新闻，2022年9月16日，https：//www.thepaper.cn/newsDetail_forward_19927150。
[2] 门洪华、刘笑阳：《中国伙伴关系战略评估与展望》，《世界经济与政治》2015年第2期，第65页。
[3] 王蔚、汪骏良：《金砖国家人文交流机制的经验与完善》，载朱天祥主编：《金砖国家国别与合作研究》（第一辑），时事出版社2019年版，第55页。
[4] 习近平：《携手努力共谱合作新篇章——习近平在金砖国家领导人巴西利亚会晤公开会议上的讲话》，《人民日报》2019年11月15日。

交流合作开展情况而言，在科教人文体等领域金砖国家已开展了一系列合作，先后举办了包括金砖国家运动会、金砖职业技能大赛、金砖女性创新大赛、开设五国媒体线上培训班在内的多元化活动。不过，由于这些活动大都是由官方主导开展的，集中在一线城市，因此如何"接地气、惠民生"，加强地方合作则是下一步金砖国家努力的方向。在这一过程中，鼓励非官方行为体开展相关合作，并给予这些行为体一定的政策引导与支持，让它们更广泛深入地参与到金砖国家合作之中，助力讲好"金砖故事"与"金砖+故事"，推动金砖国家人文交流模式朝"民众主导型"转型，为金砖国家合作走深走实，深入民心作贡献。

## 三、结语

巴西的"金砖观"在不同时期有着不同的表现形式和利益诉求，这与巴西执政党及政治家政治取向、巴西对政治大国身份追求、巴西国内经济社会情况密切相关。当前巴西的金砖战略已有止跌回暖迹象，这就要求巴西现政府和未来的新政府以及其他金砖国家一道努力。在这一过程中，作为金砖国家主要核心成员以及2022年轮值主席国的中国，就应当依托中巴现有双边关系积极发展的重要契机，努力促变。习近平主席在金砖国家领导人第十四次会晤上明确指出，"作为新兴市场国家和发展中国家代表，我们在历史发展关键当口做出正确选择，采取负责任行动，对世界至关重要"。[①] 2022 年奉行多边主义、强调金砖合作的卢拉再度当选巴西总统，我们有理由相信处于历史新起点的中巴关系以及金砖国家合作机制将以更加主动的新姿态，在政治安全、经贸财金、人文交流"三根支柱"下开展更多有价值的对话与合作，依托现有"三轮驱动"合作架构努力迈入金砖国家扩员的历史新起点。

---

[①] 习近平：《构建高质量伙伴关系 开启金砖合作新征程——在金砖国家领导人第十四次会晤上的讲话》，《人民日报》2022 年 6 月 24 日。

# 印度印地语主流报刊媒体及其报道研究

段孟洁[*]

**摘　要**：印度是世界上语言情况最为复杂的国家之一，同时印度的媒体行业十分发达，两者相结合形成了印度媒体的多语言状态。目前国内对印度媒体的动态把握以英语为主，针对这一现状，本文试图以印地语媒体为切入点，还原印度媒体中真实的中国形象，理清目前印度媒体语言构成现状，并分析这种分布现状背后的历史及社会因素。

**关键词**：印度媒体；中国形象；印地语媒体

印度国情复杂、民族众多，素有"人种博物馆"之称，与之相对应的语言情况也十分复杂。印度共有语言461种[①]，根据1950年印度宪法规定，印度的官方语言为印地语与英语，此外还承认21种地区性官方语言。印度语言情况的复杂直接导致了印度媒体的多语言状态，加之印度人口基

---

[*] 段孟洁，四川外国语大学东方语言文化学院讲师，国际传播学院博士生。本文为重庆市研究生科研创新项目"文本旅行与跨文化传播"（CYB21227）和四川外国语大学科研项目"印地语报刊镜像下的中国形象"（sisu202034）阶段性成果。

[①] 其中14种语言已经失传，数据来源："Maps of India," https://www.mapsofindia.com/culture/indian-languages.html。

数庞大、媒体行业"超级发达甚至超前发达,全国报纸杂志发行量近万份,居全球首位"①。这为我们全面客观地掌握印度媒体中的中国形象平添了许多困难,因此也要求我们在双语言,甚至多语言境况下去了解印度媒体及公众舆论对中国形象的塑造。目前国内对印度媒体的动态把握较为单一,即仅从英文媒体这一部分来了解印度媒体对中国的报道。曾任新华社驻印度首席记者的唐璐也在《印度媒体市场——不是想象的那样简单》一文中明确指出过这一点,印度各语言媒体的受众量差异巨大,中国媒体经常介绍的实际上仅仅是印度英文媒体的报道内容,但其实印地语媒体数量和读者最多,英文媒体在印度媒体市场中所占份额非常小②。印度媒体使用的语言丰富多样,这的确是一直以来影响我们对印度媒体中的中国形象的把握的一个主要难点,从下文的数据分析我们可以看出,单从印度英文媒体出发去对印度民众心中的中国形象进行研判分析是不全面甚至不准确的。在中印关系曲折动荡但积极向好的当下,全面把握印度涉华报道动态,虽不能说事关中印关系大局,但其重要作用也不容小觑。

## 一、各司其职——印度媒体的两种生态

英国在印度历时两百年的殖民统治给印度民众留下了许多难以磨灭的烙印,其中便包括了英语与读报这两项。至今,使用英文仍是印度上层阶级对外显示自己受教育程度的一把利器,也是高等教育中通用的教学语言。由于印度语言众多,南北语言差异较大,英语在一定程度上也起到了南北沟通的作用,但印度民众在日常使用中,仍以各个地方的印度语言为主。印度按语言使用划分可以划为 14 个区域③,其中北部主要通行印度官方语言印地语,区域包括北方邦、拉贾斯坦邦、比哈尔邦、哈里亚纳邦和中央邦等九个邦,同时印地语也是印度政府大力推广的官方语言,"三语

---

① 李坤:《印度媒体涉华报道及其影响研究》,复旦大学硕士论文 2012 年,第 2 页。
② 唐璐:《印度媒体市场——不是想象的那样简单》,《对外传播》2010 年第 3 期,第 58 页。
③ 此划分依据为印度国家地图网官网语言地图,数据来源:Maps of India,https://www.mapsofindia.com/culture/indian-languages.html。

方案"①中的核心语言②。此外,印度西北部旁遮普邦主要通行旁遮普语;东北部西孟加拉邦、特里普拉邦等六个邦主要通行孟加拉语;西部古吉拉特邦主要通行古吉拉特语;中西部马哈拉施特拉邦主要通行马拉地语;东部奥里萨邦主要通行奥里亚语;中东部特伦甘纳邦和安得拉邦主要通行泰卢固语;西南部卡纳塔克邦主要通行坎纳达语,喀拉拉邦主要通行马拉雅兰语;东南部泰米尔纳德邦主要通行泰米尔语,因而印度媒体也具有很强的地域性。据笔者在印度时的了解,由于国情及政策③的特殊性,印度民众的语言能力很强,普遍每人能至少掌握两种语言:印地语及当地母语,受教育程度高或家庭构成多样的印度民众甚至能掌握四到五种语言。这样特殊的多语言状态造就了印度英文媒体与印度语言媒体各司其职的"两种生态"④模式。

印度实行联邦民主制,各邦拥有较高的自治权,民众享有选举权,为了获得占选民大多数的底层民众的选票,各地区的印度语言媒体成为了政客们的宣传阵地,由此可见印度语言媒体的受众主要是基层百姓,他们关心国家政策、领导人选举、体育娱乐、当地新闻。英文媒体的受众则是以接受过良好教育的中上层阶级为主,他们关心金融股市、外交政策、留学资讯等与精英阶层自身密切相关的信息,这一阶层的人主要从事商贸行业,同时由于本身接受过相关的教育,因而对国家外交政策决策等极为关注。

印度媒体的这两种生态,圈子不同、风格不同、关注点不同,但对于印度政策决策是起到同样重要作用的,忽略任何一个都可能造成不可挽回的失误。以下的这个例子就可以很好地说明这一点,目前印度发行量最大

---

① 1963年印度政府出台的《官方语言法》规定印度的学校必须教三种语言:在非印地语地区教授印地语、英语和本地母语;在印地语地区教授印地语、英语和一种印度语言。
② 廖波:《印度的语言困局》,《东南亚南亚研究》2015年第3期,第78页。
③ 特指上文出现的"三语方案",同上。
④ "两种生态"这一说法最先由唐璐在《印度媒体市场——不是想象的那样简单》一文中提及:"一般而言,外界如果想了解印度人对外交问题的看法,应该研判印度英文报纸的观点,而要想真正理解印度政治,则需要阅读印度语言报纸。这种现象实际上折射出印度媒体的两种生态,即英语媒体和包括各地方语言在内的印度语言媒体,两者所影响的读者群完全不同,报纸关注的问题以及编辑风格也有所差异。"

的报纸《觉醒日报》的出版商、印度著名报人纳兰德拉·莫汉说过这样一段话："那些生活在德里的人都深深地被英文报纸影响着。这才是尼赫鲁错误估计了印度并且犯下悲剧性错误的原因，也是为什么英·甘地错误估计了印度而失去了大选的理由……。如果你想了解印度，只能通过地方语言报纸。"①

**表1 印度媒体使用者委员会发布的2017年日报读者量调查表（全语言）②**

| 排序 | 报纸名称 | 读者总量 | 语言 |
| --- | --- | --- | --- |
| 1 | Dainik Jagran（《觉醒日报》） | 70377 | 印地语 |
| 2 | Hindustan（《印度斯坦报》） | 52397 | 印地语 |
| 3 | Amar Ujala（《永恒之光日报》） | 46094 | 印地语 |
| 4 | Dainik Bhaskar（《太阳日报》） | 45105 | 印地语 |
| 5 | Daily Thanthi（《每日电讯报》） | 23149 | 印度地方语言 |
| 6 | Lokmat（《人民力量报》） | 18066 | 印度地方语言 |
| 7 | Rajasthan Patrika（《拉贾斯坦报》） | 16326 | 印地语 |
| 8 | Malayala Manorama（D）（《美丽马拉雅拉报》） | 15999 | 印度地方语言 |
| 9 | Eenadu（《今日报》） | 15848 | 印度地方语言 |
| 10 | Prabhat Khabar（《黎明新闻报》） | 13492 | 印地语 |

---

① 唐璐：《印度媒体市场——不是想象的那样简单》，《对外传播》2010年第3期，第58页。

② 注：印地语及地方语言报纸在国内大多没有官方中文名，表格中的中文为作者译。

续表

| 排序 | 报纸名称 | 读者总量 | 语言 |
|---|---|---|---|
| 11 | The Times Of India（《印度时报》） | 13047 | 英语 |
| 12 | Ananda Bazar Patrika（《欢喜市场报》） | 12763 | 印度地方语言 |
| 13 | Punjab Kesari（《旁遮普雄狮报》） | 12232 | 印地语 |
| 14 | Dinakaran（《迪娜卡兰报》） | 12083 | 印度地方语言 |
| 15 | Mathrubhumi（《祖国报》） | 11848 | 印度地方语言 |
| 16 | Gujarat Samachar（《古吉拉特新闻报》） | 11784 | 印度地方语言 |
| 17 | Dinamalar（《新报》） | 11659 | 印度地方语言 |
| 18 | Daily Sakal（《萨卡尔日报》） | 10498 | 印度地方语言 |
| 19 | Sandesh（《桑德什报》） | 10352 | 印度地方语言 |
| 20 | Patrika（《期刊报》） | 9823 | 印地语 |

以印度纸媒为例，从印度媒体使用者研究委员会2017年发表的报告来看，从2014年[1]到2017年期间，印度纸媒的读者人数不降反增，主要增长在农村地区，城市地区则出现了阅读人数增加，阅读模式电子化的趋势，另外印地语受众的数量一直保持领先地位。我们分析出：2017年读者数量排名前20的日报中前四位均为印地语日报，依次为《觉醒日报》《印度斯坦报》《永恒之光报》和《太阳日报》，共有8家印地语日报进入了前

---

[1] 2014年印度媒体使用者研究委员会也曾发表过一份报告，因此2017年版本的报告是与2014年的数据对比写成。

20 日报排名；其他印度语种有 11 家日报进入了前 20 的行列，但读者总量不及印地语日报；英文日报只有《印度时报》一家以第 11 位进入了前 20 日报排名。可以说，在日报读者数量上以印地语为代表的印度语言日报占有绝对比重。

表2　印度媒体使用者委员会发布的 2017 年杂志读者量调查表（全语言）①

| 杂志名称 | 读者量 |
| --- | --- |
| India Today（英语）（《今日印度》） | 7992 |
| India Today（印地语）（《今日印度》） | 7159 |
| Samanya Gyan Darpan（印地语）（《常识之镜》） | 6882 |
| Vanitha（马拉雅兰语）（《瓦尼塔》） | 6126 |
| Pratiyogita Darpan（印地语）（《竞争之镜》） | 5924 |
| Meri Saheli（印地语）（《我的朋友》） | 4623 |
| Saras Salil（印地语）（《萨拉斯·萨利尔》） | 4318 |
| Bal Bhaskar（印地语）（《少年太阳》） | 3598 |
| General Knowlege Today（英语）（《今日普通知识》） | 3493 |
| Champak（印地语）（《香普卡》） | 3336 |
| Sarita（印地语）（《萨丽塔》） | 2958 |
| The Sportstar（英语）（《体育明星》） | 2937 |
| Cricket Samrat（印地语）（《板球大帝》） | 2920 |
| Diamond Cricket Today（印地语）（《今日钻石板球》） | 2809 |
| Grish Shobha（印地语）（《格里什·索巴》） | 2759 |
| Anada Vikatan（泰米尔语）（《阿南达·维卡丹》） | 2708 |
| Diamond Cricket Today（英语）（《今日钻石板球》） | 2549 |
| Grehlakshmi（印地语）（《格雷赫拉克什米》） | 2469 |
| Jagran Josh Plus（印地语）（《觉醒热情 plus》） | 2423 |
| Filmfare（双周刊）（英语）（《电影之旅》） | 2333 |

① 注：印地语及地方语言报纸在国内大多没有官方中文名，表格中的中文为作者译。

从印度媒体使用者委员会对印度杂志读者数量调查（见表2）可以看出，英语杂志呈现出了相较于日报更大的占比，排名前20位的印度杂志中有5家是英文杂志，印地语仍然以13家杂志的数量占最大比重。这也从一个侧面说明了杂志的订阅与民众的消费习惯是息息相关的，杂志要求订阅者拥有更高的消费能力，同时也说明了印地语媒体在印度媒体中重要的地位，就其受众数量而言，印地语媒体是占比最高的，是最能反映印度普通民众及部分中上层阶级关注点的印度语言媒体，也是我们总结印度媒体如何塑造中国形象过程中不可或缺的一环。

## 二、水中望月——印地语媒体中的中国形象

印度与中国同为亚洲发展大国、人口大国与新经济体，自古以来便有着悠久的往来历史，但目前与中国媒体相较而言，印度媒体更为关注中国的相关新闻。有学者分析："由于印度的英文媒体不像地方语言媒体那样拥有大量天然的读者群，它们的生存主要依靠广告，这使得英文平面媒体以及电视台之间争夺读者（观众）的市场竞争更为惨烈。"[1] 可见印度英文媒体受到商界因素深刻的影响，因此对中国报道较多。同时英文主流媒体的观点也代表着印度中产阶级及一些青年学生对时政外交的观察，特别是某些退休的政府官员、相关精英学者和经常参加电视台辩论节目的非政府层面学者的观点，他们大多对中国持有先疑后信的态度。

那么，在印度拥有最广泛的读者，但却在中国国内鲜为人知的印地语媒体的涉华报道都是以怎样的态度进行的呢？下面笔者将以印地语主流平面媒体罗列为经线，其报道的2018年内的涉华新闻为纬线，分析主流印地语媒体上中国相关报道的措辞，以勾勒出一个近期印地语媒体中的中国形象。

《印度斯坦报》的发行量虽不及《觉醒日报》，位居印度日报第二，但可以算得上印度老牌报纸之一，由圣雄甘地创刊，1932年开始发行，在印

---

[1] 唐璐：《中印媒体在消除彼此误读中的责任》，《对外传播》2010年第5期，第6页。

度有着广泛的知名度。虽然在1942年由于"退出印度"运动①停止发行了6个月，但其仍然对印度独立运动起到了极大的推动作用，该报纸经常刊登著名作家、革命斗士耶谢巴尔的小说，是圣雄甘地与国大党的坚定拥趸。

根据《印度斯坦报》对2018年4月28日习近平主席同印度总理莫迪在武汉举行非正式会晤的相关报道②，从新闻时效性上讲，比中国相关新闻的发布晚了一天；从报道内容上讲，该图片新闻《莫迪总理中国行图赏》主要报道了习近平主席与莫迪总理就边界问题、恐怖主义问题进行了商讨并达成一致，将携手反对恐怖主义，协力减少边境冲突，建立互信机制，加强经济、教育、娱乐等多方面的合作，加大双方电影引进力度，但并未直接谈及中国的共建"一带一路"倡议。新闻的最后一段总结道，印度总理莫迪与习近平主席的谈话是积极的，由此中印关系必将得到加强。我们可以看出《印度斯坦报》的基本态度是客观积极的，对莫迪总理访华给予了极大的关注并给出了相当的肯定，当然这在一定程度上与《印度斯坦报》与国大党紧密的联系是分不开的，因此该报的观点也在一定程度上代表了当前国大党的观点，具有很强的参考性。根据笔者在印度北方邦阿格拉留学期间的了解，该报对中国相关的报道一直持有积极态度，曾经专门针对中国留学生进行过专访，并在当地发行的《印度斯坦报》头版头条进行报道。

《觉醒日报》创办于印度独立斗争关键性的一年1942年，是北印度最受欢迎的日报，也是近年来印度发行量最大的报纸，同时被世界报业联盟认定为世界上阅读人数最多的报纸，在印度具有很大的影响力。

《觉醒日报》较为关注中国投资、军事和娱乐方面的消息，从表2检索结果可以看出，《觉醒日报》近期较为关注中美局势动态、中国航母下

---

① 1942年8月8日，甘地在孟买发表演说，为了让印度尽快获得独立，发起了"退出印度"运动，该运动以非暴力抵抗为行动指南，属于公民抗命运动的重要组成部分。但演说发表后不到24小时便遭到了英属印度当局的镇压，包括甘地在内的国大党主要领导人被送往国外监禁，国大党被禁止活动，运动转移到地下。

② 新闻来源于《印度斯坦报》官网，https：//www.livehindustan.com/photos/international/see-amazing-pics-of-pm-modi-in-china-1-1931021。

海、印度电影《巴霍巴利》在中国上映、中国万达集团投资在哈里亚纳邦碰壁等新闻,从发布时间上可以看出新闻的时效性并不高,而且该报纸因本身的读者定位广泛,更偏重娱乐等版面的报道,当然其中也有一些社评。关于莫迪总理访华,《觉醒日报》5月11日曾发布一篇社评《分析:中国应认识到印度的重要性,改善地缘政治环境》,内容核心是希望中国能意识到印度地位的重要性,认为中国没有给予印度应有的平等合作的地位。另外,该报对于中国万达集团在哈里亚纳邦投资失败的分析认为,哈里亚纳邦政府未能意识到引进中国投资的重要性。

除以上两种印地语主流报纸外,还有许多读者(观众)数量众多的印地语媒体,各自关注的领域也有相通之处,就不在此一一列举了。印地语媒体对印度民众,特别是北印度民众有着极大的影响力,是他们获取外界信息、形成中国形象的主要渠道。笔者在浏览各大印地语报纸涉华新闻报道的过程中,欣喜地发现印地语媒体对于中国形象的构建整体是"中偏积极"的,但是也有种"水中望月"之感,因为某些印地语媒体的报道并不完全贴合中国实际,其中也有许多新闻利用了印度民众对中国的好奇心,只是为了满足读者的猎奇需求。

## 三、再上层楼——全面客观把握印度媒体中的中国形象

随着中印近年来高层互访和民间交往的增多,中印关系的重要性日渐凸显。印度作为中国"搬不走的邻居",中印交往自西汉开始,并且随着佛教的传播和求法运动的盛行,到唐朝达到了一个黄金期。新中国成立后,印度是第一个与中国建交的非社会主义国家,中印关系经历了大起大落、波折不断,高耸的喜马拉雅山脉暂时阻隔了中印间的相互了解,但随着中印两国各自的发展,和平友好相处是时代发展的必然,也是两国互惠互利、携手共赢的基础。中印两国皆为文明古国、文化强国,但两国民众之间知之甚少,新闻报道也多为刻板印象,因而文化互通任重而道远,中印媒体间需要增进了解、加强互通互信。

印度媒体多语言的构成状态决定了我们必须"双线作战"甚至"多线作战",想要了解印度媒体中的中国形象,是无法做到"窥一斑而知全豹"

的，必须建立在多语言的基础上进行了解和分析，必须"再上层楼"，从更高更全面的角度去观察印度媒体。英语媒体与印地语媒体就像印度音响的左右声道，缺了任何一个，听到的声音都是不完整的，得到的信息也是不全面的。"一般而言，外界如果想了解印度人对外交问题的看法，应该研判印度英文报纸的观点，而要想真正理解印度政治，则需要阅读印度语言报纸。"① 印度媒体的这两种生态就是印度媒体的突出特点，也是我们在研究印度媒体涉华报道时绕不开的关键点。

目前，随着中印企业的交流互通，许多中国互联网企业进驻印度，比如说"UC 头条"和"今日头条"已经开始在印度搭建英语及印度语言手机新闻集成平台，这为我们将来更好地宣传和塑造中国形象提供了一个很好的平台。从英语单一语言到印英双语，是全面把握印度媒体中的中国形象的客观要求，在条件更完备的情况下，可以再适当了解孟加拉语、泰米尔语等别的印度语言，以求对印度涉华报道有更加全面的把握。

---

① 唐璐：《印度媒体市场——不是想象的那样简单》，《对外传播》2010 年第 3 期，第 58 页。

# 俄罗斯贫困治理的现状、举措及前景[*]

王梓凡[**]　游　涵[***]

**摘　要**：当前，贫困问题已成为全球的重要挑战之一。"益贫性"推进不足、社会不平等、贫困线制定标准存在争议、失业率升高、外部制裁挤压等众多因素构成了俄罗斯独特的贫困现状，制约着俄罗斯贫困治理的发展潜力。普京上任以来，通过推动经济发展、合理财富分配、优化贫困指标、促进就业、参与国际减贫合作等一系列措施加速推进贫困治理。在俄罗斯政府的政策推动下，贫困治理在贫困人口数量减少、贫困群体生存发展条件改善、风险防范能力提升等领域取得了明显进展。但与此同时，经济发展疲软、特殊社会群体排斥、环境保护与经济发展失衡、新冠疫情反复以及西方制裁将持续制约俄罗斯的减贫成效。

**关键词**：俄罗斯贫困；减贫；贫困治理

贫困问题是当今全球面临的重要挑战之一，大国博弈、新冠疫情、俄

---

[*] 本文系国家社科基金青年项目"中俄全球治理战略比较研究"（19CGJ021）的阶段性成果。
[**] 王梓凡，四川外国语大学比较制度学2021级研究生。
[***] 游涵，四川外国语大学国际关系学院副教授。

乌冲突等国际因素都使得各国经济陷入不同程度的衰退，造成了一系列社会问题，减贫成为推动全球可持续发展的核心内容，更是各国参与全球治理、推动全球治理体系朝着更加公正合理方向发展的重要举措。俄罗斯作为新兴经济体，欧亚地区最有影响力的国家之一，其贫困问题有自己的独特性，一方面它直接或间接源于苏联解体后国家的政治、经济转型，另一方面俄罗斯贫困问题也受本国经济发展、国际环境的影响。因此，反贫困对于俄罗斯在国内实现可持续发展、维持政治秩序稳定、解决一系列社会问题，为居民提供良好的生活品质，参与全球治理体系改革和建设具有重要的现实意义。尽管俄罗斯声称已战胜极端贫困，但是据俄联邦统计局数据，俄罗斯当今还有相当一部分人处于贫困线下，解决与消除贫困问题依然非常迫切。

自2018年起，俄罗斯总统普京就在历年的国情咨文中反复强调减贫的重要性，提出了要在2024年使俄罗斯贫困程度至少减半的目标，扩大推行试点地区的减贫政策，指出要将消除贫困作为地方官员的政绩评估指标。[①] 不仅如此，普京还多次强调国家需要更加敏锐地意识到贫困、高失业率等问题，强化社会保障，继续为多子女、孕期和单亲家庭提供资助，实施儿童和青少年成长援助政策，并要求政府在恢复劳动力市场、提高居民收入、消除贫困方面取得进展。[②] 从连续几年俄罗斯所传递出的信息中可见，贫困问题是俄罗斯社会当前仍需面对与解决的问题。本文聚焦于俄罗斯贫困问题，从国内和国际两个层面分析俄罗斯贫困的现状，评估俄罗斯贫困治理的成效，研究其面临的挑战。

---

① 刘博玲：《俄罗斯贫困问题：现状、特点与治理》，《俄罗斯东欧中亚研究》2020年第6期，第72—88页。

② "Владимир Путин принял участие в XVIII Ежегодном заседании Международного дискуссионного клуба 《Валдай》. Стенограмма пленарной сессии," Valdaiclub, сентября. 11, 2022, https://ru.valdaiclub.com/events/posts/articles/vladimir-putin-xviii-ezhegodnoe-zasedanie-mezhdunarodnogo-diskussionnogo-kluba-valday-stenogramma/?sphrase_id=538647#masha_0=1:1, 1: 1.

# 一、俄罗斯的贫困现状

贫困现象存在于俄罗斯社会中并随着时代的发展而不断地演变。从长远来看，贫困不是只存在于经济学范围的概念，探究当今俄罗斯所面对的贫困问题须基于发展角度。

## （一）俄罗斯"益贫性"推进不足

益贫式增长理论认为经济增长和更公平的收入分配制度相组合才能实现贫困快速下降[1]，反之则不然。俄罗斯经济长期呈现产业结构单一的问题，且受世界疫情、西方制裁、战争冲突等外部冲击，经济发展不稳定、增长不足。2022年第二季度俄罗斯的国内生产总值（GDP）仅为34666亿卢布，与2021年同期相比，实际GDP下降了4.1%，平减指数相应增长了17.0%。由于最终消费支出下降4.1%和总积累下降13.8%，所以国内最终需求下降了6.4%。消费减少的原因是人民的购买力下降[2]，其直接导致的后果是国内经济发展减缓、人口问题不断加深、贫困问题加剧。[3] 据俄罗斯统计局数据，2022年第一季度，俄罗斯的贫困线为12916卢布，2090万人收入低于贫困线，占总人口的14.3%，同比增加了10万人，贫困率增长的主要原因是通货膨胀超过了人均收入的增长。[4] 据俄经济发展部预

---

[1] 张庆红：《益贫式增长的内涵及其实现路径：一个文献综述》，《新疆财经大学学报》2014年第3期，第5—12页。

[2] "Комментарий к оценке ВВП методом использования доходов и методом формирования по источникам доходов за II квартал 2022 года," Rosstat, сентября. 28, 2022, https://rosstat.gov.ru/folder/313/document/182915.

[3] Снимщикова И. В., Шамраи К. Е., "Некоторые аспекты обеспечения эконо-мическои безопасности России ской Федерации//Институциональные тренды транс-формации социально-экономической системы в условиях глобальнои нестабильности," Краснодар, 2021, pp. 432–438.

[4] "Росстат представляет информацию о границе бедности в I квартале 2022 года," Rosstat, сентября. 28, 2022, https://rosstat.gov.ru/folder/313/document/168756.

测，2022年俄居民人均可支配收入将下降6.8%，实际工资收入下降3.8%[1]，同时，鉴于俄罗斯于2001年对个人所得税由累进税率改为13%的单一税率，致使穷人的税负实际上高于富人，居民收入高度分化。[2] 因此，经济发展的不稳定以及其收入分配制度的不完善导致益贫性增长不足，贫困出现一种持续性特征。

**（二）俄罗斯的贫困问题存在巨大的社会不平等**

第一，贫富差距巨大。俄罗斯的收入不平等首先在其转型时期加剧，1998年经济危机爆发后达到顶峰，随后在1998年至2015年期间逐渐减少。[3] 然而这一差距的减少并未完全实现社会平等，2022年基于俄罗斯联邦统计局的数据，国际审计和咨询公司Fin Expertiza进行了一项调查研究，按照2021年的居民月收入水平由低到高将其分别放入5个组中，研究结果显示，2021年所有俄罗斯人的平均月收入为4万卢布。其中，最不富裕的俄罗斯人（第1组）在2021年的月平均收入为1.08万卢布，第2组为2.03万卢布，第3组为3.03万卢布，第4组为4.54万卢布，而最富裕的俄罗斯人（第5组）的月平均收入为9.35万卢布。最富裕和最贫困群体之间的收入相差达到了8.6倍，第5组人群的收入占全俄人口总收入的46.7%。而第1组人群的收入只占全俄人口总收入的5.4%。[4] 俄罗斯中产阶级比例仅为7%[5]，这显示出俄罗斯社会贫富差距巨大的现状。不仅如

---

[1] 《俄经发部预测俄居民实际可支配收入情况》，中国商务部，2022年9月3日，http://ru.mofcom.gov.cn/article/jmxw/202205/20220503313035.shtml。

[2] 郭连成、史元：《俄罗斯收入分配问题评析》，《财经问题研究》2021年第1期，第114—122页。

[3] Lisina A, Van Kerm P, "Understanding Twenty Years of Inequality and Poverty Trends in Russia," Review of Income and Wealth, Vol. 68, No. 1, 2022, pp. 108 – 130.

[4] 《俄贫富收入差距相差8.6倍 2022年会有所好转吗?》，《俄罗斯龙报》，2022年6月1日，http://www.dragonnewsru.com/static/content/home/headlines_home/2022-06-01/981635395177820160.html。

[5] Снимщикова И. В., Шамраи К. Е., "Некоторые аспекты обеспечения эконо-мической безопасности РоссийскойФедерации // Институциональные тренды транс-формации социально-экономической системы в условиях глобальной нестабильности," Краснодар, 2021, pp. 432 – 438.

此，民意也对俄罗斯所存在的收入差距鸿沟有所不满，2022年5月，全俄民意研究中心调查了1600名超过18岁的俄罗斯人，调查结果显示超过一半的俄罗斯人（55%）都认为国家应该缩小居民收入差距。①

第二，行业间的工资差异和某些经济活动的低工资是致贫的主要原因。②在俄罗斯社会中，"在业穷人"现象同样是一个尖锐的问题，低工资水平不能使相当数量的俄罗斯劳动者脱贫，对单亲家庭、多子女家庭而言，情况更是如此。尽管俄罗斯有很多人都在工作，但他们的收入却很低，甚至处于最低生活保障水平以下。③俄新社基于俄联邦统计局的数据计算了俄罗斯各个行业的收入中位数后发现，若从某些产业来看，中层员工月薪可达5万甚至6万卢布，再到收入较低的行业，中位数则不足2.5万卢布。指标最高行业的收入中位数（"采矿业"为6.5万卢布）是最低行业（"轻工业"为2.05万卢布）的三倍。④

第三，贫困人口年龄差异明显。截至2022年1月1日俄罗斯联邦统计局的数据显示，俄罗斯人均最低生活费为12654卢布，健全人口为13793卢布，养老金领取者为10882卢布，儿童为12274卢布。⑤可见，俄罗斯领取养老金的老人和儿童都没有达到人均最低生活费的标准，在贫困群体中，儿童的比率比俄罗斯总人口中儿童所占比例高1.5倍不止，低收入群体的增长主要是由于家中孩子数量众多。⑥而2013—2018年，由于俄罗斯老龄化问题严重，养老基金赤字额由17910亿卢布升至24791亿卢布，累

---

① 《民调：55%的俄罗斯人赞成国家缩小居民收入差距》，俄罗斯卫星通讯社，2022年10月12日，https://sputniknews.cn/20220621/1042059249.html。

② 李春雨：《论现代化过程中贫困的结构性前提——以俄罗斯为例》，《理论与现代化》2017年第2期，第24—30页。

③ 刁秀华：《俄罗斯贫富分化问题》，《俄罗斯学刊》2021年第6期，第59—72页。

④ 《调查：中等水平的俄罗斯人月收入为3.5万卢布》，俄罗斯卫星通讯社，2020年8月3日，https://sputniknews.cn/20200803/1031887957.html。

⑤ "Кабмин внес в Думу проект об увеличении прожиточного минимума в 2023 году до 14375 рублей," Tass, октября. 02, 2022, https://tass.ru/obschestvo/15897239？.

⑥ K. Goulin、张超：《俄罗斯居民的不平等和贫困问题》，《江西社会科学》2012年第9期，第247—248页。

计增长38.4%，其占俄罗斯GDP的比重由2.45%升至2.99%①，由此可见俄罗斯贫困人口中儿童和领取养老金的老人构成了贫困人口的主力军。

第四，贫困人口的地区分布不均。由于俄罗斯丰富的油气等自然资源分布并不均衡，因此，油气资源丰富的地区发展较好，经济总量较高，居民生活水平相对较高。同时，城乡之间也存在着贫富差距，如莫斯科和圣彼得堡的城市居民与贫穷的农村人口收入相比也有巨大的鸿沟。俄新社使用联邦统计局的数据计算居民收入中位数，发现2019年全俄人均月收入中位数与固定商品及服务成本的平均比值为1.65，全俄共有65个区域处于该平均水平以下，20个区域高于平均水平。其中，亚马尔—涅涅茨自治区排名第一，其次为北部另外的一个油气区，即涅涅茨自治区，而排名第三的莫斯科市，在这个指标上比排名第一的要落后将近30%。排在最后（第85位）的图瓦共和国，其指标只有0.97，还有四个区域的指数处于1.0—1.1区间。在全俄共有15个区，该指标不高于1.3。②

### （三）俄罗斯存在着贫困线的制定标准争议

俄罗斯将贫困线一般称为"最低生活保障"或"最低消费篮子"，消费篮子的总价值是基于俄罗斯国家统计局发布的食品、非食品商品和服务的消费者价格水平确立的，最低生活水平和贫困率是政府减贫政策的核心参考点。然而，俄罗斯的贫困线面临众多批评声音，一是最低生活水平设置过低，没有反映日常生活的实际成本③；二是贫困指标未充分考虑，如房租、服务消费等都未涵盖，如果加上这些指标，俄罗斯的贫困人口还将会有大量的增加。④ 西方学者认为，俄罗斯的贫困线之所以这样设定，是因为当贫困被定义为绝对门槛时可以一定程度上掩盖俄罗斯社会的不平等

---

① 田雅琼：《老龄化背景下俄罗斯养老保障资金筹集问题研究》，中央财经大学博士论文2020年，第113—115页。

② "Названы российские регионы с самым высоким уровнем бедности," Ria, октября. 23, 2022, https://ria.ru/20200706/1573926441.html.

③ Martin Brand, "The OECD poverty rate: Lessons from the Russian case," Global Social Policy, Vol. 21, No. 01, 2021, pp. 144–147.

④ 马蔚云：《俄罗斯贫困线：基本概念与测定方法》，《俄罗斯东欧中亚研究》2008年第5期，第26—32页。

或收入和财富分配不均等方面的问题。[①]

### (四) 失业率上升导致家庭贫困

俄罗斯科学院院士及解体后第一任总统的经济顾问阿让别扬在2022年8月接受俄罗斯"商业在线"采访时表示,俄罗斯失业率将增加一倍,其中还包括了隐性失业。从社会层面来说,一方面,由于阶层各种形式的社会排斥,缺乏就业稳定性的蓝领工人和包括单亲家庭在内的有孩子的家庭陷入极端和永久贫困的风险更高。[②] 另一方面,近年来,由于各自社会人口因素使部分俄罗斯民众陷入低收入贫困和剥夺式贫困的风险之中,性别因素、婚姻状况、抚养负担、健康状况以及居住地类型等都表明了俄罗斯贫困群体的社会人口特征与个人在劳动力市场的地位有关。[③] 除此之外,近年来除受外部因素的制约外,俄罗斯自身的科技潜力开发不足,传统能源行业面临挑战以及精英流失导致人力资源质量愈加恶化[④],尽管目前的失业率估计为3.8%,但俄媒称俄罗斯实际失业人数至少超过官方数字一倍。[⑤] 同时俄经济发展部还预测了2022年俄失业率至年底将升至6.7%,2025年才将恢复至2021年水平(4.8%)。[⑥]

### (五) 制裁挤压造成俄罗斯贫困问题加剧

从2014年乌克兰危机到2022年俄乌冲突的爆发,西方国家对俄罗斯实施了一系列经济制裁,领域从工业和农业产品到石油和天然气等能源战

---

[①] Martin Brand, "The OECD poverty rate: Lessons from the Russian case," Global Social Policy, Vol. 21, No. 01, 2021, pp. 144 – 147.

[②] Yaroshenko, S, "'New' Poverty in Russia After Socialism," Laboratorium: Russian Review of Social Research, Vol. 02, No. 02, 2012, pp. 221 – 251.

[③] 刘春怡:《俄罗斯贫困阶层的特征与分布》,《人民论坛》2017年第11期,第110—111页。

[④] 冯玉军:《俄罗斯经济的政治社会根源及国家发展前景》,《欧亚经济》2022年第1期,第1—11页。

[⑤] 《研究:俄罗斯失业率可能达到12%》,俄罗斯卫星通讯社,2022年10月16日,https://sputniknews.cn/20201001/1032239907.html。

[⑥] 《2022年俄失业率将升至》,中国商务部,2022年10月6日,http://ru.mofcom.gov.cn/article/jmxw/202205/20220503313033.shtml。

略部门，再到生活日用如婴幼儿奶粉和洗护用品①，甚至包括关闭领空②、科技封锁，导致俄罗斯经济收入减少数百亿卢布，相应的大量岗位失业增加，致使经济发展不可避免地陷入低迷。③《独立报》的负责人劳达莱斯在接受采访时指出，"西方对俄罗斯的制裁在全世界都能感受到，燃料和原材料价格上涨将导致全球贫困加剧。许多家庭将失去购买基本食物的能力，变得更加贫困和饥饿"④。

面对西方针对俄罗斯经济和军事长期的制裁与俄乌冲突的持续，俄罗斯显然把过多资源投入军事、外交领域，导致其挤占了减贫治理的空间。"据俄罗斯官方数据显示，2022年其国防预算上调约为9.2%，达到864亿美元。然而，斯德哥尔摩国际和平研究所认为这一数字仅占俄国防全年估值的78%。其中，仅"动员与额外兵力训练"专项拨款就高达2.45亿美元，较2021年同比增长约119%"。⑤ 财政面临巨额赤字的风险，进而减缓了减贫的步伐。

回顾探究俄罗斯贫困的演变发现，俄罗斯在进入社会转型期之后由于不平等的加剧和经济的猛衰加剧了卢布的通货膨胀，社会的失业率剧增，国内生产总值下滑。普京执政的两个任期内，俄罗斯贫困问题有所缓解，但是近年来，由于国际国内因素的双重影响，以及一些历史遗留问题尚未得到解决，俄罗斯当今社会存在一种"新"的贫困现象。

## 二、俄罗斯的贫困治理举措

面对贫困问题，俄罗斯政府在促进经济发展、合理财富分配、优化贫

---

① 徐坡岭：《美欧制裁压力下俄罗斯经济的韧性、根源及未来方向》，《俄罗斯学刊》2022年第4期，第22—47页。

② 《俄旅行社协会：俄旅游业因西方领空关闭损失数百亿卢布》，俄罗斯卫星通讯社，2022年10月15日，https://sputniknews.cn/20220722/1042644623.html。

③ 姜振军：《西方制裁与疫情叠加冲击下俄罗斯经济发展态势分析》，《西伯利亚研究》2022年第4期，第21—32页。

④ 《萨尔瓦多左派领导人：对俄制裁导致世界贫困加剧》，俄罗斯卫星通讯社，2022年4月2日，https://sputniknews.cn/20220402/1040446422.html。

⑤ "Trends in World Military Expenditure," 2022, Stockholm International Peace Research Institute, April, 2023, p.5.

困指标、促进就业上采取了一系列措施，并积极参与国际减贫合作。

## （一）推进经济"益贫式"增长

俄罗斯通过促进经济发展和调整收入分配制度两种有效途径来改善"益贫性"不足的问题。俄罗斯的贫困问题根本在于国家经济发展迟缓，因此需要减轻经济发展负担，治理国家腐败问题。俄罗斯不断制定和完善《国家反腐计划》，从立法的层面治理根植于俄罗斯经济运行和发展模式之中的顽疾[1]；还需要强化经济发展的韧性，俄罗斯近年来高度重视数字经济发展，调整经济结构和经济增长方式。自2016年起俄罗斯通过《俄联邦信息社会发展战略（2017—2030）》《2024年前俄联邦发展国家目标和战略任务》等文件提出了制定数字经济计划的任务[2]。除此之外，俄罗斯当局也出台大量的人才引进政策，例如，《2009—2013年创新俄罗斯科技及教育人才联邦专项计划》[3]、2014年"俄联邦青年人才支持措施"[4] 等法令都在一定程度上起到培养青年科创人才、吸引留学人员归国，进而促进国家经济的创新发展，以此实现经济可持续发展的作用。而在调整收入分配机制方面，利西纳和科姆两位学者则研究了在1994—2015年期间俄罗斯收入分配发生的显著改变，发现俄罗斯收入分配改变的主要来源是私营部门收入分散减少、养老金和公共部门收入水平增加。[5] 此外，俄罗斯在居民收入分配制度改革中也把调整个人所得税作为一项重要步骤，并实施了可以缩小居民收入差距的税收政策[6]，这些举措一定程度上使贫困人口从经济增长中间接获益，进而推动了贫困率的下降。

---

[1] 孙祁：《俄罗斯反腐新动向》，《检察风云》2021年第10期，第58—59页。
[2] 蓝庆新、汪春雨、尼古拉：《俄罗斯数字经济发展与中俄数字经济合作面临的新挑战》，《东北亚论坛》2022年第5期，第111—126页。
[3] 黎思佳：《俄罗斯政府的科技人才政策》，《中国科技信息》2013年第6期，第118页。
[4] "О мерах государственной поддержки талантливой молодёжи," normativ. kontur, октября 07, 2022, https://normativ.kontur.ru/document?moduleId=1&documentId=235515.
[5] Lisina A, Van Kerm P, "Understanding Twenty Years of Inequality and Poverty Trends in Russia," Review of Income and Wealth, Vol. 68, No. 1, 2022, pp. 108-130.
[6] 郭连成、史元：《俄罗斯收入分配问题评析》，《财经问题研究》2021年第1期，第114—122页。

## （二）调节贫富差距

第一，在行业间工资差异大的问题上，俄罗斯通过制定法律保障来缓解社会收入的不平等。俄罗斯根据宪法和劳动法出台多部法案提高最低工资标准，如《俄罗斯联邦劳动法典》中规定职工的劳动报酬不得低于国家规定的最低劳动报酬标准，[1] 又相继出台《俄罗斯联邦最低劳动报酬法》。普京于2020年还签署了关于修改最低生活费的联邦法（2020年12月29日第473-FZ号），规定2021年的法定最低工资标准，为月收入12792卢布（约合1115.21元人民币），较上一年提高5.5%。

第二，在贫困人口年龄差异明显的问题上，俄罗斯重点通过对老年人和儿童这两大贫困群体的帮扶来提高福利保障水平。在老龄化日益加剧的背景下，俄罗斯逐渐形成了"三支柱"的新型养老保障体系，分为国家养老金、强制性养老保险与个人自愿养老保险这三个不同层级的保障模式[2]，并于2022年6月1日起将俄罗斯最低工资标准、最低生活保障标准和无工作老人养老金上调10%。因此无工作养老金领取者的养老金平均将增长到19360卢布。[3] 在治理儿童贫困问题上，普京在2020年向联邦议会发表的国情咨文中强调国家对有孩子的家庭的支持将得到加强，规定国家将根据特定地区儿童的最低生活水平支付低收入家庭每月一孩和二孩的津贴[4]，并于2022年进一步修订政府决议，每月向3至8岁儿童提供补贴，并为8

---

[1] "Трудовой Кодекс Российской Федерации," Normativ. kontur, декабря31, 2001, https://normativ.kontur.ru/document?moduleId=1&documentId=454527.

[2] 田雅琼：《老龄化背景下俄罗斯养老保障资金筹集问题研究》，中央财经大学博士论文2020年，第57页。

[3] "Правительство проиндексировало пенсии, прожиточный минимум и минимальный размер оплаты труда на 10%," Government, октября. 02, 2022, http://government.ru/news/45559/.

[4] "Колесник А. П. Информационная система для мониторинга и управления материальным положением семей в Российской Федерации, предотвращения попадания их в состояние бедности и контроля за выведением из бедности (экосистема семья)," Стратегии бизнеса, No. 7, 2020, pp. 11-13.

至 17 岁的儿童分配每月福利①，对多子女家庭提供更多扶助。

第三，在贫困人口的地区分布不均的问题上，俄罗斯通过拨款资助、推动农村青年职业教育、提供法律医疗援助等行动来发展贫困地区经济。②例如 2022 年 6 月 4 日第 1435 - r 号命令，要求向一些地区如汉特—曼西、亚马洛—涅涅茨自治区以及达吉斯坦共和国等拨款超过 56 亿卢布③以推动当地经济发展，并为当地失业青年进行职业培训，为农村地区提供软贷款、法律和医疗援助以及小企业的支持计划④，都在一定程度上缓解了地区贫富不均问题。

### （三）优化贫困指标

自 2005 年起俄罗斯就由各联邦主体自主确定贫困线。国家杜马于 2006 年通过了《全俄罗斯消费篮子计划》政府法案，规定增加俄罗斯每月人均食品消费支出、文化服务消费品等指标⑤，以此完善贫困线的制定。除此之外，俄罗斯联邦统计局依据 2021 年 11 月 26 日俄罗斯联邦政府第 2049 号法令引入"基本贫困线"初始值、俄罗斯人均货币收入计算而得的"贫困率"、与家庭收入比较计算后所得的"贫困线"等指标，并规定俄罗斯联邦的整体贫困数据须每季度更新一次，各联邦主体则每年确定一次，这使得贫困指标的评估更加精细化、准确化。⑥

---

① "Правительство расширило доступ к социальной поддержке для семей с детьми," government，сентября30，2022，http：//government. ru/news/45303/.

② 李春雨：《论现代化过程中贫困的结构性前提——以俄罗斯为例》，《理论与现代化》2017 年第 2 期，第 24—30 页。

③ "Правительство направит ещё более 5，6 млрд рублей для выплат на детей от 3 до 7 лет," government，октября02，2022，http：//government. ru/news/45625/.

④ Ржаницына Л. С.，"Москва Как снизить бедность в России," Журнал новой экономической ассоциации，Vol. 2，No. 18，2013，pp. 180 – 183.

⑤ 马蔚云：《俄罗斯贫困线：基本概念与测定方法》，《俄罗斯东欧中亚研究》2008 年第 5 期，第 26—32 页。

⑥ "Об утверждении Правил определения границ бедности в целом по Российской Федерации и по субъектам Российской Федерации, используемых в оценках показателя "Уровень бедности" в целом по Российской Федерации и по субъектам Российской Федерации, и о внесении изменений в Федеральный план статистических рабо," publication. pravo，Ноября 26，2021，http：//publication. pravo. gov. ru/Document/View/0001202111270008.

## （四）政策保障提高就业率

为稳定劳动市场，俄罗斯早在 1991 年 4 月 19 日便颁布了《俄罗斯联邦居民就业法》，该法令迄今为止经历了 55 次修订，以保障包括青年、残疾人和妇女等最不受就业保护的人群实现充分就业。[①] 为充分刺激就业，俄罗斯启动多项"计划"创造工作岗位。俄罗斯联邦政府总理米哈伊尔·米舒斯京表示，2021 年 3 月"俄罗斯联邦北极地区社会经济发展"国家计划[②]的实施已创造数万个新的就业机会，增加了人民收入。与此同时，俄总理还在政府会议上表示，2022 年俄政府将划拨约 400 亿卢布（约合 3.8 亿美元）实施一系列保就业措施，其中，超过 255 亿卢布（约合 2.4 亿美元）用于为俄地方面临失业风险的公民设立临时就业岗位，以及为在就业中心登记求职人员提供公共服务工作岗位，预计 40 万人可获得上述支持。[③]

## （五）加强国际合作

贫困作为世界面临的共同挑战，近年来已被纳入全球治理的研究领域并逐渐成为全球议事日程的核心。俄罗斯积极参与推进中国提出的全球发展倡议，包括参与联合国平台"全球发展倡议之友小组"活动，与中方共同呼吁将减贫作为国际社会的重点合作领域，支持将贫困治理合作纳入金砖国家、上海合作组织、欧亚经济联盟的核心议程中，因而俄罗斯已经成为全球贫困治理的重要参与者和推动者，发挥了重振多边主义的重要作用。面对西方制裁，俄罗斯主动扩大与亚非拉国家互动来改善本国经济，同时这也将有利于促进亚非拉国家的经济发展。例如南非国防和退伍军人部部长莫迪塞表示，"在发展方面俄罗斯有潜力进行投资，成为合作伙伴，

---

[①] 朴金顺：《〈俄罗斯联邦居民就业法〉（前四章）翻译实践报告》，延边大学硕士学位论文 2021 年，第 1 页。

[②] 《俄罗斯政府批准〈北极地区社会经济发展国家计划〉》，中国海洋发展研究中心，2021 年 4 月 8 日，http://aoc.ouc.edu.cn/2021/0415/c9829a319182/pagem.htm。

[③] 《俄政府将划拨 400 亿卢布保就业》，中国商务部，2022 年 3 月 23 日，http://ru.mofcom.gov.cn/article/jmxw/202203/20220303289282.shtml。

与非洲国家的合作将有助于减少非洲大陆的贫困,并促进其发展"①。

## 三、俄罗斯的贫困治理前景

俄罗斯贫困问题在政府的努力治理下,得到了极大改善,取得了一系列建设性的成果。首先,贫困人口大量减少。自2019年到2021年底,俄罗斯贫困人口从1810万人减少至1610万人,年均减少100万人,贫困率从12.3%下降至11%。其次,贫困人群的生存发展条件得到改善。一方面,通过改革个税制度、增加民众收入、调整最低生活保障线、上调养老金,以及对有孩子家庭保障金的支持等福利政策使得贫困群体的生活获得保障。② 另一方面,政府的就业帮扶政策提升了贫困人群的脱贫能力。2022年第一季度的就业人口达到7150万人,同比增加了1.0%,平均名义应计工资为60101卢布,同比增长15.0%。③ 最后,贫困的风险防范能力提升。例如在2020年新冠疫情的影响下,世界银行的专家分析认为,俄罗斯政府的扶持措施令贫困率未因疫情出现大规模的反弹。塞利格曼指出:"根据2020年GDP下降4%的预测,2020年可能有14.2%的人口在官方贫困线以下,而当局的补救措施让该数字降到11.6%。"2020年贫困率与疫情暴发前预测的水平相当或稍低,这说明俄罗斯有关贫困治理的措施达到了目的。"俄罗斯的扶持措施规模与可比经济体相当,社会保障措施的组合彰显成效,没有让贫困因危机而增加。"④

尽管取得一系列建设性成果,但俄罗斯经济发展疲软、社会问题以及环境保护与经济发展的权衡等所引起的一系列贫困问题尚未消退。此外,近年来新冠病毒蔓延、西方对俄制裁加剧以及俄乌冲突的爆发对俄罗斯的

---

① 《南非国防部:俄罗斯在非洲国家的发展中发挥重要作用》,俄罗斯卫星通讯社,2022年8月17日,https://sputniknews.cn/20220817/1043120859.html。

② 《俄统计局:俄贫困率出现下降》,俄罗斯卫星通讯社,2021年4月15日,https://sputniknews.cn/20210415/1033488230.html。

③ "Росстат представляет информацию о границе бедности в I квартале 2022 года," Rosstat, сентября 03, 2022, https://rosstat.gov.ru/folder/313/document/168756。

④ 《世行:俄罗斯政府的扶持措施令贫困率未因疫情反弹》,俄罗斯卫星通讯社,2020年12月16日,https://sputniknews.cn/20201216/1032728783.html。

经济造成了巨大的冲击，对减贫工作造成了一定的威胁，俄罗斯的减贫事业仍旧面临众多挑战。

第一，俄罗斯经济发展疲软。俄罗斯的经济发展模式固化，长期面临产业单一、制造业竞争力低下、劳动生产率低、组织弱、科技开发不足等问题，而近年来又遭遇西方的技术封锁制裁，恐长久制约俄罗斯的经济发展。① 俄罗斯金融机构 Finam 集团宏观经济分析部负责人奥尔加·别连卡娅表示，贫困治理的挑战或与贫困地区经济潜力开发不足有关，她指出，"从战略上来看，重要的是要开发这些地区的生产潜力，建造必要的基础设施以更好地利用其自然资源和后勤优势"。②

第二，社会问题形成反贫困的挑战。首先，俄罗斯的社会排外情绪导致外来劳务融入困难。外来劳动力一定程度上解决了俄罗斯的人口问题，并为其带来了大量的适龄劳动力，但是许多俄罗斯人仍然认为，外来劳动力将导致犯罪率上升、腐败加剧、劳动力市场竞争日益激烈等负面效应。③ 其次，社会对俄罗斯北方贫困农村的排斥造成了地区贫困治理的困境。自然环境恶劣、地理位置偏远、公共投入不足等多重因素造成北方农村贫困地区经济、社会和空间上的孤立，形成了地区贫困综合征。再次，俄罗斯社会存在女性排斥问题。许多女性不仅承担家庭供养责任，还负责家务劳动，因此多从事低收入的工作，女性常常因性别和社会排斥而就业困难。④ 最后，由于国内大量的精英正在加速外流到西方发达国家，劳动市场将进一步呈现严峻的势态。对外来劳务、北方贫困农村、妇女的社会排斥以及精英外流都阻碍了俄罗斯劳动力市场的发展，激发社会矛盾，提升了贫困

---

① Богданова В. П., Родионова С. Д., "Факторы российской бедности," Современные проблемы науки и образования, Vol. 1, No. 1, 2015, p. 1494.
② 《俄贫富收入差距相差 8.6 倍 2022 年会有所好转吗？》，《俄罗斯龙报》，2022 年 6 月 1 日，http://www.dragonnewsru.com/static/content/home/headlines_home/2022-06-01/981635395177820160.html.
③ 宋志芹、蒲晨晨：《俄罗斯外来劳务移民发展的现状及影响》，《欧亚人文研究》（中俄文）2022 年第 3 期，第 21—32 页。
④ Ярошенко, Светлана Владимировна, "Женская занятость в условиях гендерного и социального исключения," Социологический журнал, No. 3, 2002, pp. 137–150.

治理的难度。①

第三，环境保护与经济发展的权衡也对俄罗斯减贫构成新挑战。全球气候变化所导致的干旱、洪水和森林大火等自然灾害频发，给俄罗斯社会和经济造成重大损害，致使俄罗斯对能源转型的立场发生了动摇。低碳转型将是俄罗斯未来发展的重点方向之一，但出于当前俄罗斯经济过于依赖化石能源的现实，实现碳中和将致使俄罗斯经济发展陷入困境，进而影响贫困治理。② 俄罗斯卫星通讯社援引俄罗斯专家们在"各种形式的碳定价对减少温室气体排放和社会经济发展的影响"报告中的观点指出，2030年俄罗斯碳价将达每吨10美元，到2050年增加到每吨50美元，这将使GDP年均增长率降低1.5个百分点。因此俄罗斯的碳监管可能导致经济增长放缓、通货膨胀和失业率加剧、投资减少，最终可能伴随贫困率上升。③

第四，疫情之下全球减贫的不确定性增加。新冠疫情暴发以来，各国经济发展受到严重阻碍，社会贫富差距进一步拉大，全球绝对贫困人口激增。同时，新冠疫情封锁扰乱了国际贸易，世贸组织发布贸易数据预测时表示将2022年商品贸易量的增长预期从4.7%下调至3%。④ 因此，新冠疫情造成了国际贸易的前景黯淡，这可能导致世界新的原材料短缺和更高的通货膨胀。疫情给俄罗斯本已不稳定的经济发展带来严重的负面冲击，不仅使俄罗斯"突破性增长"和"投资新周期"计划被迫搁置，疫情长期化的发展还使得居民消费储蓄倾向改变以及能源行情持续低迷。⑤

第五，制裁加剧俄罗斯贫困问题。俄乌冲突后美欧对俄罗斯发起了一

---

① Ярошенко, Светлана Владимировна, "Женская занятость в условиях гендерного и социального исключения," Социологический журнал, No. 3, 2002, pp. 137–150.
② 刘乾:《低碳转型背景下俄罗斯能源行业面临的挑战》，《欧亚经济》2022年第1期，第12—26页。
③ 《俄专家：俄罗斯碳监管政策或导致贫困和价格上涨，但放弃将更糟》，俄罗斯卫星通讯社，2022年7月15日，https://sputniknews.cn/20220715/1042512623.html。
④ "Russia – Ukraine Conflict Puts Fragile Global Trade Recovery at Risk," WTO, April 12, 2022, https://www.wto.org/english/news_e/pres22_e/pr902_e.htm.
⑤ 徐坡岭：《新冠肺炎疫情对俄罗斯经济的影响：抗疫反危机措施、经济运行状况与增长前景》，《新疆财经》2020年第4期，第57—68页。

系列范围更广、规模更大的制裁[1]，大批跨国公司都带着产品和服务撤出了俄罗斯，大量工作岗位被削减，失业率增高，并且由于卢布贬值，俄罗斯公民的购买力和生计大幅下降，俄罗斯将面对与国际金融体系迅速且广泛的脱钩所带来的困难。从长远来看，美西方的制裁将对俄罗斯经济造成严重冲击，进而影响俄罗斯的反贫困发展。

总的来看，俄罗斯经济发展的不稳定性影响了减贫效应，社会排斥、环境保护与经济发展的权衡等一系列问题都是其减贫所面临的重要挑战，而疫情和西方世界的制裁则加大了减贫的不确定性。俄罗斯的脱贫之路还很长，俄罗斯需要调整其发展战略，争取实现减贫效应的最大化。

---

[1] 陈文林、吕蕴谋、赵宏图：《西方对俄能源制裁特点、影响及启示》，《国际石油经济》2022年第9期，第1—10页。

# 新时代中国与金砖国家深化人文交流的路径思考

游雨频[*]

**摘　要**：人文交流已成为金砖国家政治、经济、人文"三轮驱动"合作机制中的关键一环，巩固和深化金砖国家在人文交流领域的合作对建设持久稳定的金砖国家伙伴关系具有重要意义。现有研究对中外人文交流的理论与相关实践已有较充分的讨论，本文主要聚焦中国深化与金砖国家人文交流的两大要素——主体与领域，在描述现状与不足的基础上，提出有助于深化金砖成员国之间人文交流的新路径和新举措。

**关键词**：金砖国家；人文交流；路径

## 一、引言

2021年9月9日，习近平主席出席金砖国家领导人第十三次会晤并发表题为《携手金砖合作应对共同挑战》的讲话。在讲话中，习近平主席倡议金砖国家坚持互学互鉴，加强人文交流合作，以推动金砖务实合作朝着

---

[*] 游雨频，四川外国语大学西方语言文化学院葡萄牙语专业教师，澳门大学葡文系硕士，主要从事葡汉翻译和葡语国家相关研究。

更高质量方向前进。①从2013年3月习近平作为中国国家主席首次出席金砖国家领导人第五次会晤至今，习近平主席对推动金砖五国人文交流的重视与期许始终如一。这不仅因为人文交流已成为金砖国家政治、经济、人文"三轮驱动"合作机制的关键一环②，也因为"国之交在于民相亲"，巩固和深化金砖国家在人文交流领域的合作对建设与发展持久而稳定的金砖国家伙伴关系具有重要意义。

当前国际形势复杂多变，地区局势变幻动荡，百年未有之大变局导致各种矛盾错综交织，唱衰金砖的各种言论和观点也时有所闻。③ 2021年是"金砖国家"概念提出二十周年，这一概念所构建的"金砖"政治身份和共同利益决定了金砖国家深化务实合作的共识不会改变，"金砖"的价值与潜力不容置疑。然而毋庸讳言，相比政治联系和经贸往来，人文交流仍是当前金砖国家合作的短板，面临基础薄弱、进展缓慢、各国参与不平衡、机制建设不完善等诸多问题与挑战。因此，必须充分认识当前国际环境下坚持深化金砖国家人文交流合作对于推动金砖各国高质量务实合作不可或缺的作用。2022年中国接棒印度担任金砖国家轮值主席国。在新时代、新形势下，中国如何以身作则，为推动中国与金砖国家人文交流的制度创新、方法创新和内容创新提出中国方案，为增强金砖国家人文交流领域的广度、厚度和深度贡献中国智慧，为百年未有之大变局和新冠疫情影响下的金砖国家人文交流合作注入中国活力，是我们当下需要认真思考、谨慎作答的问题。

现有研究对中外人文交流的理论与实践已有较为充分的讨论④，从宏观

---

① 《习近平在金砖国家领导人第十三次会晤上的讲话》，中国政府网，2021年9月10日，http://www.gov.cn/xinwen/2021-09/10/content_5636527.htm。
② 吴兵、刘洪宇：《金砖国家人文交流的进展、挑战与路径》，《当代世界》2019年第12期，第26—32页。
③ "Twenty years on, the Brics have disappointed," Financial Times, November 29, 2021, https://www.ft.com/content/034ba0e7-7518-437e-854c-7c0dd5d74e34.
④ 有关中外人文交流理论与实践的新近讨论可见张骥、邢丽菊主编：《百年未有之大变局与中外人文交流》，世界知识出版社2021年版。

层面探讨金砖国家人文交流合作机制建设的研究也较常见[①],本书中亦有专门的章节讨论当前金砖国家人文交流面临的困难与阻碍。有鉴于此,本文将主要围绕中国与金砖国家深化人文交流合作的两大要素——主体与领域,在描述现状与不足的基础上,尝试提出一些有助于中国深化与金砖成员国之间人文交流的新路径和新举措。

## 二、推动金砖国家人文交流主体多元化

随着中国继续坚定不移扩大对外开放,传统意义上的单一人文交流模式显然已无法充分满足新形势的要求。既然中国的对外开放是全方位的,那么中国开展人文交流的主体也应当是多元化的。因此,实现新时代中国与金砖国家人文交流的"提质增效",必须坚定不移地推动人文交流主体的多元化,必须在发挥好高层引领的示范作用、利用好顶层设计的指导作用的同时,真正做到人文交流的重心下移,通过充分调动地方力量、民间力量、海外力量等一切可以调动的力量,引导和鼓励更多主体参与到中国与金砖国家的人文交流活动中来,形成全方位、全社会合力。在此过程中,应当着重选择具有巨大人文交流潜力的主体,探索中国深化与金砖国家人文交流的新思路、新模式、新作为。各级政府则需要加强对多元主体参与金砖国家人文交流的政策引导、平台搭建和资源整合,为推动金砖国家人文交流主体的日益多元化创造条件、提供支持与保障。

具体而言,新时代有意愿、有能力在中国深化与金砖国家人文交流的过程中扮演"主角"的主体主要包括:"出海"的中国企业,"在地"的华人华侨,从事国际学术交流的中国学者,与金砖国家缔结了友好城市关系的中国城市以及中国的青年一代。

### (一)中国企业的人文交流角色

根据商务部国际贸易经济合作研究院、商务部对外投资和经济合作司

---

① 代表性研究例如蒲公英:《金砖国家人文交流合作机制分析》,《俄罗斯东欧中亚研究》2017年第4期,第46—56页;徐秀军:《金砖国家人文交流机制建设:作用、挑战及对策》,《当代世界》2018年第8期,第26—29页。

等相关机构编撰的中国《对外投资合作国别（地区）指南》等相关研究，中国与巴西2020年双边贸易额已达1190.40亿美元，中国企业在巴投资规模不断扩大，目前涉及石油、电力、新能源、基础设施、农业、制造业、通信、电子商务等众多领域，中国企业同年在巴新签承包工程合同77份，新签合同额达32.50亿美元，完成营业额高达16.37亿美元。[1]中国与南非2020年双边贸易额则接近360亿美元，中国对南非直接投资存量现位列非洲首位，南非已成为中资企业非洲区域总部的首选之地，顺丰快递、滴滴打车等中国知名企业已落地南非。[2]据商务部统计，2019年中国企业在印度新签承包工程合同209份，新签合同额51.73亿美元，完成营业额25.39亿美元，累计派出各类劳务人员1419人，年末在印劳务人员2073人。[3]中国与俄罗斯2019年贸易额达1107.9亿美元，中国企业在俄新签承包工程合同160份，新签合同额169.18亿美元，完成营业额27.67亿美元，累计派出各类劳务人员3486人，年末在俄罗斯联邦劳务人员6694人。[4]

毫无疑问，中国企业在金砖国家进行跨国投资和经营过程中，实际上已成为代表中国的国际组织，不仅承担着促进金砖国家经贸"互联互通"的建设任务，也承担了推动中国人民与金砖国家人民"民心相通"的人文交流职责。同时，中国企业在金砖国家的茁壮成长和可喜成就，本身就是中国故事的重要素材。另外，中国企业的"出海"之路绝非一帆风顺，它们在金砖国家的项目往往涉及基础设施建设、能源和信息技术等高敏感领域，因此其正常的经济活动经常成为部分西方媒体对华负面关注和不实报道的重点，甚至被冠以所谓的"新殖民主义"称号，严重影响中国企业海外业务的正常开展。因此，中国企业积极参与人文交流，讲好自己的中国故事，也是自身发展的内在需求。换言之，中国在金砖国家经营投资的企

---

[1] 《对外投资合作国别（地区）指南：巴西（2024年版）》，商务部网站，http://www.mofcom.gov.cn/dl/gbdqzn/upload/baxi.pdf.

[2] 《对外投资合作国别（地区）指南：南非（2024年版）》，商务部网站，http://www.mofcom.gov.cn/dl/gbdqzn/upload/nanfei.pdf.

[3] 《对外投资合作国别（地区）指南：印度（2024年版）》，商务部网站，http://www.mofcom.gov.cn/dl/gbdqzn/upload/yindu.pdf.

[4] 《对外投资合作国别（地区）指南：俄罗斯（2024年版）》，商务部网站，http://www.mofcom.gov.cn/dl/gbdqzn/upload/eluosi.pdf.

业通过发挥人文交流的主体作用，不仅有利于提升企业形象和中国的国际形象，也有助于增进中国企业与金砖各国人民之间的相互认知与了解，减少或消除误解与偏见，在确保工程项目顺利实施的同时，塑造区域文化认同和价值认同，最终提升中国企业在金砖国家经济活动的合法性和支持度。

因此，深化中国与金砖国家人文交流，必须发掘中国企业的人文交流潜力，唤醒中国企业对外讲好中国故事、参与人文交流的主体意识。在此过程中，相关政府部门应当有意识地针对中国在金砖国家的企业开展多样化、全方位的培训，通过形成完整的企业培训机制，帮助中国企业在"出海"过程中逐渐成长为中国对外人文交流最有力的国际生力军。①当前中国在金砖国家开展人文交流仍面临积极性与参与度较低，企业投入不足，交流对象错位，以及尚未形成常态化人文交流机制与互动模式等问题。因此，建议金砖国家的中资企业和相关民间组织，在政府参与协调和提供一定保障的情况下，积极发挥人文交流的主体作用，根据自身经营的实际需求，主动寻找或自主搭建以当地人民为主要对象的交流平台，同时积极参与当地的各类社会公益活动，通过成立金砖国家人文交流企业基金会等形式，探索中国企业"现身说法"参与金砖国家人文交流的新模式。

### （二）华侨华人的人文交流角色

2018年，时任巴西总统特梅尔签署法令，正式将每年8月15日设立为巴西"中国移民日"，该纪念日的设立不仅体现了巴西各界对华侨华人200多年拼搏奉献的认可、对发展中巴关系的高度重视，也体现了中巴两国人民的深情厚谊，体现出巴西华侨华人社会地位的提高。②据相关统计与估算，目前中国在巴西的华侨华人数量为30万左右③，巴西已成为仅次于

---

① 王文：《后疫情时代的中外人文交流：机遇与挑战》，载张骥、邢丽菊主编：《百年未有之大变局与中外人文交流》，世界知识出版社2021年版，第62页。
② 《东西问丨中国前外交官刘正勤：巴西缘何设立"中国移民日"?》，中国新闻网，2021年10月15日，https://www.chinanews.com.cn/gn/2021/10-15/9587365.shtml。
③ 束长生：《巴西华侨华人研究文献综述与人口统计》，《华侨华人历史研究》2018年第1期，第36页。需要指出的是，巴西华侨华人的人口精确统计一直是困扰研究者的难题，因此本文的相关数据是基于现有研究的合理推算。

秘鲁的南美华侨华人第二大聚居地。根据中国华侨华人研究所最新出版的《世界侨情报告（2021）》，俄罗斯境内目前约有15万中国公民，持长期居住证在俄的中国公民有3600多人，留学生大概2.7万人[1]，俄罗斯华侨华人总数在35万人左右。根据相关统计，南非华侨华人总数在30万人左右[2]，南非同时也是拥有最大规模华侨华人社团的非洲国家。由于各种原因，印度的华侨华人数量一直较少，据不完全统计，在印华侨华人总数不足万人。由此可见，中国在金砖四国的华侨华人总数可观，广大华侨华人能够在推动人文交流、增进金砖各国民心相通上发挥更大作用。

国家间人文交流的开展需要广泛的社会基础。金砖五国社会文明形态和文化习惯各具特色，各国民生民情中的复杂性与差异性往往成为深入开展人文交流的阻碍。随着华人华侨在金砖国家人数的增长以及经济实力和社会地位的不断提高，他们对于推动中国与金砖国家人文交流具有不可替代的优势。华人华侨本身就是中华文化的载体，更是中国形象在金砖国家的代言人和塑造者，对于在金砖四国传播中华文化和讲好中国故事、促进金砖国家人文交流和民间外交具有巨大潜力。因此，深化中国与金砖国家人文交流，必须发挥华人华侨的人文交流作用与影响，引导并鼓励他们利用其特殊的"在地"主体身份，积极参与和塑造中国与金砖国家的人文交流。

有鉴于此，相关部门与各地政府在开展侨务工作中，应积极推动在金砖国家的华侨华人发挥人文交流纽带作用，鼓励他们发挥自身横跨不同文明的独特桥梁作用，把人文交流的主体意识主动融入"在地"生活和工作中，用所在国和地区的语言与当地民众和政府沟通交流，以当地人民的文化习俗和思维习惯讲述金砖国家人民能够听懂的中国故事。在此过程中，民间人文交流应当成为主要途径，当地的华侨华人团体应当成为交流活动的主要载体，通过"以民促官"丰富金砖国家人文交流的内涵。同时，在发掘海外侨胞参与人文交流的潜力过程中，应当注重维系他们与祖国的血

---

[1] 王祎：《2020年俄罗斯侨情分析》，载张春旺、张秀明主编：《世界侨情报告（2021）》，社会科学文献出版社2022年版，第167页。

[2] 吕挺：《非洲华侨华人新移民教育需求分析与供给模式探索》，载贾益民主编：《华侨华人研究报告（2016）》，社会科学文献出版社2017年版，第260页。

脉联系，尤其需要增进他们与新时代中国的现实接触，增加他们对新时代祖国发展成就的感性认识，唯此才可能真正增强金砖国家华侨华人主动服务人文交流的意愿。

### （三）中国学者的人文交流角色

学术研究被视为"最具深度和使命感的人文交流和文明对话方式"[1]，从事学术研究的学者因此在人文交流活动中也扮演着重要角色。就增进金砖国家对华认知、科学系统地向金砖国家人民讲述中国新时代发展故事的意义而言，中国的学者不仅是对外人文交流的一线参与者，也是新时代深化与金砖国家人文交流的重要突破口。[2]另外，中国学者通过开展金砖国家研究，不仅能以知识生产的方式为政治、经贸、人文等领域的广泛交流与合作提供知识供给和理论支撑，而且对增进金砖五国相互的认知和理解、夯实金砖人文交流的基础，也具有不可忽视的推动作用。

中国高度重视金砖国家研究，目前国内已有一批发展迅速、各有特色的金砖国家研究机构，分布在相关高校和政府部门。然而现阶段的中国金砖研究国际化的程度还有待提高，中国学者的声音和成果在金砖国家传播的速度与力度还远远不够。由于语言和学术研究模式等差异，来自金砖国家的学者与他们的中国同行之间学术交流的频度和程度都尚有不足，尤其在信息共享、经验交流和合作研究等方面还有较大提升空间。新冠疫情的全球蔓延更加阻隔了金砖国家之间的现实学术交流，极大增加了中国学者到金砖各国实地考察调研、开展田野调查的难度。中国学者如何在新形势下充分发挥自身作为人文交流主体的作用，提升学术层面金砖人文交流的质与量，是中国在深化与金砖国家人文交流过程中必须认真思考的问题。

为切实推进金砖国家学术交流，充分调动和发挥中国学者参与金砖国家人文交流的主体作用，增进中国学者与金砖国家同行的学术互动与交流，建议构建"金砖国家学术共同体"，推动中国的金砖国家研究与俄罗

---

[1] 张凡等：《中国与拉美：软实力视域下的人文交流》，朝华出版社2020年版，第162页。
[2] 黄昊等：《学术领域中外高级别人文交流机制中的模式构建研究》，载张骥、邢丽菊主编：《百年未有之大变局与中外人文交流》，世界知识出版社2021年版，第121页。

斯、印度、南非和巴西四国的中国研究融合发展。"金砖国家学术共同体"的构建不仅能够有力拓展中国对金砖国家研究的内涵与外延，而且能够快速提升中国学者开展金砖研究国际化的程度。一旦"金砖国家学术共同体"形成常态化的交流机制，金砖国家内部研究资源的交换与共享则有望实现。此外，打造"金砖国家学术共同体"事实上是探索中国与金砖国家在学术交流层面的实质性合作关系，有助于提升金砖国家整体的学术话语权，突破西方学术话语霸权。为鼓励中国学者积极参与金砖国家人文交流，建议在学术考核和奖励机制等方面提高国际化相关指标的权重，以此鼓励中国学者"走出去"，到金砖国家参加学术研讨会、发表文章和接受媒体采访，以更具说服力和权威性的人文交流主体身份发出中国声音、讲好中国故事。同时，"金砖国家学术共同体"应当吸引更多金砖国家的学者到中国来开展"在地"研究，相关机构和高校应当为此设立专门的项目和奖金，鼓励他们扎根中国、实地研究。

必须指出，近年来我国越发重视金砖国家智库的建设与交流工作，原因在于发挥智库的专业优势和协作效应，有利于服务金砖国家决策与合作的开展。因此，主要由学者和研究人员构成、专职为政府部门提供政策咨询的智库，也应被视作一种特殊而重要的人文交流主体。事实上，随着金砖国家合作的全面深化，金砖国家智库之间交流与合作的机制也在不断发展与演进。[1]在深化与金砖国家人文交流的过程中，应当重视智库对金砖国家合作的智力支持，尤其是需要有关完善金砖国家人文交流机制、增进金砖国家战略互信等方面的建议与举措。

### （四）友好城市的人文交流角色

在中国对外开放的新时代，城市作为外交主体的地位与角色日益重要，城市外交的兴起可以说正在重塑国家间人文交流的路径与渠道。作为一种独特的外交主体，城市外交是在中央政府的授权和指导下，具体由某一具备合法身份和代表能力的城市当局及其附属机构，出于谋求城市安

---

[1] 蒲公英：《金砖国家人文交流合作机制分析》，《俄罗斯东欧中亚研究》2017年第4期，第49页。

全、繁荣和价值等目的，与其他国家的官方和非官方机构围绕非主权事务所开展的制度化的交流活动。[1]换言之，作为外交主体的城市因其天生具备的"次政府"性质，在对外交往中往往更容易发挥人文交流的桥梁和纽带作用。在具体实践中，作为人文交流重要主体的城市越发受到重视。2014年5月，国家主席习近平在中国人民对外友好协会成立60周年纪念活动上首次使用了"城市外交"一词。截至2024年，中国已同世界上147个国家缔结了3054对友好城市。作为金砖国家领导人会晤的配套活动，金砖国家友好城市暨地方政府合作论坛自2011年在海南三亚首次举办以来，已成为金砖国家成员加强城市间合作、推动人文交流的重要舞台。2011年以来，中国与其他金砖四国以每年10对以上的频率建立起城市友好关系。[2]由此可见，友好城市作为金砖国家人文交流的特殊主体，既是对现有金砖国家人文交流机制的有益补充，也能为推动金砖国家人文交流向纵深发展提供有力支撑。

在不断深化中国与金砖国家友好城市合作与交流的过程中，不仅需要以各种方式和活动保持城与城、人与人之间交流的热度，还需要挖掘金砖国家友好城市交流的潜力，尤其需要增强与金砖国家建立了友城关系的中国城市作为人文交流主体的活力，切实提升友城人文交流的质量。2021年，《金砖国家领导人第十三次会晤新德里宣言》肯定了金砖国家在应对城市发展新挑战方面取得的进展，着重强调了智慧城市研讨会、城镇化论坛、友好城市暨地方政府合作论坛等活动在深化金砖国家人文交流中的作用。[3]在继续开展金砖国家友好城市常态化交流和合作之外，有必要充分利用城市外交的优势，挖掘中国与金砖国家友好城市在地方文化特色上的共同之处、互补之处，开展重点领域和空白领域的合作，尤其在新冠疫情背景下注重发展友好城市之间的"云交往"与数字化合作。在友好城市个体

---

[1] 赵可金、陈维：《城市外交：探寻全球都市的外交角色》，《外交评论》2013年第6期，第69页。

[2] 《金砖五国友好城市与地方政府共同发布"成都倡议"》，新华网，2017年7月13日，http://www.xinhuanet.com//world/2017-07/13/c_1121315796.htm。

[3] 《金砖国家领导人第十三次会晤新德里宣言》，中国政府网，2021年9月10日，http://www.gov.cn/xinwen/2021-09/10/content_5636528.htm。

交往基础上，需要更好发挥金砖国家城市之间类型、规模、资源的互通性与互补性，扩大友城"朋友圈"，逐步形成金砖国家友好城市"人文交流群"，真正实现人文交流规模化发展和共享式成长。在此过程中，应当鼓励国内各级地方政府增强主体意识，不断完善金砖国家友城间的联络与对话机制，通过互设办事处、办公室等方式，加强友城之间的跨国沟通，建立内外联动的友城人文交流互动机制，从制度保障上切实提升金砖国家友城关系质量，同时通过友城间的务实合作，为助推金砖国家人文交流贡献城市力量、城市智慧。

### （五）青年一代的人文交流角色

青年兴则世界兴，青年强则世界强。青年一代不仅是金砖国家参与全球治理和解决全球问题的生力军，也是推动各国文明互鉴和文化交流的主力军。作为新时代最富朝气和创造力的群体，青年一代能够为金砖五国探索人文交流的新路径提供新思路，为深化金砖国家人文交流作出新贡献，同时也能从中受益、提升自我。目前，金砖国家青年交流已形成以金砖国家青年外交官论坛、金砖国家青年峰会、金砖国家青年部长会、金砖国家青年创新创业合作伙伴关系以及金砖国家科学家论坛等为代表的常态化机制，这无疑有助于从培养未来领袖的角度发挥青年一代在形塑金砖国家发展前景上的关键作用。然而总体看来，青年一代在参与和推动中国与金砖国家人文交流的进程中发挥的主体作用仍然相对较小，影响力仍然较弱。随着金砖国家人文交流的不断深入，金砖国家青年势必会对参与和引领人文交流产生更强的需求。有鉴于此，有必要高度重视青年一代在深化金砖国家人文交流过程中的主体作用，在帮助广大青年树立"主人翁"意识的同时，创新金砖国家青年人文交流渠道，充分发挥青年一代在金砖各国文明互鉴、民心互通中的桥梁与纽带作用。

要更充分发挥青年参与和推动中国与金砖国家人文交流的主体角色，首先要增加金砖国家青年之间的相互认知与了解，尤其需要增加金砖国家青年对新时代中国发展的客观真实交流，这就需要切实增进中国与金砖国家青年之间的实质接触与交流。为此，有必要投入更多资源支持金砖国家青年留学互访项目，并通过培育"金砖青年看中国""金砖青年中国行"

"金砖青年文化嘉年华"以及金砖青年研修班、夏令营等人文交流项目，吸引更多金砖国家青年来华留学和访学，亲身体验中国发展、感受中国文化。另外，应当鼓励中国青年一代不断拓宽自身全球视野、参与金砖国家间的文明对话与互鉴，加大力度培养熟练掌握金砖国家语言、熟谙金砖国家文化习俗的复合型国际化青年人才，推动中国青年到金砖国家和人民中去，用他们的语言和方式传播中国青年好声音。需要注意的是，青年创新创业已经成为金砖国家青年追求理想抱负、实现人生价值的重要途径，因此应当利用各国青年来华创业的发展机遇，创造性发挥青年创新创业对深化中国与金砖国家人文交流的正向引导作用，以"润物细无声"的方式，将人文交流融入青年创新创业活动中去，在帮助金砖国家青年把握新时代中国发展机遇的同时，增进彼此交流和相互理解。

## 三、拓展金砖国家人文交流领域新内涵

随着人文交流在金砖国家合作中的地位与作用得到显著提升，金砖国家人文交流涉及的领域也在不断增多，各成员国对于不同领域人文交流的成效与收获也有了新的期待。本节将结合金砖国家人文交流的最新发展趋势，从教育、科技、文化、体育四大人文交流领域的发展现状入手，探讨在深化金砖国家人文交流过程中推动上述领域内涵式发展的新思路和新举措。

### （一）教育领域的人文交流

教育领域向来是金砖国家开展人文交流与合作的重点领域，这不仅因为金砖各国在教育领域的合作起步较早、互补性强，也因为教育交流与合作内涵丰富、前景广阔。迄今为止，金砖五国已成功构建了以金砖国家教育部长会议为代表的高级别、高层次人文交流机制，通过《北京教育宣言》等一系列部长宣言构筑了金砖五国深化教育合作的共识，还打造了金砖国家大学联盟、金砖国家网络大学等高等教育多边合作机制以及金砖国家—教科文组织集团等教育领域的常设机制。可以说，金砖国家在教育领域的人文交流取得了丰硕的合作成果，合作的形式和内容都可圈可点，教

育合作已成为金砖人文交流的"金字招牌"。在新冠疫情的特殊形势下，深化中国与金砖国家在教育领域的人文交流，必须完善机制建设，坚持共建共享，深挖合作潜力，充实合作内涵。事实上，能否切实拓展教育领域人文交流的内涵，将成为金砖国家打造第二个"金色十年"的关键。

习近平主席在金砖国家领导人第十三次会晤上的讲话中提出倡议，建立金砖国家职业教育联盟，举办职业技能大赛，并为五国职业院校和企业搭建交流合作平台，[1]这表明金砖国家在教育领域的人文交流正在由高等教育向职业教育延展，职业教育和相关技能培训将会成为后疫情时期金砖教育合作的新方向与新热点。为响应习近平主席倡议，切实推动金砖国家在职业教育与技能方面的内涵式发展，应加强金砖国家职校师生的互访交流与实习实训基地建设，通过搭建开放包容的职教互联互通平台，提升金砖国家职业院校国际化办学水平和国际核心竞争力。[2]此外，应当聚焦金砖各国职业教育的优势领域，在共建共享和互补互利等原则指导下，开展多边务实合作，推动中国与金砖国家合作培养更多高水平、高技能职业人才，鼓励金砖国家间共享职业教育发展成果与宝贵经验。在拓展职业教育合作内涵的过程中，金砖国家可借鉴鲁班工坊等具有代表性的职业教育国际化办学品牌和平台的成功经验，注重打造职业教育合作的金砖国家间品牌，以带动金砖国家间职业教育的海外办学实践创新，为推动金砖国家间服务各自产业发展和产能合作培养更多优秀的职业技能人才。[3]

同时，金砖国家在教育领域的人文交流应当以坚持开放包容、超越文化差异为核心，聚焦推动全球教育治理、实现教育公平、提升教育品质和国际化程度等合作重点，利用现有机制平台开展更为广泛深入的教育合作，在凝心聚力应对全球性教育挑战的同时，加强金砖国家间的相互认同与协作，以此实现真正的民心相通。作为推动金砖国家人文交流的中坚力

---

[1] 《习近平在金砖国家领导人第十三次会晤上的讲话》，中国政府网，2021年9月10日，http://www.gov.cn/xinwen/2021-09/10/content_5636527.htm。
[2] 《2021中国—印度职业教育合作研讨会成功举办》，中国教育国际交流协会网站，2021年12月29日，http://www.ceaie.edu.cn/dist/#/detail?id=1574594141592018945&active=news。
[3] 《全国政协委员金永伟：打造职业教育国际化品牌》，鲁班工坊网站，2022年3月9日，http://www.lubanworkshop.cn/html/2022/rmgf-lb_0309/426.html。

量,中国应积极营造有利于深化金砖国家教育合作的政策环境,鼓励国内相关高校参与金砖国家教育联盟,升级与金砖国家现有教育合作的层次,推动金砖国家人才培养的多边合作,促进金砖国家间在人员互访、学术交流、科研合作等多领域的创新合作,尤其要注重培养掌握金砖国家语言的国际组织复合型人才和涉外复合型人才,让金砖国家间的师生与教育领袖在频繁交流、定期沟通中增进相互理解与认知。

### (二) 科技领域的人文交流

科技领域人文交流的主要目的,在于通过人员互动、学术合作、科研攻关、政策协调等一系列活动,扩大国家之间民意友善的基础,在提升科技水平的同时增强政治互信,进而对国家间总体关系产生积极影响。[1]由此可见,科技人文交流是金砖国家人文交流中不可或缺的重要组成部分。正如金砖国家领导人在新德里宣言中所指出的,金砖成员国研究人员开展科技创新合作、共同应对新挑战十分重要,为推动金砖国家科技进步和促进成员国之间相互信任创造了有利条件。[2]经过十余年的发展,金砖国家科技人文交流已经初步形成了以金砖国家科技创新部长级会议为主要机制、以《金砖国家科技创新活动计划》为行动方案的交流框架,并在科技人文交流等方面取得了丰硕的成果。例如2021年10月由中国科学技术交流中心主办的金砖国家科普论坛,正是为了落实2020年第八届金砖国家科技创新部长级会议通过的《金砖国家科技创新活动计划(2020—2021年)》的具体举措。[3]最新的《金砖国家创新合作行动计划(2021—2024年)》已于2021年11月在第九届金砖国家科技创新部长级会议上通过。[4]从长远来看,以开放、创新和互利为主要特征的科技合作潜力巨大,必然能在深化中国

---

[1] 毛瑞鹏:《新型大国关系构建中的中美科技人文交流》,载张骥、邢丽菊主编:《百年未有之大变局与中外人文交流》,世界知识出版社2021年版,第181页。
[2]《金砖国家领导人第十三次会晤新德里宣言》,中国政府网,2021年9月10日,http://www.gov.cn/xinwen/2021-09/10/content_5636528.htm。
[3]《30名中方代表参加金砖国家科普论坛》,科技部网站,2021年10月22日,http://www.most.gov.cn/kjbgz/202110/t20211022_177433.html。
[4]《科技部副部长张广军出席第九届金砖国家科技创新部长级会议》,科技部网站,2021年11月30日,http://www.most.gov.cn/kjbgz/202111/t20211130_178263.html。

与金砖国家人文交流的进程中发挥更强大的支撑与引领作用,让科技创新成果通过人文交流惠及金砖国家间和人民。

加强科技创新合作既体现了金砖国家间合力应对全球挑战的共同意愿,也为中国充实与金砖国家人文交流的内涵指明了方向。在共商、共建、共享理念指引下,中国应围绕全球挑战下科技创新的动力与需求,推动完善金砖国家科技伙伴关系网络,助力构建多维度金砖国家科技交流体系,同时聚焦金砖国家间的科技优先发展领域,深化与金砖国家在科学传播、科普推广、科技服务等方面的交流合作。此外,应当推动金砖国家更全面地融入全球科技治理体系,加强中国与重要国际科技组织的合作交流,尤其是通过民间科技交流渠道服务以联合国为核心的全球多边治理体系。中国应与金砖国家加强在医药卫生、清洁能源、航空航天等前沿领域的交流合作,并推动构建金砖国家科学技术转移协作网络。中国还应通过设立金砖国家科技人员交流计划、继续举办金砖国家青年科学家论坛、打造金砖科技创新孵化平台等一系列务实举措,推动金砖国家科技人才交流互访,同时组织"金砖科技人才中国行"等相关活动,为推动金砖国家优秀科技人才来华交流和从事研究搭建服务平台。

### (三)文化领域的人文交流

文化领域的交流与合作从来都是金砖国家人文交流的重中之重,这不仅因为国与国、人与人之间的理解和尊重首先来自不同文化之间的好奇与相互欣赏,也因为文化领域的交流对话究其性质而言,是与人文交流本身最为契合的。在金砖国家文化部长会议等高级别、高层次机制的引领下,金砖国家人文交流在文化、文艺等领域蓬勃发展。在《金砖国家政府间文化合作协定》以及相关行动计划的指引下,中国与金砖国家以文化遗产保护、民间艺术交流、创意经济发展为重点,以金砖国家博物馆、美术馆、图书馆等专业机构联盟以及金砖国家电影节等文化活动为抓手,在文化领域开展了全方位、多层次、宽领域的务实合作,通过文化交往编织起了民心相通的友好纽带。①事实上，在新冠疫情和全球形势不确定的大背景下，通过文化领域深化中国与金砖国家人文交流的作用与重要意义正日益凸显。正如里约热内卢联邦大学教授安德烈·海勒-洛佩兹一针见血指出的，"在当前的新形势下，文化是我们的唯一出路，因为只有文化与艺术才能够恒久地唤醒我们的人性。我们要继续巩固金砖国家之间的文化纽带，同舟共济，携手与共"②。因此，新时代中国深化与金砖国家人文交流，必须充分挖掘文化领域的巨大潜力，尤其是丰富文化合作的形式与内涵，用丰富多彩、引人入胜的文化交流夯实金砖国家人文交流的民意基础。

为推动金砖国家在文化等相关领域的人文交流，不仅需要继续举办各类有声有色的常规性、常态化人文交流活动，还需要创造性地充实金砖国家文化交流的内涵。具体而言，中国应充分利用电影、电视、文学、音乐以及新媒体等金砖国家人民喜闻乐见的文化产品和艺术形式，从不同题材、不同维度探索文化交流的内容与表现形式，借助文艺作品的共情力，激发金砖国家间人民的文化共鸣感。应当利用网络和社交平台等新兴传播媒介，缩短金砖国家间人民体验对方文化的距离感，让文化直指人心。应当鼓励金砖国家间在传媒和传播领域的合作与资源共享，加速文化产品在各国的流通，同时支持文创人员跨国跨界合作，产出更多诸如《时间去哪儿了》《半边天》等的文化作品。中国还应当进一步推动金砖国家间的传统文化合作与世界遗产旅游合作，开发金砖特色旅游路线，推动金砖文旅合作再上新台阶。此外，有必要在金砖国家内部设立更多类似北京俄罗斯文化中心的文化中心，作为承载和推进各成员国人文交流活动、有效推介本国文化的重要平台，以此在对象国树立本国的良好形象，夯实两国人民之间的心灵沟通基础。

---

① 《金砖国家召开第六届文化部长视频会议》，文旅部网站，2021年7月6日，https://www.mct.gov.cn/whzx/whyw/202107/t20210706_926239.htm。

② "BRICS em perspectiva: Intercâmbios culturais e interpessoais, o estado da Arte," Coordenadoria de Estudos da Ásia da Universidade Federal de Pernambuco, 22 de junho de 2021, https://ceasiaufpe.com.br/?p=2648。

## （四）体育领域的人文交流

以中国为首的金砖国家对举办世界性的体育盛会并不陌生，尤其是两次北京奥运会，更是极大促进了中国与世界各国的人文交流。体育一直是金砖国家开展人文交流的重要领域。从 2017 年 6 月首届金砖国家运动会在广州举行至今，以金砖国家运动会为代表的金砖国家体育领域友好合作已取得丰硕成果，金砖国家体育交流已从双边向多边、从单一比赛向综合赛事延展。竞技场上的同场切磋与竞技，不仅体现了"开放、包容、合作、共赢"的金砖国家合作伙伴精神，也增进了金砖国家间人民的友谊、拉近了情感，为推动金砖国家人文交流发挥了积极独特的作用。在深化中国与金砖国家人文交流的过程中，应当鼓励金砖国家间在体育领域开展形式更加广泛、内涵更加丰富的合作。众所周知，足球是中国体育"永远的痛"，而夺得世界杯足球赛冠军最多的巴西则被誉为"足球王国"，两国在足球领域合作、开展人文交流的潜力可谓巨大。正如拉娜——曾经的女子足球世界冠军和现在的巴西中巴足球交流中心副主席所观察到的，"中国目前正在大力发展足球，特别是足球青训和校园足球。巴西作为世界足球强国，可以帮助中国培养高水平教练，并将巴西领先的青训体系引入到中国。中国有巨大的足球市场，并且在足球领域进行了大规模投资，与中国的合作可以帮助巴西足球获得更多的国际资金支持"[1]。由此可见，中国与巴西等金砖国家在体育领域开展人文交流互补性极强，具有巨大的挖掘潜力。

2020 年 8 月，金砖国家举行了首次部长级会晤，并通过了合作谅解备忘录。在深化金砖国家人文交流合作的过程中，中国将与金砖各国在谅解备忘录的框架下加强体育合作，落实好金砖国家领导人就加强体育交流达成的重要共识，促进金砖国家民心相通。[2] 未来中国与金砖国家有必要加强

---

[1] 《拉紧人文交流纽带 筑牢金砖合作第三支柱——来自金砖国家人文交流论坛的声音》，光明日报网，2019 年 12 月 3 日，https：//epaper.gmw.cn/gmrb/html/2019 - 12/03/nw.D110000gmrb_20191203_1 - 07.htm。

[2] 《金砖国家体育部长会通过合作谅解备忘录》，搜狐网，2020 年 8 月 25 日，https：//www.sohu.com/a/414874138_267106。

体育领域的机制化合作和交流，在足球、橄榄球、曲棍球、花样游泳、艺术体操以及冰雪运动等关键体育领域开展更广泛、更深入的合作，同时加大金砖国家运动员交流互访的支持力度，推动武术等中国传统体育竞技项目在金砖国家的传播与开展。

## 四、结语

当今全球面临百年未有之大变局，世界各国间的关系也正在发生重大变化。"明者因时而变，知者随事而制。"越是在国家间合作阻力增大、交流面临困境的时候，越是需要我们加强人文交流，"需要不同文化体之间加强沟通的力度、拓宽沟通的渠道，不断加强共识、建构认同"。[1]金砖国家人文交流在不同文化、不同语言、不同地域中进行，金砖国家之间组织开展人文交流的体制与机制不可避免存在差异，各国对人文交流活动的效果与影响也各有期待。然而，无论面对什么样的困难和挑战，只要金砖国家间能够做到顺时而变、顺势而为，坚持不懈推动金砖国家人文交流的深化与进展，推动人类命运共同体的构建，金砖国家人文交流就一定能够行稳致远，在新时代焕发新的生机与活力，点亮金砖国家合作共赢的未来！

---

[1] 秦亚青：《百年变局与新型文化间关系》，载张骥、邢丽菊主编：《百年未有之大变局与中外人文交流》，世界知识出版社2021年版，第7页。

# 金砖国家命运共同体的构建：
## 基于危机管理理论的视角

张 庆* 陈 果** 孙昊洋***

**摘 要**：危机管理理论为构建金砖国家命运共同体提供了独到见解。鉴于危机管理可被划分为危机前预防、危机处置和危机后应对三个阶段，因此在各个阶段都应做出相应的努力。在危机前预防阶段，我们必须着重于内部准备及外部立场的协调。在危机处置阶段，需要通过强大的领导力与凝聚力来协调内部的思想和行动，而外部努力应聚焦于争取其他利益相关方的支持。危机后的应对包括通过对危机的回顾来加强内部学习，以及在外部环境中塑造积极的社会评价，从而达成更广泛、更高层次的共识。从这一视角来看，危机管理的三个阶段性要求与金砖国家构建命运共同体的多个任务一致，也为其提供了参考价值。

**关键词**：命运共同体；金砖国家；危机管理理论

---

\* 张庆，四川外国语大学教授、博士，金砖国家研究院人文交流研究所所长。
\*\* 陈果，四川外国语大学国际关系学院比较制度学硕士，建筑结构高级工程师。
\*\*\* 孙昊洋，四川外国语大学国际关系学院比较制度学在读硕士。

## 一、前言

随着21世纪到来，人类社会面临三大全球性挑战——和平、发展和治理。在一个全球一体化不断加速的时代，没有哪个国家可以单方应对这些挑战。国际社会需要以持久和平与繁荣为目标，绘制出蓝图并制定出实施方案。中国国家主席习近平提出了"人类命运共同体"的理念，这一理念已从内涵、特性和思想渊源等角度得到了研究。作为一个初步框架，本文试图从危机管理理论的角度来探讨构建金砖国家命运共同体，丰富研究方法和实施策略。

## 二、危机与危机管理

危机是指任何会或预期可能会导致个人、团体、社区或整个社会陷入不稳定和危险局面的事件。危机被认为是安全、经济、政治、社会或环境事务中的负面变化，尤其是它们会在几乎没有预警的情况下突然发生。

查尔斯·赫尔曼认为[1]，外交政策危机是威胁政治单元最重要也是主要的因素，它限制了思考、计划和响应的时间来改变可能的结果。赫尔曼强调，危机是由政府单位所应察觉的状况。罗森塔尔认为这个定义仅涉及"政府单位"，所以它太狭窄。相反，他更倾向于将危机视为一个过程："危机与具有严重威胁、不确定性和紧迫性等因素有关。可以从这些角度出发来研究各种现象，比如：自然和技术灾害、冲突和骚乱以及恐怖行动等。"[2] 洛格兰试图从目标人群的角度理解危机。[3] 他将其定义为由不同事务组成的谱系，这些事务对某些群体来说是危机，但对另外一些群体来说

---

[1] Hermann C. F., "International Crises: Insights from Behavioral Research," New York: Free Press, 1972, p. 13.

[2] Rosenthal U. and Pijnenburg B. eds., "Crisis Management and Decision Making: Simulation Oriented Scenarios," New York: Springer, 1991, p. 3.

[3] Loughran H., "Understanding Crisis Therapies: An Integrative Approach to Crisis Intervention and Post Traumatic Stress," London: Jessica Kingsley Publishers, 2011.

不是。

全球化时代的危机具有独特的特点。首先，危机发生的频率日益增高，因而逐渐成为人们生活中的常态。其次，国家之间的频繁交流加大了彼此的相互依赖，导致危机不再是孤立的事件，而是一系列事件的集合。各种原因都可能触发危机，而危机后的相对稳定可能会酝酿出新的危机。同时，危机代表着风险和机遇并存。"无论他们是否承认，当局和决策者常常真切地知道，危机除了是一种威胁，也可能是一种机遇。"[1] 根据功能主义的观点，危机可有效促进社会协调。危机可以作为"安全阀"，以地震的形式偶尔释放地壳下的能量，缓解政治、经济和社会的紧张与不安。

危机管理普遍被视为一种过程，涉及组织领导者的行动和沟通，试图减少危机发生的可能性，最大程度地减少危机造成的损害，并在危机后努力重建秩序。[2][3][4] 具体而言，危机管理意味着政府和其他社会组织采取监测、预警、预控和评估的措施，以防止潜在的危机，处理不间断的危机，减轻损害，甚至将危机转化为机遇。因此，危机管理具有以下特点：

第一，危机管理旨在保障利益。危机管理的根本目标是通过维护社会秩序、安全和稳定，来保障各种组织和个人的广泛利益。

第二，危机管理的逻辑前提在于其可预防性。危机带来的严重后果会促使人们认识到预防危机的需要和重要性。在一项事件被视为严重危机时，领导者有义务动员人民群众以防止危机。"我们已经从自己的研究中提炼出了一套实用的步骤，管理者可以通过采取这些步骤来更好地发现新问题，设定适当的优先级，并进行有效的预防性应对。"[5]

---

[1] Rosenthal U. and Pijnenburg B. eds., "Crisis Management and Decision Making: Simulation Oriented Scenarios," New York: Springer, 1991, p. 2.

[2] Bundy J. and Pfarrer M. D., "A Burden of Responsibility: The Role of Social Approval at the Onset of a Crisis," Academy of Management Review, Vol. 40, 2015, pp. 345 – 369.

[3] Kahn W. A., Barton M. A. and Fellows S., "Organizational Crises and the Disturbance of Relational Systems," Academy of Management Review, Vol. 38, 2013, pp. 377 – 396.

[4] Pearson C. M. and Clair J. A., "Reframing Crisis Management," Academy of Management Review, Vol. 23, 1998, pp. 59 – 76.

[5] Watkins Michael D. and Bazerman Max H., "Predictable Surprises: The Disasters you Should Have Seen Coming," Harvard Economic Review, Vol. 81, 2003, pp. 72 – 80, p. 140.

第三，危机管理的外部环境具有开放性和非竞争性的特征。危机的爆发危及所有相关方的利益，需要所有组织和个人交互合作。这同样适用于国际社会。面对危机，所有相关国家都很难独善其身。所有政府、企业、非政府组织和平民都应该参与危机管理，共渡难关。

第四，危机管理采取了总体化和系统化的措施。危机的时间线包括萌芽、预警、爆发、进行和消退阶段。而且，一场危机往往会引发另一场，具有复杂性效应。因此，危机管理需要综合系统的策略来协调不同部门之间的关系，以保证紧急管理的统一指挥。

第五，危机管理既可以在国内也可以在国际上发挥作用。传统意义上，国际危机被定义为这样一种局面：事件的发生范围扩大了破坏母系统结构稳定性的影响力，并激活了子系统中同类型的要素，同时还增加了使用武力进而造成危害的可能性[1]，或者是发生在竞争对手之间的行动中的"情势变化"，影响到整个国际政治系统。[2] 显然，这些定义都在强调国际行动者之间的争端和冲突。实际上，全球化时代还有另一种需要所有国家联手共同努力解决的危机，如恐怖主义、气候变化和经济增长放缓。

在国际政治领域，采取不同的方法来解决危机会导致相关各方面临不同的情况。一种情况是由于缺乏预先安排的计划和有效的措施，一些国家无法承受危机带来的沉重打击，决策者的形象和威望受到损害，陷入合法性危机。另一种情况是在危机的初期，决策者不仅要承受各种压力，还要采取积极有效的策略，从而良好地控制危机的势头，实质性地巩固和提高了他们的地位和竞争优势。因此，从国家利益的角度出发，在国内和国际上，有必要探讨如何通过危机管理确保共同立场来应对国际社会面临的普遍危机。

---

[1] Young Oran R., "The Intermediaries: Third Parties in International Crises," Princeton: Princeton University Press, 1967, p. 10.

[2] McClelland Charles A., "The Anticipation of International Crises: Prospects for Theory and Research," International Studies Quarterly, Vol. 21, 1977, pp. 15 – 16.

## 三、金砖国家与危机管理之间的内在联系

BRICS 是由当时的高盛资产管理公司主席吉姆·奥尼尔创造的金砖五国的缩写，代表五个主要的新兴经济体。① 这五个国家共同追求一个不同于美国及其盟友主导的世界秩序的愿景，反映了它们对现有全球体系的负面影响的共同诉求。通过将亚洲、非洲、欧洲和拉丁美洲的重要国家的联合力量汇聚在一个小型战略性组织中，它们有更大的机会实现这一愿景。②

实际上，金砖国家的发展并非一帆风顺。五个成员国在政治和经济上有着巨大的差异，这导致它们价值观对立、利益立场不同。③ 在 BRICS 内部，因互相视对方为潜在的威胁和竞争对手，它们的双边关系里存在着巨大的不信任和紧张关系，诸如此类的种种因素限制了它们的合作。④ 这一现象在中国和印度在南亚地区的竞争中尤为显著。

金砖国家命运共同体是中国政府反复强调的一个新理念，旨在最大程度保证国家利益的同时考虑他国的诉求。这一概念的核心是平衡与协调一个国家的发展与金砖国家的共同发展。在这一背景下，危机管理理论与构建金砖国家命运共同体的内容有类似之处，即基本目标、逻辑前提、外部环境、实施措施和影响范围。

第一，构建金砖国家命运共同体的基本目标是保障五国人民，甚至（是）全世界人民的福祉，如和平、合作和发展。金砖国家命运共同体的首要目标是维持世界和平和各国人民的基本需求。因此，平等的伙伴关系是实现这一目标的有效手段。五个国家需要在建设命运共同体的过程中，通过合作追求安全、发展和互利共赢。同时，共同繁荣是五个国家的共同

---

① O'Neill Jim, "Building Better Global Economic BRICs," Goldman Sachs Global Economics, 2001, https：//www.goldmansachs.com/insights/archive/building-better.html.

② De Coning C., Mandrup, T. and Odgaard L. eds., "The BRICS and Coexistence: An Alternative Vision of World Order," New York: Routledge, 2015, p.25.

③ Mottet Laetitia, "Cooperation and Competition among the BRICS Countries and other Emerging Powers," French Centre for Research on Contemporary China (CEFC), 2013.

④ Glosny Michael, "China and the BRICs: A real (but limited) partnership in a unipolar world," Polity, Vol.42, 2010, pp.100-129.

梦想，应该在确保国家利益的同时考虑他国的诉求。

第二，构建金砖国家命运共同体的逻辑前提是，人类所面临的各种挑战和威胁可以检测、预见和控制。"危机预防是危机管理的一个广泛概念，可作为一种管理控制类型，危机管理可以在（以下）三个广泛的领域为任何环境的危机预防发挥作用：一是系统解决潜在危机的潜在原因；二是建立信号机制以预见潜在的危机；三是学习并理解任何危机持续的（须具备的）基本条件。"[1] 1962年的古巴导弹危机标志着国际危机管理的新阶段。当时的美国国防部长罗伯特·麦克纳马拉评论说，此后的战略可能会被危机管理所取代。[2] 随着20世纪90年代经济全球化的加速，非传统安全问题，如流行病、生态恶化和恐怖主义的持续上升，促使学者需从危机预防和管理的角度来解决这些问题。

第三，构建金砖国家命运共同体需要一个开放且非竞争的外部环境。面对复杂的全球问题，五个国家中的任何一个都无法保证孤立发展。金砖国家命运共同体的理念超越国籍、种族和文化的界限，提供了一种探索共同利益和价值观的新观点。它要求所有国家共同努力，以开放和非排他性的精神，共同应对全球威胁。

第四，在计划实施方面，构建金砖国家命运共同体需要采取全面和系统的方法。从本质上讲，构建金砖国家命运共同体是一项宏伟的设计，涉及各个团体在不同层次上的利益。它寻求公平和正义的国际政治、互惠的经济合作、绿色发展的生态系统和全方位的文化交流。因此，其系统性的实施计划高度复杂。

第五，在危机管理方面，金砖国家命运共同体的影响范围涵盖了国内和国际事务。在国内，人们需要达成共识并携手应对各种社会问题，如失业和社会安全。在国际上，为解决共同利益的问题，金砖国家应该共同努力，缩小意识形态差距，加强相互信任并争取互利共赢。

---

[1] Penuel K. B. Statler M. and Hagen R.，"Encyclopedia of Crisis Management," Los Angeles：SAGE Publications，2013，p. 375.

[2] Bell C.，"The Conventions of Crisis：A Study of Diplomatic Management," London：Oxford University Press，1971，p. 2.

因此,我们可以得出结论,危机管理的理论框架与构建金砖国家命运共同体的理念在逻辑上呈现出一致性。

**表3　构建金砖命运共同体与危机管理的内在逻辑比较**

|  | 危机管理 | 构建金砖国家命运共同体 |
| --- | --- | --- |
| 基本目标 | 利益保护 | 各国人民福祉 |
| 逻辑前提 | 危机可控性 | 人类面临各种危机的可察觉性和可控性 |
| 外部环境 | 开放和非竞争性 | 开放和非排他性 |
| 实施方法 | 综合性和系统性 | 综合性和系统性 |
| 影响范围 | 国内和国际 | 国内和国际 |

资料来源:笔者自制。

## 四、构建金砖国家命运共同体的核心方法:加强危机管理合作

通常,危机管理可以分为三个阶段:危机前预防、危机应对和危机后处理,每个阶段都应从内部和外部的角度来看待。在危机前预防阶段,应侧重从内部角度组织准备工作,而从外部角度则应侧重于利益相关者的关系,以减少危机发生的可能性。危机应对阶段涉及危机发生后管理者采取的行动,其中内部注重于危机领导力,外部角度注重于利益相关者对危机的看法。在危机后处理阶段,内部角度强调危机后组织性学习的作用,而外部角度强调社会评估作为结果。[1]

---

[1] Bundy J, Pfarrer M. D., Short C. E and W. Coombs T., "Crises and Crisis Management: Integration, Interpretation, and Research Development," Journal of Management, Vol. 43, No. 6, 2017, pp. 1661 – 1692.

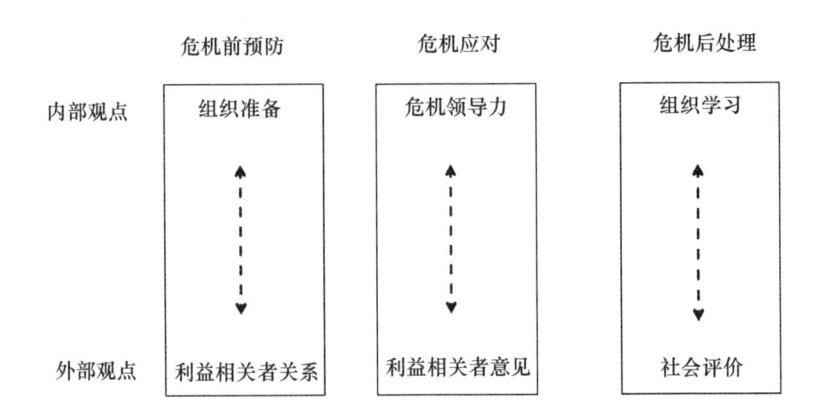

**图 1　危机过程中的内部和外部观点**

资料来源：Bundy, J., Pfarrer, M. D. Short, C. E. & W. Coombs, T., "Crises and Crisis Management: Integration, Interpretation, and Research Development," Journal of Management, Vol. 43, No. 6, 2017, pp. 1661 – 1692。

## 阶段一：危机前预防

从内部角度看，这个阶段应当涵盖两个主题：组织的可靠性和组织文化及结构在组织如何为危机做准备中的角色。[1] 高度可靠的组织被定义为具有处理意外事件能力的组织，这种能力源于集体管理的"正念"的认知和行为过程。[2] 为详细描述高度可靠性组织的定义，比格利和罗伯茨[3]进一步关注了该概念的三个方面：允许更改正式结构的机制、领导对即兴创作的支持以及增强意义构建的方法。与此同时，内部的准备需要文化和结构

---

[1] Bundy J, Pfarrer M. D., Short C. E and W. Coombs T., "Crises and Crisis Management: Integration, Interpretation, and Research Development," Journal of Management, Vol. 43, No. 6, 2017, pp. 1664 – 1667.

[2] Weick K. E., Sutfcliffe K. M. and Obstfeld D. eds., "Organizing for High Reliability: Processes of Collective Mindfulness," In B. M. Staw and L. L. Cummings eds., "Research in Organizational Behavior," pp. 81 – 123. Greenwich, CT: J AI Press. 1999, p. 37.

[3] Bigley G. A. and Roberts K. H., "The Incident Command System: High – Reliability Organizing for Complex and Volatile Task Environments," Academy of Management Journal, Vol. 44, 2001, pp. 1281 – 1299.

的构建。格雷夫、帕尔默和波兹纳认为[1]，一个组织的文化可能更容易接受不当行为，这往往是管理者的个人抱负或权力竞争导致的。相似地，施纳特利[2]发现，某些治理实践——包括政策和沟通的明确性——在预防白领犯罪方面比其他治理结构更为有效，例如增加董事会外部人员的比例。

相比之下，从外部角度看，危机前的预防重点在于与利益相关者的关系。做到这一点的关键是与利益相关者保持积极的关系。克莱尔和瓦多克[3]提出的"全责任管理"方法强调了认识到组织对利益相关者的责任的重要性，以增强危机的检测和预防。同样地，库姆斯[4]指出，"利益相关者应该是预防思维和过程的一部分"，并且利益相关者可以帮助识别以及减轻可能导致危机的风险。

按照相似的逻辑，构建金砖国家命运共同体也需要内部准备和外部利益相关者关系的协调。从内部来看，这五个国家都希望通过提高政治和经济的可靠性来增强各自制度的可靠性，并通过五国人民的共同努力实现更高的统一标准。从外部来看，构建金砖国家命运共同体需要整体的安全观，与克莱尔和瓦多克提出的"全责任管理"方法的逻辑相一致。每个国家都应该摒弃孤立主义的自保行为，主动拥抱全球化时代，成为全球治理的参与者和建设者。每个国家都应该通过与世界上其他国家沟通和合作来建立一个全球安全网。金砖五国都是地区大国，我们应该抵制损害他人来追求安全的行为，充分尊重其他国家的利益，考虑到他人的安全关切，并通过实质性措施实践义务和责任。以生态安全为例，这是一个超出任何国家单独处理能力的全球性问题。地区大国凭借各自的地区影响力，要呼吁

---

[1] Greve H., Palmer D. and Pozner J. E., "Organizations Gone Wild: The Causes, Processes, and Consequences of Organizational Misconduct," Academy of Management Annals, Vol. 4, 2010, pp. 53 – 107.

[2] Schnatterly K., "Increasing Firm Value Through Detection and Prevention of White – Collar Crime," Strategic Management Journal, Vol. 24, 2003, pp. 587 – 614.

[3] Clair J. A. and Waddock S. A., "'Total' Responsibility Management Approach to Crisis Management and Signal Detection in Organizations," In C. M. Pearson, C., Roux – Dufort and J. A. Clair eds., "International Handbook of Organizational Crisis Management: Thousand Oaks," CA: Sage, 2007, pp. 299 – 314.

[4] Coombs W. T., "Ongoing Crisis Communication: Planning, Managing, and Responding (4th ed.)," Thousand Oaks, CA: Sage, 2015, p. 107.

各国人民既认识到它对人类生产和生活方式的影响，也要启动联动机制努力执行顶层设计的计划。

### 阶段二：危机应对

当危机变得不可避免时，危机管理进入第二阶段——危机应对。传统意义上，危机管理的特点是"典型的工程使命"——识别并修复导致无效输出的问题。[1] 虽然现代危机管理研究不一定与这个使命相一致，但从国际角度看，危机应对仍侧重于"解决问题"的方法，经常强调影响组织内危机的领导因素，特别是危机感知与危机领导力之间的关系。[2] 具体来说，詹姆斯及其同事[3]认为，那些将危机视为威胁的领导者在反应上更为情绪化，努力更为有限，但是那些将危机视为机会的领导者在思维上则更为开放和灵活。此外，危机领导者的个性，如魅力，可能会影响危机应对中的内部凝聚力。[4][5][6]

从危机应对的外部角度来看，大量研究集中在利益相关者如何看待和应对危机，以及组织如何影响这些看法。为实现这一目标，需要完成四项任务。首先，应努力建立组织或国家的积极形象，以消除其他方对其的疑虑和不信任。应明确传达一个信息，即积极努力的最终目标是联合多边力量，共同努力，控制事态的发展势头和影响，这有助于增强各相关方的责任感。其次，应采取合理的危机反应策略，及时交换信息并与其他方协调

---

[1] Kahn W. A., Barton M. A. and Fellows S., "Organizational Crises and the Disturbance of Relational Systems," Academy of Management Review, Vol. 38, 2013, p. 377.

[2] Bundy J., Pfarrer M. D., Short C. E. and W. Coombs T., "Crises and Crisis Management: Integration, Interpretation, and Research Development," Journal of Management, Vol. 43, No. 6, 2017, p. 1671.

[3] James E. H., Wooten L. P. and Dushek K., "Crisis Management: Informing a New Leadership Research Agenda," Academy of Management Annals, Vol. 5, 2011, p. 458.

[4] Howell J. M. and Shamir B., "The Role of Followers in the Charismatic Leadership Process: Relationships and their Consequences," Academy of Management Review, Vol. 30, 2005, pp. 96 – 112.

[5] James E. H., Wooten L. P. and Dushek K., "Crisis Management: Informing a New Leadership Research Agenda," Academy of Management Annals, Vol. 5, 2011, pp. 455 – 493.

[6] Pillai R. and Meindl J. R., "Context and Charisma: A 'Meso' Level Examination of the Relationship of Organic Structure, Collectivism, and Crisis to Charismatic Leadership," Journal of Management, Vol. 24, 1998, pp. 643 – 671.

行动。例如,应该与其他方分享不同阶段的危机信息,如受灾地区、受影响人数和灾害规模,以减少危机造成的损失。[1] 再次,有必要提高相关方的认知水平和识别能力,这对危机的判断和分析至关重要。一般来说,具有较高识别能力的组织或国家可以更早地意识到危机发展的严重性和方向。[2] 最后,媒体在危机管理中的作用值得认可。众所周知,媒体在危机的看法和解释中起到了核心作用。[3][4][5][6][7] 例如,格拉芬[8]及其同事演示了媒体如何理解一个丑闻。

  危机应对为构建金砖国家命运共同体带来的启示是:从内部角度加强领导和团结,从外部角度完善形象、优化策略、提高认知能力并强调媒体的功能。首先,构建金砖国家命运共同体的大计划离不开有力的领导,这是团结国内外人民并汲取其智慧的前提。就外部关系而言,金砖五国首先需要建立一个负责任和有问责制的形象。例如,习近平在联合国大会第七十届会议的一般性辩论中发表了题为《携手构建合作共赢的新伙伴,同心打造人类命运共同体》的演讲,在此次演讲中他首次提出了中国的三重身份:世界和平的建设者、全球发展的贡献者、国际秩序的维护者。习近平

---

[1] Bundy J. and Pfarrer M. D., "A Burden of Responsibility: The Role of Social Approval at the Onset of a Crisis," Academy of Management Review, Vol. 40, 2015, pp. 345–369.

[2] Zavyalova A., Pfarrer M. D., Reger R. K. and Hubbard T. D., "Reputation as a Benefit and a Burden? How Stakeholders' Organizational Identification Affects the Role of Reputation Following a Negative Event," Academy of Management Journal, Vol. 59, 2016, pp. 253–276.

[3] Adut A. A., "Theory of Scandal: Victorians, Homosexuality, and the Fall of Oscar Wilde," American Journal of Sociology, Vol. 111, 2005, pp. 213–248.

[4] Greve H., Palmer D. and Pozner J. E., "Organizations Gone Wild: The Causes, Processes, and Consequences of Organizational Misconduct," Academy of Management Annals, Vol. 4, 2010, pp. 53–107.

[5] Hoffman A. and Ocasio W., "Not All Events Are Attended Equally: Toward a Middle-Range Theory of Industry Attention to External Events," Organization Science, Vol. 12, 2001, pp. 414–434.

[6] Rhee M. and Valdez M. E., "Contextual Factors Surrounding Reputation Damage with Potential Implications for Reputation Repair," Academy of Management Review, Vol. 34, 2009, pp. 146–168.

[7] Wiersema M. F. and Zhang Y., "Executive Turnover in the Stock Option Backdating Wave: The Impact of Social Context," Strategic Management Journal, Vol. 34, 2013, pp. 590–609.

[8] Graffin S. D., Bundy J., Porac J. F., Wade J. B. and Quinn D. P., "Falls from Grace and the Hazards of High Status: The 2009 British MP Expense Scandal and its Impact on Parliamentary Elites," Administrative Science Quarterly, Vol. 58, 2013, pp. 313–345.

表示："中国将继续维护以联合国宪章宗旨和原则为核心的国际秩序和国际体系。中国将继续同广大发展中国家站在一起。"① 其次，金砖国家都需要采用这样的合理和积极策略，如信息共享平台、多层次的对话机制和智库合作，与其他方建立有效的沟通机制。再次，有必要通过人与人之间的交往提高公民对危机的认知水平。以全球金融危机引发的贸易保护主义为例，自2008年经济衰退以来，不少国家的经济发展陷入停滞，失业率上升，消费能力减弱，实体经济投资不足。为追求短期利益，一些国家通过贸易保护主义和非贸易壁垒将危机转嫁给其他国家。这种投机取巧的做法是不长久的，金砖国家应该警惕。最后，金砖国家应促进成员国之间的媒体合作。每天，在不同文化背景的人们之间会发生许多生动的故事。媒体应以开放和包容的态度报道和讲述这些故事，促进不同文化之间的对话和交流，最终为金砖国家以及整个世界的进步作出贡献。

### 第三阶段：危机后处理

危机管理的第三阶段是危机后处理。从内部角度看，它需要增强认知学习，而外部角度主要侧重于通过社会评价来扩大共识。

就组织学习作为关键的危机后处理而言，先前的经验可以很好地减少未来危机的可能性。② 兰佩尔和他的同事③将其描述为一个既关注事件本身，也关注发展组织能力的有意和应急过程。同样地，从危机中学习，超越现状以创造新的竞争机会是非常重要的。④

---

① Xi Jinping. "Working Together to Forge a New Partnership of Win – Win Cooperation and Create a Community of Shared Future for Mankind," 2015, http://www.xinhuanet.com//politics/2015 - 09/29/c_1116703645.htm.

② Madsen P. M., "These Lives Will Not Be Lost in Vain: Organizational Learning from Disaster in U. S. Coal Mining," Organization Science, Vol. 20, 2009, pp. 861 - 875.

③ Lampel J, Shamsie J. and Shapira Z, "Experiencing the Improbable: Rare Events and Organizational Learning," Organization Science, Vol. 20, 2009, pp. 835 - 845.

④ James E. H, Wooten L. P. and Dushek K., "Crisis Management: Informing a New Leadership Research Agenda," Academy of Management Annals, Vol. 5, 2011, pp. 455 - 493.

从外部角度看，社会评价包括对组织声誉、合法性和信任的评估。[1]之前的研究已经反复论述了利益相关者的认知和组织的应对策略之间的关联。[2][3][4] 例如，当感知到高度的危机责任时，建议组织提供更加宽容的应对策略让利益相关者的负面反应最小化。

危机后处理为金砖国家命运共同体的构建提供了一些启示。以中印关系为例，2017年9月，第九届金砖国家领导人在厦门峰会受中印之间长期的边界争端的影响，导致双方的外交处于紧张状态。就在峰会开始前的几天，两国都从喜马拉雅的对峙中撤回了军队。在《金砖国家领导人厦门宣言》中，金砖五国都表示愿意坚定信念，在以前峰会的成果和共识的基础上，来迎接金砖国家合作和团结的第二个"金色十年"。同样，在《金砖国家领导人第十五次会晤约翰内斯堡宣言》中，金砖国家重申了对相互尊重、主权平等、民主、包容和加强合作原则的承诺。为实现这一目标，各方应努力完善学习过程并优化社会评价。首先，需要摒弃制度偏见。制度设计植根于每个国家独特的历史、文化和传统，这意味着每个国家都有权选择自己的发展道路和制度模式。其次，在意识形态和价值观上求同存异是很重要的。在当今世界，意识形态不应被用作对抗的借口或政治合作的障碍。再次，金砖国家和其他发展中的经济体需要通过结构转型和经济创新以更深入参与全球化进程。传统的国际经济秩序需要通过增加新兴经济体的权重来更新，以实现世界经济中管理主体的多样化。最后，金砖国家应坚守文明的新理念，加强不同文明之间的沟通和交流。应鼓励在体育、青年、电影、文化、教育和旅游等领域的稳定进展和交流。例如，金砖国

---

[1] Bundy J., Pfarrer M. D., Short C. E. and W. Coombs T., "Crises and Crisis Management: Integration, Interpretation, and Research Development," Journal of Management, Vol. 43, No. 6, 2017, pp. 1661 - 1692.

[2] Bundy J. and Pfarrer M. D., "A Burden of Responsibility: The Role of Social Approval at the Onset of a Crisis," Academy of Management Review, Vol. 40, 2015, pp. 345 - 369.

[3] Claeys A. S. and Cauberghe V., "What Makes Crisis Response Strategies Work? The Impact of Crisis Involvement and Message Framing," Journal of Business Research, Vol. 67, 2014, pp. 182 - 189.

[4] Coombs W. T., "Choosing the Right Words: The Development of Guidelines for the Selection of the 'Appropriate' Crisis - Response Strategies," Management Communication Quarterly, Vol. 8, 1995, pp. 447 - 476.

家间可以在旅游贸易、航空联通性、旅游基础设施和旅游安全等领域交流知识、经验和讨论最佳做法，以此增强旅游合作。

## 五、结语

自2017年1月中国国家主席习近平在日内瓦联合国办事处发表题为《共同构建人类命运共同体》的主旨演讲以来，因其提供了应对全球挑战的中国方案，这一理念获得了更广泛的国际认同。同样地，构建金砖国家命运共同体的精神也是在追求一个开放、包容、干净和美丽的世界。在该理念的指引下，这个世界将享有长期和平、全球安全和共同繁荣。根据这一理念，金砖国家应相互尊重，平等协商，杜绝冷战心态和强权政治。各国应采取新的方式来发展国家之间的关系，即沟通而非对抗，建立伙伴关系而非结盟。

危机管理理论为金砖国家构建命运共同体提供了启示。全球危机的可能性，如经济增长放缓、气候变化和恐怖主义，客观上为团结各国人民提供了机会，这也要求各利益相关者摒弃狭隘的民族主义，并肩对抗威胁到金砖国家甚至整个世界的危机。

根据危机管理理论，整个危机管理过程可以分为危机前预防、危机应对和危机后处理阶段。因此，应该在不同阶段采取相应的措施。在危机前阶段，必须在针对内部的准备和外部立场的协调上努力。在危机应对阶段，应该通过强有力的领导和凝聚力同步内部的意识形态和行动，并从外部努力获得其他利益相关者的支持。危机后处理的反思包括通过危机回顾来增强内部学习和在外部环境中建立积极的社会评价，以达到更高层次和更大范围的共识。从这个角度看，危机管理的三个阶段与为金砖国家构建命运共同体的各种使命相吻合，并为其提供了参考意义。在危机前预防阶段，从内部来看，金砖五国都期望通过政治和经济表现提高各自政权的可靠性，并通过汇集人民的努力实现更高标准的团结。从外部来看，构建金砖国家命运共同体需要一个整体的安全观念，这与克莱尔和瓦多克提出的"全责任管理"方法相吻合。在危机应对阶段，金砖国家需要从内部角度增强领导力和凝聚力，并从外部角度提高形象、优化策略、提高认知能力并强调媒体的作用。在危机后处理阶段，金砖国家应该重视学习过程，并提高对共同经历过的危机的社会评价。

希望在危机管理理论的原则指导下，金砖国家的合作将得到加强和巩固，从而为金砖国家构建命运共同体提供坚实的基础。

# 金砖国家地方合作的发展现状与未来趋势

郑佳宝[*]

**摘　要**：近年来，国际形势风云迭起，地缘政治动荡不断，全球经济衰退加剧，公共卫生危机频发，对以金砖国家为代表的新兴市场国家的生存和发展提出了更高的要求。金砖国家起初被质疑为虚有其表的"漂亮摆设"，后逐步探索出多层次、多领域的合作机制，力求建立和维护更加公平、公正的国际秩序的功能性机制。笔者认为，金砖国家合作深入到地方，成员国间的地方合作逐渐呈现开放化、务实化和多元化趋势，但仍存在许多亟待解决的问题和挑战，借此研究对金砖国家地方合作的成绩进行反思和预测。

**关键词**：金砖国家；地方合作；机制化合作

在全球化深入的背景下，世界正处在一个发展和变革交织的时代。伴随着全球范围内的政治、经济、文化和宗教冲突，以及区域发展不均衡的问题，追求和平与发展的呼声也愈发强劲。如何在变革中找规律，在冲突中寻和平，是当下各国对外战略的重中之重。金砖国家机制起初是为了应

---

[*] 郑佳宝，四川外国语大学西方语言文化学院讲师。

对国际金融危机,逐渐成为建立和维护更加公平、公正的国际秩序的功能性合作机制。金砖国家间地方合作逐渐呈现开放化、务实化和多元化趋势,发展与挑战并存,但前景基本看好。

## 一、金砖国家地方合作的背景

2017年9月举行的金砖国家工商论坛上,金砖五国领导人就发展更紧密、更广泛、更全面的战略伙伴关系达成一致,巩固政治安全、经贸财金、人文交流"三轮驱动"合作框架,确立"金砖+"合作理念。开幕式上习近平强调,要从两个维度观察金砖国家的合作发展:既要把金砖合作放在世界发展和国际格局演变的历史进程中来看,又要把金砖合作放在五国各自和共同发展的历史进程中来看。2021年9月9日,金砖国家领导人第十三次会晤以视频会议形式在线上召开,中国国家主席习近平、南非总统拉马福萨、巴西总统博索纳罗、俄罗斯总统普京出席,印度总理莫迪主持会晤。本次会晤围绕"金砖15周年:开展金砖合作,促进延续、巩固与共识"的主题进行深入交流,通过了《金砖国家领导人第十三次会晤新德里宣言》,标志着金砖国家合作进入新时期。[①] 2022年,中国接任金砖国家主席国,并于6月23日成功主办金砖国家领导人第十四次会晤。盛事共襄,金砖五国领导人推心置腹,就金砖国家各领域合作和共同关心的重大问题深入交换意见,达成许多重要共识,为构建高质量伙伴关系,共创全球发展新时代注入动力。

时值金砖国家合作第二个"金色十年",随着金砖五国国力不断增强,金砖国家合作走深走实,合作影响力已经超越金砖五国范畴,金砖国家机制的影响力和吸引力持续提升,成为促进世界经济增长、完善全球治理、推动国际关系民主化的建设性力量。金砖国家热爱和珍视和平,坚持主张公平正义,积极推动全球治理体系改革,就国际和地区热点问题发出"金砖"声音,一方面提升了新兴市场国家和发展中国家的国际话语权,另一

---

[①] 黄茂兴主编:《金砖国家新工业革命伙伴关系创新基地发展报告(2021)》,社会科学文献出版社2022年版,第281页。

方面也成为推动南南合作的重要平台。①

面对世界政治经济形势发展的新格局，金砖国家寻求在动荡与合作共存的新环境下站稳脚跟，同谋出路，就需要金砖五国建立健全合作机制，从上而下贯彻合作理念，深化拓展合作领域，在政治安全、经贸财金、人文交流"三轮驱动"合作框架下，加强在核心领域的合作。

## 二、金砖国家地方合作的现状与特点

近年来，金砖五国各自的综合国力和国际影响力愈发强大，金砖五国联合行动的影响力与日俱增，金砖国家合作机制不断完善。尽管国际地缘政治动荡，疫情和经济衰退的影响持续，反全球化和民族主义等思潮回流，但金砖国家各成员国仍在艰难的国际局势中保持开放、包容的态度，积极推进务实合作，开展多领域的互助与合作，逐渐形成了开放、务实和多元的地方合作机制。

金砖国家已然形成多层次、多领域的合作架构，地方合作取得多方面的重要成果，涵盖政治、经济、金融、贸易、社会、人文等多个方面，成员国之间地方合作的推进，也使得金砖国家合作机制不断深入，助力推动全球治理体系改革。

本文将列举几个典型的实例，展示在金砖国家合作"第二十个金色十年"过半之后，各国在地方合作方面取得的重大成果，借此对金砖国家地方合作机制及其成效进行反思和预测。

### （一）推动基础设施建设

目前，以金砖国家为代表的新兴经济体大多都存在基础设施老旧和不足的问题。例如印度，其一半以上的国土尚未开通公路，铁路系统运力严重不足；俄罗斯虽有一定的公路和铁路设施基础，但普遍设施陈旧，不能满足实现新经济发展的需求；南非电力设施急需更新换代，全国大部分公

---

① 2022 年金砖国家领导人会晤筹备工作秘书处：《金砖国家简介》，2022 年 2 月 21 日，http://brics2022.mfa.gov.cn/chn/gyjzgj/jzgjjj/。

路路况很差；巴西交通基础设施非常不完善；中国虽在基础设施建设方面做出了举世瞩目的成就，但也存在着区域分布不均的问题，部分落后偏远地区的设施与人口密集地区相去甚远。①

新兴经济体的基础设施投资需求巨大，政府预算是其资金的主要来源，然而当前大部分新兴国家政府以及相关金融类国际组织所能提供的资金都有限。中国作为金砖国家组织和共建"一带一路"倡议的积极维护者和推动者，在协助成员国发展基础设施方面投入了大量资金，以投资的形式分享发展成果，实现互助共赢。

2021年4月9日，金砖国家灾害管理工作组会议在线上举行，邀请金砖五国代表就多灾害早期预警系统、志愿服务与灾害管理、灾害韧性基础设施等议题进行交流，金砖各国代表慷慨分享了本国经验和反思，表达了进一步加强相关领域务实交流与合作、不断提高各国灾害管理能力和防灾基础设施建设的强烈愿望。

### （二）促进社会文化交流

金砖国家拥有悠久的历史与文化渊源，人文交流是金砖国家合作的重要支柱之一，在金砖国家合作中发挥着基础性作用，同时是潜力巨大的金砖国家合作增长点。金砖国家在人文交流领域达成了一系列合作文件，不断加强议会、政党、青年、智库和地方合作，金砖国家大学联盟、金砖国家网络大学等的成立，进一步推动金砖国家人文交流合作迈入新的阶段。②

2015年6月，首届金砖国家文化部长会议在俄罗斯莫斯科举行，7月，在金砖国家领导人第七次会晤上，《金砖国家政府间文化合作协定》的签署为金砖国家开展文化交流与合作夯实基础。

2017年7月25日，金砖国家青年论坛在北京开幕，为期三天的会议上，来自金砖五国的50名青年代表就"构建伙伴关系，促进青年发展"的主题展开热烈讨论，他们当中有青年公务员、青年学者、青年企业家、

---

① 国家开发银行、对外经济贸易大学：《金砖国家可持续发展战略报告：创新金砖国家投融资机制，促进务实合作互利共赢（2018）》，中国社会科学出版社2019年版，第44页。
② 黄茂兴主编：《金砖国家新工业革命伙伴关系创新基地发展报告（2021）》，社会科学文献出版社2022年版，第160—161页。

青年艺术工作者、青年媒体工作者以及大学生等，最终形成《2017年金砖国家青年论坛行动计划》。① 2017年，金砖国家达成《落实〈金砖国家政府间文化合作协定〉行动计划（2017—2021年）》《金砖国家加强媒体合作行动计划》《金砖国家青年论坛行动计划》《金砖国家电影合作拍摄2017—2021年计划》等一系列文件，并成立图书馆联盟、博物馆联盟、美术馆联盟和青少年儿童戏剧联盟，人文交流合作领域不断拓展；同年7月，金砖国家教育部长共同签署的《北京教育宣言》提出，支持"金砖国家网络大学"成员开展教育、科研和创新相关领域的合作。

2018年6月，在金砖国家智库国际研讨会暨第二十一届万寿论坛上，与会嘉宾就金砖国家人文交流的机制创新等议题达成广泛共识。

2019年11月，在金砖国家人文交流论坛上，首部金砖国家联拍纪录片《孩童和荣耀》的全球首映式同时举办。②

2020年12月3日，金砖国家治国理政研讨会暨人文交流论坛开幕式以线上形式举行，中共中央政治局常委、中宣部部长黄坤明出席并发表主旨演讲，正式启动了第二届金砖国家联拍联播纪录片主题全球征集活动。本次活动是金砖国家交流治国理政经验的重要契机，为深化人文交往与合作，促进金砖伙伴关系走深走实，推动构建人类命运共同体提供良好机会。③

2021年6月10日，以"携手共建创新基地打造金砖合作典范"为主题的2021金砖国家智库国际研讨会在厦门举行，本次会议是由金砖国家智库合作中方理事会和厦门市人民政府共同主办的，来自金砖国家的智库专家学者以及业界代表齐聚厦门，共商金砖创新基地建设，共谋金砖国家务实合作。2021年8月25日，第十三届金砖国家知识产权局局长会议以线上形式举行，通过本次视频会议，金砖各国知识产权局局长共同听取了各

---

① 黄茂兴主编：《金砖国家新工业革命伙伴关系创新基地发展报告（2021）》，社会科学文献出版社2022年版，第266页。

② 黄茂兴主编：《金砖国家新工业革命伙伴关系创新基地发展报告（2021）》，社会科学文献出版社2022年版，第160—161页。

③ 黄茂兴主编：《金砖国家新工业革命伙伴关系创新基地发展报告（2021）》，社会科学文献出版社2022年版，第278页。

局牵头的围绕"金砖国家知识产权合作路线图"进行的项目的进展情况，讨论下一步的工作计划。重点围绕数字化技术和其他新兴技术应用，分享了各自的成功实践经验，对未来可能开展合作的领域进行了积极讨论。[①] 2021年9月，《金砖国家领导人第十三次会晤新德里宣言》指出，运用数字解决方案确保包容和公平的优质教育，加强教育与培训领域的合作，发出在开发、分配和获取公开数字内容等方面进行合作的倡议。

### （三）推进人才培养合作

第一，孔子学院和鲁班工坊项目：作为金砖国家之间人才培养合作的主要载体，孔子学院已在金砖国家遍地开花，为传播中华文化，促进中外人文教育交流作出杰出贡献，当中，数俄罗斯的孔子学院数量最多。鲁班工坊作为中国职业教育国际化发展的先驱，建立起了中外人文交流的知名品牌，在金砖国家——尤其是印度和南非——职业教育中有出色表现，输出中国优秀的职业教育经验和先进的生产技术，帮助金砖国家成员国借鉴中国经验，培养更多能顺应时代要求的优秀职业技能人才。

第二，金砖国家法律院校联盟：2015年10月，由圣保罗天主教大学、乌拉尔国立法律大学、莫斯科国立法律大学、阿米提大学、印度法律研究院、华东政法大学和开普敦大学签署的金砖国家法律院校联盟协议，宣告金砖国家法律院校联盟成立。该联盟旨在落实成员国大学之间的双边、多边法律合作，开展合作教育和培训计划，共同培养一批具有全球化视野、通晓国际规则、具备参与国际法律事务的能力、能为金砖国家成员国政府、法律人士和跨国企业提供人才支持的法学家和律师。[②]

第三，金砖国家标准化研究中心：2017年9月，浙江省政府与国家标准委签署方案，筹建金砖国家标准化（浙江）研究中心，推动中国标准"走出去"。2018年12月22日，新工业革命伙伴关系背景下金砖国家标准化国际交流与人才队伍建设暨第二届"之江标准"研讨会在义乌召开，金

---

[①] 黄茂兴主编：《金砖国家新工业革命伙伴关系创新基地发展报告（2021）》，社会科学文献出版社2022年版，第280页。

[②] 黄茂兴主编：《金砖国家新工业革命伙伴关系创新基地发展报告（2021）》，社会科学文献出版社2022年版，第63页。

砖国家专家共同围绕国际标准化合作、人才队伍建设、人才教育等问题展开研讨。2019年5月金砖国家标准化中心通过验收，在家电、纺织、皮革等领域形成一批研究成果，搭建了金砖国家标准化信息共享和服务平台，组建了多个相关研究联盟，推动金砖国家标准化交流与合作。

第四，金砖国家技能发展与技术创新大赛：2017年，中国作为金砖国家轮值主席国，于6—8月成功举办首届金砖国家技能发展与技术创新大赛，涵盖数控大赛、3D打印与智能制造大赛、创客大赛、智能制造挑战赛、焊接大赛等多项赛事，共吸引了4500余人参加。2018年第二届大赛举办赛事23场，近5万人次参与，赛区分布在中国、南非和俄罗斯。第三届和第四届大赛也都成功举办，截至2021年，累计近10万人参加相关竞赛和会议。金砖国家大赛成为金砖国家和友好国家间人才交流的重要活动，搭建了一个国际化的人才合作平台。[1]

第五，金砖国家大学联盟与金砖国家网络大学：在共建"一带一路"倡议之下，金砖国家高等教育多边合作领域建立了这两大机制，作为金砖国家之间文化教育和人才培养的合作载体。其中，金砖国家网络大学指集散在五个国家的高水平新型网络状大学实体。2022年，金砖国家网络大学年会以线上线下相结合的方式在北京召开。截至目前，已有55所来自金砖国家的大学被纳为成员。[2] 通过共同推进以联盟高校优势学科研究为载体的基础合作，利用信息网络平台推动信息技术和教学相融合的长线合作，以建立联合学院为载体推动联盟高校深度合作。这些合作方式被称作"点状合作""线状合作"和"面状合作"，体现了该组织多样化的合作途径和创新的合作精神。[3]

---

[1] 黄茂兴主编：《金砖国家新工业革命伙伴关系创新基地发展报告（2021）》，社会科学文献出版社2022年版，第65—66页。

[2] 《2022年金砖国家网络大学年会在北师大召开》，人民网，2022年04月28日，http://news.bnu.edu.cn/zx/ttgz/127374.htm。

[3] 黄茂兴主编：《金砖国家新工业革命伙伴关系创新基地发展报告（2021）》，社会科学文献出版社2022年版，第65—66页。

## 三、金砖国家地方合作面临的问题与挑战

在金砖国家合作关系建立初期，外界曾普遍担忧其可持续性，认为金砖国家可能会成为一个新兴大国自娱自乐的小团体，不过是形式主义的空心组织。"金砖国家在发展合作方面造成的影响，传统上分为南北合作和南南合作两个维度，两者是同时进行、相互混合的。而金砖各国都各有不同的议程，使得国家之间的合作更加有效。"[1] "影响金砖国家未来发展的另一个因素是其最重要的双边关系，即印度与中国之间的关系。最近两国在一些问题上出现了分歧，如恐怖主义、边界问题、印度与美国和日本的亲近等。"[2] 诸如此类对金砖国家的运作机制和发展前景持悲观态度的声音实际上并不罕见，其观点集中在对其组织的稳定性、合作的务实程度、成员国地缘政治冲突、行动的集体性等方面的担忧和质疑。

在地方合作方面，金砖国家虽取得了一定成果，但仍存在许多亟待解决的问题，面临来自内部和外界的多重挑战。

### （一）缺乏长效机制

目前金砖国家的合作仍以论坛形式为主，缺乏稳定、正式的长效机制，缺乏有力的常设平台以深化合作。例如仅有国家层面的领导人高峰会议等高层会晤机制，但没有设立常设机构以监督落实会议决议；成员国各级地方政府或社会机构缺乏有效平台进行沟通，难以调动资源，发挥协同作用等。[3]

### （二）各国经济增长放缓

近年来国际经济持续低迷，2019年底新冠疫情席卷全球，中印边界问

---

[1] Ricxhard Carey and Xiaoyun Li, "The BRICS in International Development: The New Landscape," IDS Evidence Report 189, 2016, p. 12.

[2] Rajiv Bhatia, "Whither BRICS?," Eurasia Review, 2017, https://www.eurasiareview.com/02052016-whither-brics-analysis/.

[3] 魏建国、李锋等：《金砖国家合作机制研究》，社会科学文献出版社2018年版，第162页。

题引发冲突，俄乌冲突引发能源博弈，全球经济形势雪上加霜，新一轮的金融危机可能来袭。金砖国家首当其冲，作为全球主要的几大新兴经济体，却不是最具有抗压力的经济体，产业改革、能源贸易、就业和基础建设都备受打击，经济增速显著降低。金砖国家地方财政也因此普遍承受巨大压力，不得不降低合作力度，以求平缓渡过危机。

### （三）合作基础不稳固

地区经济一体化的程度从根本上决定了区域合作的程度，而金砖国家在地缘经济结构上并不很紧密，除了受地理位置的限制以外，还因为成员国的经济发展主要都是外延型的，缺乏可持续性发展的动力。成员国处于相似的发展阶段，对外依存度高，据统计，2020年南非货物和服务进出口总额为1692亿美元，俄罗斯、印度和中国分别达到6838亿美元、6847亿美元和50951亿美元，[1] 出口依赖型的经济模式以及贸易保护主义容易引发竞争和利益冲突。

成员国拥有截然不同的历史背景和发展趋势，虽同为新兴市场国家，但经济实力差距明显，中国和印度的发展潜力普遍比俄罗斯、南非和巴西看好；各国之间的金融体系发展也不平衡，难以实现金融资源的优化配置，制约了金砖国家金融合作的深入。[2]

### （四）严峻的外部挑战

全球和区域经济发展放缓、金融危机步步逼近的大环境下，金砖国家也面临着来自外部的严峻挑战。世界各国都在竞相吸引外资，引导制造业和就业机会回流，弱化了金砖国家原有的国际竞争力，制约其发展国际合作。

新一轮技术和产业革命使得发达国家获得了更大的技术领先，金砖国家等新兴市场总体不占优势，即使合作也难以抵御发达经济体的技术冲

---

[1] 中国国家统计局等编：《金砖国家联合统计手册2021》，中国统计出版社2022年版，第168页。

[2] 魏建国、李锋等：《金砖国家合作机制研究》，社会科学文献出版社2018年版，第164页。

击，存在再次陷入落后境地的可能。新的技术条件下，原有的原材料、劳动力等生产要素禀赋和价格优势可能不再有经济意义，全球分工和贸易体系面临重构，金砖国家的经济地位和发展潜力面临巨大的不稳定性。[1]

## 四、金砖国家地方合作的趋势预测[2]

金砖国家的合作机制经过十余年的发展，正在经历一个重要转型，即从一个"侧重经济治理、务虚为主的对话论坛"向"政治经济治理并重、务虚和务实相结合的全方位协调机制"转型。金砖国家成员国间的合作愈发注重实践性而非理论性，期望给各国政府和人民带来切实的利益。金砖国家各国政府都鼓励"项目化"合作，其合作机制的转型也推动许多实实在在的地方合作项目落地，使金砖国家成为一个为金砖成员国政府和国民提供交流、发展机会的机构，借助"接地气"的项目将资源和构想落实到社会根基中去。

当前国际政治形势严峻，经济危机一触即发，民族主义和"右翼"思想回潮，金砖国家作为一个新兴国际组织，金砖国家间的合作也极有可能受其影响，造成一定程度的收缩和保守。中国作为金砖国家当前经济体量最大的国家，在政治、经济、军事、文化、卫生等多领域都取得了瞩目成就，总体竞争力在金砖国家中名列前茅。虽然中国对内和对外不需要处理其他金砖成员国面临的某些严峻问题，但同处全球化浪潮之中，中国不可能独善其身，寻求片面的"自保"，可以通过金砖国家合作机制和国际组织向他国提供帮助，追求共同发展，实现互惠互利，深化务实成员国合作机制。金砖国家在贸易投资、科技、金融、环境、能源、农业、信息通信技术、人文交流等关键领域有极大的合作潜力和发展空间，在关键领域的合作将提高金砖国家在国际社会上的话语权，将在全球经济复苏中唱响"金砖"声音。

---

[1] 魏建国、李锋等：《金砖国家合作机制研究》，社会科学文献出版社2018年版，第163页。

[2] 黄茂兴主编：《金砖国家新工业革命伙伴关系创新基地发展报告（2021）》，社会科学文献出版社2022年版，第168页。

笔者认为，在金砖国家合作新的阶段，各国之间的地方合作将在以下重点领域继续推进。

### （一）进一步深化地方经贸财金合作

经贸合作一直是金砖国家合作的重要动力，促进金砖国家的全面经贸财金合作对深化金砖国家战略伙伴关系具有重要的作用和战略价值。在金砖国家经贸合作体系下，金砖国家间已经形成了重要且良好的贸易合作伙伴关系，尽管2020年开始，全球贸易深受疫情影响，但在金砖国家经贸合作机制的引导与推动下，金砖国家加强经贸务实合作，不仅保障了当前疫情关键物资的供应，未来还将进一步扩大贸易往来，为金砖国家经济复苏、全球产业链供应链安全高效运行筑牢基础。已达成的多个合作协议框架成果有效推动了成员国间的贸易投资合作，比如《金砖国家贸易投资与可持续发展倡议》《金砖国家专业服务合作框架》《金砖国家经济伙伴战略2025》等。

新开发银行是金砖国家财金合作的旗舰项目。在金砖国家领导人第六次会晤上，各国代表一致决定成立金砖国家新开发银行，2015年金砖国家新开发银行开业，为金砖国家及其他新兴经济体和发展中国家在融资、抵御金融风险、双边及多边金融合作、基础设施建设、可持续发展项目等方面提供合作平台、拓宽合作路径。

### （二）进一步强化能源和环境可持续合作

化石能源在第一次工业革命后开始成为社会生产生活发展的重要动力能源。随着化石能源的广泛使用，其带来的环境和资源问题逐渐引起全球关注。当前，金砖国家汇集了能源需求和供给两侧举足轻重的国家，对于资源和能源的需求将在未来的经济和社会发展进程中不断增多，能源和环境问题将成为金砖国家实现可持续发展和高质量发展过程中不容忽略的问题，因此金砖国家地方之间以及其与其他新兴市场和发展中国家进行的能源清洁转型和环境污染防治合作、绿色金融等将成为未来能源和环境合作的主旋律。

金砖国家领导人第十一次会晤和第十二次会晤通过了《金砖国家能源

研究合作平台工作章程》《金砖国家能源合作路线图》《第六次金砖国家环境部长会议联合声明》，金砖国家各国领导人表示，未来将进一步加强能源和环境合作，巩固已有的成果，推动能源研究平台和环境友好技术合作平台的建设，强化扩大能源联合研究范围、实施能源联合项目、能源研究平台建设、建立环境友好技术平台架构模型等方面的工作，对进一步强化金砖国家能源和环境保护领域的战略伙伴关系有坚定的信心和决心。

### （三）进一步推动共建卫生健康事业

疫情发生以来，金砖国家深入开展卫生领域合作，将进一步促进金砖国家卫生健康共同体的构建，共同参与全球抗疫，巩固抗疫成果，共同应对疫情及其连锁负面影响等全球性挑战和威胁。

新冠疫情期间，中国与南非通过举办多次抗疫经验视频交流会，围绕病毒检测、疫情防控经验、疫苗研发等九大主题展开交流；2020年4月28日，在金砖国家应对新冠疫情特别外长会上，各国代表围绕抗击疫情、深化金砖合作等主题进行深入探讨，就坚持密切疫情信息分享和经验交流、开展药物和疫苗研发合作、坚定支持世界卫生组织等国际组织在国际抗疫中的领导作用等议题展开讨论，并达成共识；截至5月，中国已向柬埔寨等19个国家派出了21个医疗专家组，向这些国家提供疫情防控工作援助、指导与咨询。其他金砖国家与别国的抗疫合作以疫苗研发合作方式为主。

金砖国家可推动成员国间的应急医疗卫生合作和嵌入型医疗卫生合作相融合，同时设立医疗卫生合作的短期目标和中长期目标。短期合作目标有助于针对突发疫情采取应急协调、磋商和合作，中长期目标则有助于金砖国家间、金砖国家与其他国家、国际机构在疫苗研发、传统医药合作、卫生人才培养等领域展开的中长期交流合作，提高医疗卫生能力，降低疫情对国际社会的潜在风险。

### （四）进一步推进人文交流合作

人文交流作为金砖国家合作三大支柱之一，对于金砖五国合作始终发挥积极的促进作用。教育、文化、体育、科技等人文领域的广泛交流与合作为增进金砖五国人民相互理解与友谊、夯实民意基础，发挥了重要作用。不同国情、社会背景下的金砖国家文化、文明各具特色和优势，互补性强，为金砖国家间的相互学习、借鉴奠定了基础。金砖国家的政治、经济和社会制度也因此存在较大的差异，构建人文交流纽带才能做好民心工程，增进金砖国家间的相互了解与信任，进而推动金砖合作走深走实。

在金砖国家合作机制成立的较长一段时间内，金砖国家合作的着力点主要集中于经济领域，而人文交流合作的进程相对缓慢，人文交流机制缺乏顶层设计，人文交流机制间的协调性不足、约束力与执行力较弱。此外，金砖国家间的文化与文明的优势互补尚未充分挖掘，如何实现金砖国家各自文化与文明的优势互补仍然是金砖国家合作需要研究的重要课题。

随着金砖国家合作迈入新阶段，金砖国家应发挥政府的引导和统筹作用，充分调动和整合各种资源，为人文交流合作搭建平台，同时要发挥政府与民间机制的联动效应；在资源有限的情况下，金砖国家人文交流合作机制要立足于金砖五国人文交流合作的切实需要和满足人民的迫切需求，将资源投入有效增进金砖国家间相互了解和信任的人文交流合作领域，优先进行人文交流重点领域的机制建设，打造示范性成果；发挥智库合作的专业优势和协同效应，针对金砖国家人文交流机制建设开展基础性和对策性研究。

# 《世界贸易组织中的金砖五国：巴西、俄罗斯、印度、中国和南非的贸易比较》书评

裴尹琦[*] 谢小丽[**] 周心语[***]

**摘 要**：金砖五国的国际贸易是当前全球经济和贸易议题的焦点之一。与此同时，在全球经济形势不断变化的背景下，金砖五国作为世贸组织的成员，依然展现出引人注目的经济活力，并且在国际机构和全球贸易领域不断扩大政策实施的空间。近年来，金砖国家不断加强成员国间以及其他发展中国家之间的贸易合作，但由于金砖五国的国情不同，在某些方面仍存在利益分歧。因此，深入研究"金砖五国在世贸组织中的比较贸易政策"对于应对多样风险挑战，强化新兴市场国家和发展中国家的团结合作，具有重要的现实意义。本文旨在通过对金砖五国贸易政策的综合比较分析，根据各国国情的差异，探寻更有效实现广泛领域深层次合作的途径。通过分析，我们可以得出结论，这种合作将为金砖五国及其他发展中国家在国际贸易舞台上发挥更大作用提供有力支持。

**关键词**：金砖国家；世界贸易组织；贸易政策比较；多边贸易体制；

---

[*] 裴尹琦，四川外国语大学西方语言文化学院葡萄牙语专业本科在读学生。
[**] 谢小丽，四川外国语大学西方语言文化学院葡萄牙语专业本科在读学生。
[***] 周心语，四川外国语大学西方语言文化学院葡萄牙语专业教师、葡萄牙里斯本大学博士研究生。

争端解决机制；利益分歧与合作。

## 一、内容简介

当前政治和经济形势具有巨大的不确定性，随着金砖国家凭借庞大的国内市场和不断增长的经济脱颖而出，学术界也加强了对金砖国家在主要国际政治和经济论坛上的关系演变的研究。世贸组织是多边领域最相关的论坛之一，它为研究金砖各国作为国际参与者的作用提供了充足的空间。在此背景下，巴西应用经济研究院和国际经济关系局发起了全球贸易监管项目，出版了有关金砖国家贸易政策比较分析的书籍——《世界贸易组织中的金砖五国：巴西、俄罗斯、印度、中国和南非的贸易比较》(*OS BRICS NA OMC: Políticas Comerciais Comparadas de Brasil, Rússia, Índia, China e África do Sul*)[1]。

本书的目的是以世贸组织为参考框架，对金砖各国的贸易政策进行比较分析。通过研究金砖各国在国际贸易中的地位，以及在多边贸易制度中的参与（包括其外交与法律支柱、争端解决制度以及其政治与谈判支柱、多哈回合谈判等），呈现金砖国家在多边贸易制度框架中的重要衔接工作。

本书各章将通过主要贸易工具的使用概况，介绍每个金砖国家的贸易政策，各国的相似性和对比性，以及它们在世贸组织中扮演的角色。这一分析将提供金砖国家成员利益趋同和分歧领域的证据，并提供金砖国家在多边贸易中可能的合作概况。其目的是要证明，即使有巨大的商业和政治差异，金砖国家也有为共同利益而进行战略衔接的空间。这本书可以帮助我们更加了解金砖国家的贸易动态及其在世贸组织中的行动，对于分析该集团经济议程中的合作和冲突可能性至关重要。

---

[1] *OS BRICS NA OMC: Políticas Comerciais Comparadas de Brasil, Rússia, Índia, China e África do Sul*（《世界贸易组织中的金砖五国：巴西、俄罗斯、印度、中国和南非的贸易政策比较》）是2012年在巴西利亚由巴西应用经济研究院和国际经济关系局发起的全球贸易监管项目出版的有关金砖国家的贸易比较分析的书籍。组织者为维拉－索斯滕森和伊万－蒂亚戈－马查多－奥利维拉，由巴西应用经济研究院和赫图利奥－瓦加斯基金会圣保罗经济学院全球贸易和投资中心有关的研究人员共同承担了本书的分析与写作。

《世界贸易组织中的金砖五国：巴西、俄罗斯、印度、中国和南非的贸易比较》书评

本书分为五个部分，分别介绍金砖国家在世贸组织中的表现特点分析与金砖国家之间政治互动发展的主要时刻，金砖各国国际贸易状况分析，金砖各国主要贸易政策议题研究，金砖国家在世贸组织争端解决机构中的作用和金砖国家参加的多哈回合谈判。

## 二、主要观点简述

书中对金砖各国活动的总结清楚地表明，金砖各国在政治上的合作一直在加速，其合作也落实到各领域的具体行动上。[1] 国际舞台上的新事物是金砖国家的共同关注，为了加强在全球治理中的力量，金砖各国主要通过参与国际组织的决策论坛，在寻求当前重大问题的解决方案时发出自己的声音。

金砖国家在世贸组织背景下的政策衔接方向面临着巨大和复杂的挑战，因为这种合作的基础是基于它们经济政策的不同优先事项和它们经济增长的不同阶段的国际贸易政策，因此对每个金砖成员国的贸易政策的比较分析有很大意义。通过主要政策工具的综合分析揭示的趋同和分歧的要点，可以确定金砖国家内部合作可能增长的领域，以及这种合作需要它们之间做出更大努力的领域。

始于2001年的多哈回合谈判是金砖各间合作的一个独特范例，巩固了它们作为新兴国家集团在国际舞台上的政治存在。在多哈回合谈判的漫长岁月中，世贸组织成为有效协调各方立场的舞台，尤其是在农业领域。这一成功的实践表明，在国际贸易议程中，各种利益的结合使金砖各国衔接成为可能。但它也提出了其他一些利益分歧的地方，使这种合作更加困难。正是在这些领域，金砖国家必须做出更大的努力，以巩固自己在国际舞台上的主要角色。

---

[1] Vera Thorstensen and Ivan Tiago Machado Oliveira, "OS BRICS NA OMC: Políticas Comerciais Comparadas de Brasil, Rússia, Índia, China e África do Sul," Brasília: Ipea, 2012, p. 23.

## 三、章节主要内容简述

### （一）金砖国家在世贸组织活动中的表现特点分析

书中指出，金砖各国在世贸组织的表现一直呈现出自己的特点，通过分析能够得到其国际贸易政策中的优先事项，以及确定它们在国际舞台上所捍卫的利益。[①]

书中提到了金砖国家的国际贸易在其增长模式中代表了不同的优先事项。对中国来说，三十年来，国际贸易一直是建立在资本主义基础上的经济政策的核心要素。中国此前优先考虑通过国有与外资企业进出口商品自由化，直到2011年初，中国才发出信号，表示将对国内市场的增长给予更大的关注。而对巴西、印度和南非来说，国际贸易是一个不太重要的因素，它们的优先事项是通过扩大需求和控制通货膨胀来发展国内市场。印度和南非保持经济封闭，直到20世纪90年代才开始开放其活动，对国际贸易给予更大的重视。印度优先考虑出口服务，但即使在今天印度仍然对其各领域呈现出高水平的保护，特别在农业领域。巴西选择了内部发展模式，但自20世纪80年代末以来，巴西开放了经济。对于处于从计划经济向市场经济过渡阶段的俄罗斯来说，贸易已成为减少对能源产品（如石油和天然气）相关活动依赖的最快方式。因此，俄罗斯有兴趣加入世贸组织，目的是使其国际贸易多样化并促进其经济发展。

此外，金砖五国对参与世贸组织也显示出不同的优先程度。巴西、印度和南非是1948年《关税及贸易总协定》（General Agreement on Tariffs and Trade），（简称"关贸总协定"）生效前的23个缔约国中的三个。巴西、印度和南非已经参加了关于建立关贸总协定的最初讨论和所有的谈判回合，还参加了关于建立世贸组织的谈判，在发展中国家发挥了领导作用。中国也是关贸总协定的缔约国，2001年12月中国正式加入世贸组织。1991年苏联解体后，俄罗斯申请关贸总协定缔约国地位，经过近二十年的

---

[①] Vera Thorstensen and Ivan Tiago Machado Oliveira, "OS BRICS NA OMC: Políticas Comerciais Comparadas de Brasil, Rússia, Índia, China e África do Sul," Brasília: Ipea, 2012, p.24.

谈判，俄罗斯于 2012 年 8 月完成了加入世贸组织的进程。

在中国加入世贸组织之前，中国进行了彻底的经济调整，这代表了中国政府的一项重要政治决定，即将中国重新纳入世界贸易舞台，从而能够将贸易转变为其发展的驱动轴。中国的加入使自身与世贸组织成员双方的利益都得到了满足。

中国和俄罗斯加入世贸组织引起了学者们对经济和政治原因的日益关注，他们认为加入该组织的漫长而复杂的过程有其经济和政治原因以及此类决定的成本和收益平衡是合理的。

## （二）金砖国家国际贸易概况分析

2010 年起国际贸易形势发生了深刻的变化，根据世贸组织的数据，2009 年是一个里程碑，中国以 1.2 万亿美元的出口额成为世界货物出口的领导者，取代了德国和美国，而在进口方面，美国仍然引领着国际贸易。2000 年至 2010 年十年间，中国的出口量增长了 6.4 倍，进口增长了 6.2 倍。俄罗斯也是世界主要出口国之一，在 2010 年占据了第 12 位，在 2012 年 8 月加入世贸组织后，其国际贸易有望大幅增加。与 2000 年相比，俄罗斯的出口额翻了 3.8 倍，进口额翻了 5.3 倍。印度在国际贸易中一直呈现出重大发展，十年来，印度的出口量增加了 5.2 倍，进口量增加了 6.2 倍。与 2000 年相比，巴西 2010 年出口额翻了 3.7 倍，进口额翻了 3.2 倍，南非的进口量翻了 2.7 倍，进口量翻了 3.1 倍。[①]

就参与全球贸易而言，从 2000 年到 2010 年，中国从占出口总额 5% 的第 5 位上升到占出口总额 13.3% 的第 2 位。俄罗斯从第 11 位上升到第 7 位，占出口总额的 3.4%。印度从占出口总额 0.9% 的第 20 位上升到占出口总额 1.8% 的第 14 位。巴西从第 19 位上升到第 16 位，占出口总额的 1.7%。而南非则从第 27 位升至第 24 位，占出口总额的 0.7%。[②]

在服务领域，根据世贸组织的数据，2000 年至 2010 年期间的结果也

---

[①] Vera Thorstensen and Ivan Tiago Machado Oliveira, "OS BRICS NA OMC: Políticas Comerciais Comparadas de Brasil, Rússia, Índia, China e África do Sul," Brasília: Ipea, 2012, p.29.

[②] Vera Thorstensen and Ivan Tiago Machado Oliveira, "OS BRICS NA OMC: Políticas Comerciais Comparadas de Brasil, Rússia, Índia, China e África do Sul," Brasília: Ipea, 2012, p.30.

很显著。十年间，中国增长了5.6倍，印度增长了6.1倍，俄罗斯增长了4.4倍，巴西增长了3.3倍，南非增长了2.8倍。[①]

就参与全球服务出口而言，数据分析表明中国和印度在该领域一直在增长，俄罗斯的增长略显不足，巴西保持在同一水平，而南非在该领域失去了相对的重要性。

根据各国的开放程度来看，巴西在金砖国家中的贸易占国内生产总值（GDP）的比例最低。2008年至2010年间，对外贸易占巴西GDP的24%，而俄罗斯占52%，印度占48%，中国占55%，南非占61%。[②] 巴西是更接近美国、法国和德国等发达经济体，而不是最具活力的新兴国家。

### （三）金砖国家主要贸易政策议题研究

#### 1. 金砖国家关税概况

本书通过对金砖国家的关税政策分析与简要比较研究，得出金砖国家的关税政策有一个共同特点，即经济自由化。所有国家过去都采取了保护主义措施，重点放在国内市场，以鼓励工业化。中国是该集团中唯一一个制定以外国市场为重点的经济发展战略的成员。巴西和南非将其关税政策从属于其区域集团南方共同市场和南部非洲关税联盟，因此，它们修改政策的自主权有限。其中，印度是关税合并程度最低的国家。巴西是金砖国家中唯一一个平均农业关税低于非农产品的国家。总的来说，其他成员国，尤其是印度的农业关税相对较高。书中特别提到，2008年10月金融危机后，金砖国家寻求协调立场，以避免国际保护主义升级。在此背景下，金融危机对金砖各国的关税政策产生了多种影响：印度、中国和南非在自由化和限制性措施之间保持平衡，巴西采取了相当多的开放政策，俄罗斯选择加强保护主义措施。[③]

---

[①] Vera Thorstensen and Ivan Tiago Machado Oliveira, "OS BRICS NA OMC: Políticas Comerciais Comparadas de Brasil, Rússia, Índia, China e África do Sul," Brasília: Ipea, 2012, p. 30.

[②] Vera Thorstensen and Ivan Tiago Machado Oliveira, "OS BRICS NA OMC: Políticas Comerciais Comparadas de Brasil, Rússia, Índia, China e África do Sul," Brasília: Ipea, 2012, p. 450.

[③] Vera Thorstensen and Ivan Tiago Machado Oliveira, "OS BRICS NA OMC: Políticas Comerciais Comparadas de Brasil, Rússia, Índia, China e África do Sul," Brasília: Ipea, 2012, p. 88.

## 2. 金砖国家农业概况

本书对主要农业指标的分析表明，金砖各国的国情和目标是明确的，具有各自的特点。巴西是一个农业自给自足的国家，也是资本密集型农产品的出口国。由于具有竞争力，该国适度使用其关税政策，采用平均关税。巴西作为主要农产品出口国的潜力导致该国在谈判中寻求更大的进入发达国家市场的机会，减少农业补贴和其他对其产品施加的壁垒。中国是农产品的主要进口国，尽管能够自给自足，但农产品生产力低，依赖于政府的支持措施，以确保粮食安全和保持农村人口的稳定。印度是一个农村国家，一半以上的人口在农村工作。它分为自给农业和出口生产，旨在保护家庭农业、低生产率、高关税，并通过最低价格和低于市场利率的信贷提供补贴。对该国来说，最好的解决方案是开放进入欧洲和美国市场的机会，同时维持统一关税。南非存在缺乏基础设施和土地分配的周期性问题。政府的主要重点是通过土地改革、基础设施现代化和鼓励私人投资，让中小农民企业参与出口生产。尽管南非的农业生产潜力有限，但对出口其产品有着浓厚的兴趣，同时也寻求国际农业贸易的自由化。俄罗斯是一个以谷物出口为主的强大农业经济体。

根据世贸组织的说法，金砖各国在 2008 年金融危机后期增加了农业补贴，但也放松了在多哈回合谈判中的立场和限制，以遏制发达国家更为保护主义的态度。金砖国家间还有其他共同点，例如使用特殊和差别待遇下宣布的政府援助措施，以及发放大量补贴。

在多哈回合谈判中，巴西等出口国在谈判中采取了更加开放的立场，而印度和中国等国家则有意维持其关税。利益的汇合将使金砖国家之间在农业领域开展合作，巩固该集团在多边谈判中的地位。

## 3. 技术、卫生和植物健康障碍

随着进口关税的降低，在过去几年中，技术标准和卫生与植物检疫控制措施已成为进口控制的手段。尽管它的使用受到世贸组织的监管，但进口国对人类、动物和植物健康的复杂衡量和不断呼吁，使得这种形式的商业保护很难控制。

2010 年金砖国家开始规范了技术和质量标准，扩大了相互承认协议的数量，并使国内立法与国际惯例相一致。中国最近实现了卫生检查制度、标准化和技术标准的现代化。然而，通过立法使其与国际标准相协调以及修改公司的生产技术之间还有很长的路要走。在这方面，印度比中国先进得多。对国内生产的技术和卫生检查更为普遍，这可以减少产品在欧洲和美国等市场面临的障碍。巴西在实施技术和卫生控制方面拥有更大的行政能力，尽管它最近才表示可以增加检查，以确保遵守强制性标准。与印度和南非相比，巴西和中国拥有更广泛的措施监管框架，他们更积极地参与世贸组织委员会，其目的包括保护其利益免受其他成员可能实施的保护主义措施的影响。

金砖国家间在这一领域可能进行广泛合作，因为金砖国家都认识到技术、卫生和植物健康障碍壁垒在出口活动中的重要性，且各国都处于该领域发展的密切阶段，利益的汇合使金砖各国在处理这一问题的多边论坛上表达各自的立场。

4. 金砖国家贸易防御

多年来，国际贸易政策的基本工具一直是关税和关税配额，这是世贸组织在《关税与贸易总协定》中允许的唯一保护性要素。然而，随着多轮谈判的进行，关税正在降低，部分关税被技术、卫生和植物检疫壁垒等透明度较低的非关税壁垒所取代，包括汇率、出口利率，甚至劳动力或环境壁垒在内的部分金融机制没有多边协议的支持但也被使用。针对不公平贸易或进口爆发，其他包括反倾销、针对补贴的反补贴措施和保障措施在内的相关贸易政策资源是商品的贸易防御工具。

大多数国家倾向于将反倾销措施作为贸易防御手段，同时金砖各国也拥有不同的特殊性。书中特别提到，中国是金砖国家国家中乃至所有世贸组织成员反倾销的主要目标，因为中国的出口具有高度竞争力，劳动力成本低且货币贬值政策积极。印度是金砖国家中利用贸易防御机制最多的国家。此外，印度是世贸组织成员国中对中国采取的反倾销措施更多的国家，甚至超过美国与欧盟。[1]

本书对金砖国家成员使用贸易防御工具的情况和世贸组织贸易防御框

---

[1] Vera Thorstensen and Ivan Tiago Machado Oliveira, "OS BRICS NA OMC: Políticas Comerciais Comparadas de Brasil, Rússia, Índia, China e África do Sul," Brasília: Ipea, 2012, p. 140.

架进行了详细的分析,得到以下结论:世贸组织各成员国都在积极使用贸易防御工具,多年来,中国作为主要出口国,不仅受到发达国家的反倾销措施,也受到发展中国家的反倾销;据数据分析,巴西在捍卫国家利益方面表现不佳,书中提出巴西在贸易防御领域的立场应该更加积极,同时巴西不能也不应该将贸易防御机制的使用政治化,贸易防御不应被用作政治博弈中的筹码①。

5. 金砖国家服务业概况

服务业在金砖国家经济中的重要性一直在急剧增长。目前,该行业占巴西、印度、南非和俄罗斯 GDP 的一半以上,服务业在中国的重要性也在持续上升。在巴西、南非和俄罗斯,服务业生产力的增加伴随着工业在 GDP 中的份额下降,而在印度和中国,工业和服务业的增长则损害了农业生产力发展。

由于服务贸易对世界经济的重要性,书中介绍了金砖国家成员国迄今在世贸组织中所作的承诺,并指出了在世贸组织服务贸易法律框架下,在服务贸易监管方面可能出现的变化。

金砖各国一直在迈向服务贸易自由化。2001 年中国和 2012 年俄罗斯加入世贸组织期间,中国和俄罗斯就服务自由化进行了谈判并作出承诺,双方都致力于在更多的部门实现市场准入和国民待遇优化。此外,各国有着明显的特征。在印度和中国,在相当多的行业中外资参与和合资企业都存在着限制。在金砖国家成员中,巴西是对本国服务提供商的限制最高的国家。而南非尽管在电信等重要部门保持限制,但对市场准入的限制比巴西和印度少。

服务领域为金砖国家间的政治交流提供了一个可能的领域,以期未来在多边体系中进行谈判。

6. 知识产权管理

国家的经济发展水平对科学发展有着促进作用,而以专利为表征的技术进步同时也促进了经济的发展。随着知识经济的发展和国际知识产权保

---

① Vera Thorstensen and Ivan Tiago Machado Oliveira, "OS BRICS NA OMC: Políticas Comerciais Comparadas de Brasil, Rússia, Índia, China e África do Sul," Brasília: Ipea, 2012, p.164.

护的加强，知识产权举措已经日益成为金砖各国政府促进技术、经济和文化领域的发展，增强国际竞争力的手段。随着更多外国资本的涌入，金砖各国对知识产权的保护愈加重视，其知识产权保护主要体现在专利、品牌和工业设计方面，金砖国家根据国情的不同，完善了国内法规和执行规则：中国改进其知识产权保护制度，作为吸引外国投资和促进技术转让的一种方式；印度也一直在改进其知识产权保护体系，主要体现在化学和生物制品方面；巴西立法承认在国家紧急状况下，可以不遵守市场要求，暂停知识产权的应用；俄罗斯对海关立法以及药物流通的许可进行了改革；南非在知识产权立法方面相较其他金砖四国是比较规范的，并无重大变化。

此外，金砖国家的参与情况也发生了重大变化。在专利注册领域，1990年，巴西、印度、中国和南非的专利注册量还不到美国年度注册量的2%，而2010年，中国向世界知识产权组织通报的申请数量约为美国的一半。巴西、印度和南非仍然没有达到美国总量的1%。俄罗斯在20世纪90年代初的年注册量占美国总量的21%，到2010年下降到12%。[1] 这可能会改变金砖各国在多边层面对知识产权监管的立场，针对金砖国家的快速发展，金砖各国应该健全专利的运行机制，对专利技术进行管理和保护。鉴于在该领域的复杂关系，金砖国家在知识产权领域还有很长的路要走。

7. 投资

随着经济全球化趋势的不断加深，促进贸易投资有助于拉紧国内外企业利益纽带、推动国际经贸往来、促进国家关系发展。投资领域也成为金砖国家合作的主要议题之一。在2000年，金砖国家经济增长就呈现出较高的经济增长率，吸引了大量的投资，并用于资助生产和国际贸易。为了给本国提供更多市场机遇、投资机遇、增长机遇，所有金砖国家都或多或少地制定和实施了鼓励资本流入的政策。虽然金砖五国的共同点是努力在吸纳新技术的政策下吸引投资，并且鼓励金砖国家在经济增长阶段进行内部合作，但在政策实施方面仍然存在较大差异，这些政策与它们在工业领域

---

[1] Vera Thorstensen and Ivan Tiago Machado Oliveira, "OS BRICS NA OMC: Políticas Comerciais Comparadas de Brasil, Rússia, Índia, China e África do Sul," Brasília: Ipea, 2012, p. 212.

基础设施及服务领域发展政策的不同战略相关：中国的投资重点主要是在基础设施领域和农业领域，要求投资的技术含量高，并将其活动领域和地点限制在欠发达地区；印度优先考虑信息技术部门的发展；俄罗斯寻求吸引投资进入其能源产业部门，以实现能源多样化；巴西的投资主要与石油和天然气勘探领域有关，也涉及基础设施领域，如机场和港口；南非的投资主要集中于矿业开采和旅游业，多数投资都来源于发达国家。金砖五国都有各自不同的投资优势。

8. 诸边贸易协定

金砖国家参与世贸组织的诸边协议，是这些国家在国际舞台上利益多样性的一个例子，这也证明了因为它们各自的经济发展具有不同的特征，集团成员在经济谈判舞台上的立场协调具有局限性。金砖国家间唯一的共同点是将政府采购和信息技术作为促进发展和创造就业的公共政策。[①] 从《信息技术协定》来看，金砖五国在这方面的发展极不平衡，存在着严重的利益不平衡，甚至有金砖成员没有加入《信息技术协定》，所以金砖国家间还没有对这个方面进行过谈论和协商。就《政府采购协定》来看，金砖各国的立场也各不相同：巴西主张将多边协议置于诸边协议之上；南非若加入诸边协议，因黑人在历史中的特殊地位，该国则很难坚持国民待遇原则；印度对加入《政府采购协定》表现出了极大的兴趣，但仍在考虑中；俄罗斯和中国因为经济体制的特殊性，加入《政府采购协定》则会产生利益分歧。综上，可以得出结论，金砖国家间仍然存在一些利益差异，而由于利益的不对称性，一些可能的协调立场最终限制了合作的领域。

9. 新议题

随着国际贸易领域的不断扩大和深化，世贸组织承受着适应当今世界要求的强大压力，面临着新的多边谈判的挑战，尤其是国际贸易谈判议程中出现的"新议题"的挑战。金砖国家对于世贸组织引入新议题的反应多为抵制，认为新规则的建立将更加有利于发达国家的发展。然而随着这些新议题在其他国际论坛上的逐步发展以及关于相同主题的国家规则的演

---

① Vera Thorstensen and Ivan Tiago Machado Oliveira, "OS BRICS NA OMC: Políticas Comerciais Comparadas de Brasil, Rússia, Índia, China e África do Sul," Brasília: Ipea, 2012, p. 462.

变，金砖国家对所提出的新议题并不反感，因为它们也试图加入和应用新议题。其中最具有代表性的两个新议题便是环境和贸易便利化，这二者都取得了重要进展，贸易便利化是成员之间最可能达成共识的议题之一。[1] 但重点仍然在发展问题上。这可以被看作是世贸组织多边谈判动态的一个转折点，发展中国家在几个金砖国家的带领下，努力协调，改变了自身路线和方法。同时，围绕新议题的讨论将为金砖国家提供机会，为实现共同利益建立非常规的联盟。

### （四）金砖国家在世贸组织争端解决机制中的作用

从书中描述的金砖国家在世贸组织争端解决机制中的参与情况，我们可以得出以下结论：金砖国家在世贸组织争端中的话语权不断随着经济水平和国家综合实力的发展而提升，在此过程中也极大地保障了发展中国家的合法权益。争端解决机制中的参与程度极大地保障了发展中国家的合法权益，在世贸组织中的话语权也在不断随着经济水平和国家综合实力的发展而提升。除了南非之外，所有其他的金砖国家都表现出积极和成功地参与到维护部门和系统的利益中。金砖国家中的巴西、中国和印度，已经将世贸组织争端解决机制作为促进其在多边贸易体系中的利益的战略工具，并在解决争端中强行界定模糊点。其中特别提到，巴西已将世贸组织争端解决机制作为其外贸政策的战略支柱，并且似乎已经找到了最平衡和成功的参与系统的动力，即依靠政府、私营部门和第三方咨询形成了三足鼎立。印度和中国已经制定了类似的模式，但在与生产部门的互动以及在公共和私营部门的能力创建方面仍需要调整。[2] 就南非而言，它应该扭转其被动的姿态，探索其他的方法来积累经验并作为索赔者进行干预。总的来说，金砖国家对以协商一致的方式解决争端表现出积极的态度，并在诉讼

---

[1] "Ver discurso do diretor – geral da OMC," Pascal Lamy, em 24 de junho de 2011. Disponível em：http：//www.wto.org/english/news_e/sppl_e/sppl197_e.htm.

[2] Vera Thorstensen and Ivan Tiago Machado Oliveira, "OS BRICS NA OMC: Políticas Comerciais Comparadas de Brasil, Rússia, Índia, China e África do Sul," Brasília: Ipea, 2012, p.466.

失败时，选择了遵守争端解决机构的仲裁结果。①

世贸组织向争端解决机构提起诉讼的案件数量激增，反映出了相关成员方越来越重视和依赖世贸组织争端解决机制来处理成员间的贸易争端，维护其贸易权益，从侧面推动了世贸组织争端解决机制的程序趋于完善。

在金砖五国中，巴西和印度在积极利用世贸组织机制来取得双方满意的解决方案方面取得了显著的成功。其中一些典型案例为世贸组织应对类似问题的解释树立了先例，为世贸组织争端解决机制提供了确定性和可预测性，并且可以通过获胜经验的不断积累，进一步影响和深化世贸组织的各轮谈判，促进了多边贸易体系的完善。这很大程度上归功于国家在谈判模式方面的不断优化，形成了政府—私营部门—第三方咨询的三足鼎立的模式。

从金砖国家诉讼胜利的经验来看，利用世贸组织争端解决机制，有利于金砖国家同各国际贸易伙伴磋商和解决贸易争端，改善自身国家的谈判地位和贸易待遇，也将为国家带来巨大机遇。它们敢于挑战美国、欧盟等发达成员无视世贸组织规则的行为，维护其产业与贸易权益，正在形成主流和一股新兴的力量。

近年来，随着全球经济一体化程度的加深和金砖国家的不断崛起，国际社会对金砖国家的期望值越来越高，要求金砖国家承担更多国际义务的呼声也日益强烈，金砖国家也将在世贸组织争端解决机制中发挥更重要的作用。

数据显示，金砖国家在国际贸易方面，主要受到来自以美国（33%）和欧盟（32%）为代表的发达国家的起诉。② 面对挑战，金砖国家多选择以外交手段解决矛盾，通过和解的方式避免将冲突司法化，反映了金砖国家对多边贸易体系的维护，巩固和保障了争端解决机制在解决贸易冲突方面的地位；金砖国家也在维护自身权益的过程中，不断完善和加强了国际贸易法规的能力建设，以便适应争端解决机制的裁决方案，在贸易冲突中

---

① Vera Thorstensen and Ivan Tiago Machado Oliveira, "OS BRICS NA OMC: Políticas Comerciais Comparadas de Brasil, Rússia, Índia, China e África do Sul," Brasília: Ipea, 2012, pp. 390 – 391.

② Vera Thorstensen and Ivan Tiago Machado Oliveira, "OS BRICS NA OMC: Políticas Comerciais Comparadas de Brasil, Rússia, Índia, China e África do Sul," Brasília: Ipea, 2012, p. 382.

的保障贸易权益最大化。

在金砖五国中，中国是受到起诉最多的国家，其次是巴西、印度和南非。产生这种数量差异的主要原因是国家资源的丰富程度以及参与国际贸易的比重。随着金砖国家贸易量和在全球贸易中所占份额的不断增长，金砖国家面临的贸易争端形势不容乐观，更凸显了全球贸易保护主义不断抬头。在这种情况下，金砖各国通过完善本国国际贸易法规，依靠政府、私营部门和第三方咨询的力量以维护自身正当贸易权利。

为了避免将贸易分歧政治化，金砖国家在面临辩护失败时采取了尊重和维护争端解决机制的决定，承诺在合理的时间内遵守这些决定。采取这种方式的原因主要是金砖国家清楚争端解决机制能够确切保证它们在未来争端中的权利，也理解维护一个有效的争端解决机制的系统性好处。

中国、巴西和印度作为第三方广泛参与世贸组织争端解决机构磋商、小组讨论和上诉程序，试图丰富其在世贸组织争端解决机制中的经验，并扩大其对欧洲安全与合作组织通过的决定的影响范围。中国还制定了优先雇佣当地公司协助其政府进行这些活动的战略，这有助于提高中国律师和专家在争端解决方面的水平。印度和巴西也很好地利用了第三方机构，分别解决了 71 个和 65 个争端。只有南非对这一特权的利用非常少，仅有两次参与。因此，该国错过了一个在正在进行的争端中加强其利益，并发展其民间组织的技能的重要机会。[1]

综上，金砖国家虽然在世贸组织争端解决机制中的参与程度不同，涉及贸易的范围也不尽相同，但主要目标都是一致的：在不将分歧政治化的情况下解决贸易冲突，寻求各国的共同利益点。金砖国家积极利用世贸组织的争端解决机制，有效地排除贸易障碍，保障本国的贸易地位，维护本国利益，进一步发展与其他国家的贸易经济关系。

### （五）金砖国家参与多哈回合谈判

书中指出，金砖国家先后尝试在各谈判回合中发挥主导作用，积极提

---

[1] Vera Thorstensen and Ivan Tiago Machado Oliveira, "OS BRICS NA OMC: Políticas Comerciais Comparadas de Brasil, Rússia, Índia, China e África do Sul," Brasília: Ipea, 2012, p.387.

出建议，在多哈回合谈判中取得了成功经验，改变了世贸组织谈判的几何结构①，对提升金砖国家在国际组织中的话语权和维护发展中国家的利益具有积极意义。金砖国家参与各谈判小组，并在关于农业、非农产品市场准入、反倾销、补偿措施、服务和知识产权的谈判中寻求共同利益，协调各方立场，发挥了突出作用。②

一是在关于农业的谈判中，同意考虑给予发展中国家特殊和差别待遇的原则，并为其承诺提供更有利的条件。巴西在谈判中坚持进攻立场，谈判涉及范围广；印度和中国以家庭农业为主，在许多问题上采取了防御立场。尽管金砖国家在经济结构上存在差异，但积极通过 G20 与发达国家进行谈判，以达到降低关税、减少出口和国内生产补贴的目的。通过在整个回合中始终保持中间和建设性的立场，在复杂利益格局中把握和处理与金砖国家间的利益关系，实现金砖各国的共同发展。

二是在关于非农产品市场准入的谈判中，金砖各国积极参与了解决非关税壁垒的机制设计。中国在谈判中保持了进攻立场，而巴西、印度和南非则通过非农产品市场准入小组（Nama-11）集团采取了更为谨慎的立场。关于削减关税的主题中，中国、巴西和印度都提出了比发达国家可以减少更多关税的公式，最后确定削减应按照瑞士公式进行，并且对待发达国家和发展中国家应有不同的标准系数，提升了关税削减的灵活度；还通过 Nama-11 积极参与了关于消除非关税壁垒的谈判，为成员们解决非关税贸易壁垒创造了一种新模式。但在多哈回合谈判中仍然存在利益冲突，即发达国家和发展中国家关于汽车和汽车零件、纺织品和化学品等一系列产品的关税谈判，并且已经成为多哈回合当前僵局的中心点。

三是在关于反倾销的谈判中，金砖国家通过辩论进一步澄清和改进了《反倾销协定》中存在的不合理概念。由于金砖国家在这一领域涉及的利益广泛，巴西通过"反倾销之友"小组，就几乎所有主题提出了提案，为实施这些措施制定更为严格的标准；中国由于其特殊经济地位，已经成为

---

① Vera Thorstensen and Ivan Tiago Machado Oliveira, "OS BRICS NA OMC: Políticas Comerciais Comparadas de Brasil, Rússia, Índia, China e África do Sul," Brasília: Ipea, 2012, p. 401.

② Vera Thorstensen and Ivan Tiago Machado Oliveira, "OS BRICS NA OMC: Políticas Comerciais Comparadas de Brasil, Rússia, Índia, China e África do Sul," Brasília: Ipea, 2012, p. 402.

大多数发达国家和发展中国家反倾销措施的目标国家，因此在谈判中保持了比较谨慎的态度，批评了非市场经济条款的应用，并反对引入反规避规则；印度和南非在此谈判中参与程度较小，印度则公开反对归零的做法，赞成小额关税规则。

四是就补偿措施的谈判中，巴西发挥了主导作用。巴西首先是提出了旨在减轻发展中国家在对发达国家补贴提起诉讼时举证责任的建议，还提出了一项建议以捍卫出口与利益、严重损害和出口补贴定义相关的更高附加值商品的发展中国家的利益；其次是在印度的支持下，捍卫了基准概念的应用，确定了发展中国家的补贴限额；还参与了被禁止的出口补贴和信贷的定义。

五是至于在服务领域对发展中国家的特殊和差别待遇，金砖国家捍卫了《服务贸易总协定》的目标，通过谈判具体承诺发展中国家的参与，制定服务市场准入和当地市场供应商许可的规则，以促进经济增长和发展。中国和印度参与了几个发达国家和发展中国家的联合提案，以支持进一步自由化。

六是在关于知识产权的谈判中，就《与贸易有关的知识产权协定》和《生物多样性公约》两个主题进行谈判。由于中国在乌拉圭回合中不是缔约方，并且巴西和印度因为国际收支危机而立场不坚定，金砖国家受到了以美国为首的发达国家的施压。由于发达国家与发展中国家在利益上的不协调性，双方就多哈回合中的知识产权授权的解释上仍然存在分歧。

综上，可以看出金砖国家一直是多边贸易体制的积极维护者，在维护发展中国家的利益方面发挥了突出作用。金砖国家清楚发展中国家的利益在很大程度上受到多边谈判演变的影响，知道如何克服特定谈判部门的重要分歧，阐明本国的利益诉求，积极通过寻求利益交汇点，推动金砖国家间密切合作。从历史经验来看，金砖国家在多哈回合中对各方利益的协调是很成功的。

## 四、启示

国际形势中的不稳定因素日益突出，在全球性挑战增多的背景下，以金砖国家为代表的新兴市场国家和发展中国家群体不断崛起，它们对于推动国际秩序朝着更加公正合理的方向转变具有重要作用。这也意味着，金砖国家是维护多边贸易体制的重要实践者，对于维护新兴市场和发展中国家的共同利益和发展空间具有重要作用。因此，如何在政治与经济形势面临着巨大不确定性的形势下，具体分析金砖各国在世贸组织中的表现特点以及金砖各国国际贸易状况，并对金砖各国主要贸易政策议题进行研究，对于努力突破金砖国家间的利益分歧，寻求更广阔领域的共同发展具有极大的现实意义。

本书对金砖国家在世贸组织中的表现特点与金砖国家间政治互动发展的主要时刻、金砖各国的国际贸易状况、金砖各国主要贸易政策议题、金砖国家在世贸组织争端解决机构中的作用和金砖国家参与的多哈回合谈判的情况进行了系统且全面的介绍与分析，可以帮助相关研究人员更加了解金砖国家的国际贸易动态以及其在世贸组织中的作用，对于寻求金砖国家在多边贸易合作中的更大可能性以及共同利益的衔接具有积极意义。

可以看出，金砖五国因其经济水平的发展程度不一，对待和处理国际贸易问题的方式也不尽相同，虽然在一些方面存在着利益分歧，同时也存在着很多短板，但这并不代表金砖五国间就无法进行贸易合作和经济交流。金砖五国作为新兴经济体和发展中国家的成员，在利益方面也存在着许多共同点，未来将会有更深的发展空间，这已成为时代大势。把握金砖国家合作机遇，加强金砖五国之间的经济政策沟通以及务实合作，对于提升发展中国家在多边贸易体制下的国际话语权和维护发展中国家的利益具有重要作用。

# The Analysis of BRICS Transregionalism

## Pu Gongying[*]

**Abstract**: Under the impacts of COVID – 19 pandemic and the trend of deglobalization, the BRICS countries face dual challenges from external realities and internal growth, which also come along with opportunities to further participate in global and regional governance. Since BRICS is formed as a transregional partnership grouped by different emerging economies worldwide, the theory of transregionalism can help BRICS explore the pathway for their development in a new perspective. Stretching beyond traditional geographic and cultural limitations, the BRICS countries have established an open, pluralistic and inclusive relation beneficial to cross – border dialogues and cooperation. Working through transregional mechanism, BRICS partnership echoes the world's aspirational vision of connectivity and is present as an important breakthrough for building a community with a shared future for humanity. So, the practices of BRICS transregionalism need to be fueled by strong national power. In view of that, China should make

---

\* Pu Gongying, College of Russian Studies, Sichuan International Studies University, Chongqing, China.

efforts to make BRICS countries a transregional platform for all – round mutually beneficial cooperations among emerging market economies and developing countries, thereby becoming the exemplary model for regional and global governances.

**Keywords**: BRICS; transregionalism; regional governance; global governance

# I. Challenges and Opportunities for the Development of BRICS Countries

BRICS countries, as representative of a transregional grouping and emerging economies with global influences, are the unwavering upholders for multilateralism and are committed to playing an active role in global governance. Starting their pragmatic cooperation since the global financial crisis in 2008, BRICS countries, faced with the crisis – induced challenges and opportunities, have shown strong dynamism. Since the BRICS summit in Yekaterinburg in 2009, the mechanism by which BRICS countries cooperate with each other has been constantly improved, the areas of cooperation have been continuously expanded especially in the fields of finance, economy and trade, people – to – people exchange, and global and regional governance. These partners have worked in concert traversing the first golden decade of growth. However, in the grip of the outbreak of the COVID – 19 pandemic in early 2020 which triggered another global crisis, that swept across through the world, how should BRICS economies tackle the daunting challenges brought by the pandemic, and how should they grasp the historical opportunities behind the crisis to sustain their success into the next decade?

The global outbreak of COVID – 19 has not only crimped personal contacts and economic and trade exchanges worldwide, but also sowed the seeds of deglobalization or anti – globalization with the rapid cross – border spread of the virus—albeit a manifestation of globalization. As a result, the process of globalizing got hampered. In fact, since the beginning of globalization, anti‑globalization has emerged, and deglobalization will be subsequently supercharged by such global crises—evolving from a small ripple to tidal waves. Deglobalization after the global financial crisis in 2008 has continued. Additionally, under the Trump Administration, the United States has become the major force against globalization in the world with a series of actions featuring unilateralism and protectionism. During the pandemic, the world is handicapped by both anti‑globalization and deglobalization. The resolve of the BRICS countries, wholly and individually, is being severely tested, and their common commitment to globalization and multilateralism underlying BRICS partnership is risky in cracking. At the same time, when seeking future growth, BRICS countries are also faced with multiple challenges from and between the member states, as well as from their own national systems. Under increasing pressure from economic growth that comes with the pandemic, economic conflicts and deficit of political mutual trust among some members have sporadically turned up, and the grouping is occasionally split on dealing with some international issues. In a word, their multilateral cooperations maintain a precarious equilibrium with increasing risk of division, and the effectiveness of such cooperations is also being questioned. In post‑pandemic period, as a grouping of emerging market economies that constantly share the benefits of economic globalization, it is imperative for BRICS to promote cohesion and consensus inside and further explore potential cooperations through innovation and development.

Despite being handicapped by the widespread pandemic, we have reason to believe that globalization remains an irreversible historical trend worldwide. With the advancement of science and technology and the establishment of cyberspace, the pandemic did not hinder global transmission of information and data. Rather, it makes people have the sense that global non‑traditional security threats have great negative impacts on national economies and individual lives. In the wake of pandemic, no country or region can be isolated from the virus—a warning that forces human to reflect and change. A variety of emerging global issues call for a higher level of global governance as well as transnational and interregional coordinative mechanisms. Therefore, with the increasing overall strength and international influences, BRICS retains more international responsibilities and is expected more by emerging market economies and developing countries. The tide is turning, since the BRICS countries are no longer the lagging responders but the active shapers of the new international order. Therefore, their reflection on the current international economic and political order and their practical exploration of new dialogue and cooperation models among actors in international relations all highlight its significance. At present, due to the existing weak and ineffective global governance, coupled with the influences of unilateralism and protectionism, power vacuum in global and regional governance has formed after the "withdrawal" of some developed countries—a rare and precious historical opportunity for BRICS countries.

As globalization is plowing ahead and regionalism is flourishing, the concepts of new regionalism, interregionalism and transregionalism are seen, coupled with more multi-layered cooperations. Therefore, it is necessary to raise the questions "can BRICS, asa transregional grouping, consider their own development from a novel perspective in the face of the opportunities and challenges? And have the advantages of BRICS transregional cooperation been fully implemented and utilized?" To answer the questions, we can resort to the theory of transregionalism that may provide a wide-reaching vision for BRICS partners in pursuit of growth, thereby making them amenable to detecting feasible ideas and pathways.

## II. The Review of Transregionalism Theory

Transregionalism[①] is an objective phenomenon in international relations that

---

① It is also known as "crossregionalism".

comes with globalization and regionalization. The studies on transregionalism are often intertwined with interregionalism, but no conceptual consensus has been reached in academic community at present and the debate continues.

(1) **The Definition of Transregionalism**

After the Cold War, with rising regionalism and regional integration and development, region – based cooperation have gradually been in the spotlight in international relations, followed by the emergence of interregionalism. Transregionalism is deemed one of the forms of interregionalism, according to some scholars. Heiner Hänggi, for example, defines interregionalism as institutionalized links between regions in the world, and divides it into five: relations among biregional organizations or groupings (e. g., EU – ASEAN dialogue), relations between regional organizations or forums and regional integrated groups (e. g., ASEM – EU dialogue), relationship between transregional state groupings (e. g., the East Asia – Latin America Forum), relations between regional organizations or groupings and single powers in other regions (e. g., EU – US relations), and links between countries from different regions worldwide (e. g., APEC) .[1] From Heiner's point of view, only ties between biregional groupings or organizations constitute pure interregionalism, the relationship between regional organizations or groupings and single powers in other regions is considered as quasi – interregionalism, and the relations between more than two countries from different regions worldwide are perceived as transregionalism—a kind of mega – regionalism.[2] Further, in considering the diversity of interregional actors and the levels of institutionalization, Xianwu Zheng categorizes interregionalism into three: semi – interregionalism—the relations between regional organizations,

---

[1] Heiner Hänggi, Ralf Roloff, Jùrgen Rùland, "Interregionalism and Interational Relations," Oxon: Routledge, 2006, p. 40.

[2] Heiner Hänggi, "Interregionalism as a Multifaceted Phenomenon: In Search of a Typology," Heiner Hänggi and Ralf Roloff and Jùrgen Rùland, "Interregionalism and International Relations: A stepping Stone to Global Governance?" London: Routledge. 2005, pp. 31 – 62.

groupings or state groupings in one region and single powers in other regions; bi-interregionalism—the links among biregional organizations, groupings or state groupings; and transregionalism—the relationship among state groupings, regional organizations and groupings or non-state actors from more than two regions. [1] In analyzing interregional and transregional ties, Zongyi Liu suggests that, although it is important to distinguish regions geographically or strategically, the conceptual divisions mainly depend on functional basis, that is, it is non-geographical factors that actually work as a major driving force to fuel the establishment of interactions between regions. Therefore, interregionalism can be divided into bilateral interregionalism, transregionalism and hybrid interregionalism. [2] Zhimin Chen notes that North Atlantic Treaty Organization (NATO) and Asia-Pacific Economic Cooperation (APEC) should be perceived as transregional relations since the linkages between or across regions constitute interregional relations. [3] Bin Xiao classifies East Asian interregionalism into three: transregional group-to-group relations, bilateral and transregional arrangements and hybrid forms. [4]

On the other hand, some researchers suggest that interregionalism and transregionalism be clearly distinguished. Christopher Dent considers interregionalism to be the relationship between two independent regions, while transregionalism refers to the common spaces between regions or the actors in the regions. [5] Jürgen Rüland also believes that it is necessary to divide the interactions between

---

[1] Xianwu Zheng, "A New Level in International Studies: Theory and Practice of Interregionalism," World Economics and Politics, No. 8, 2008. p. 63 [in Chinese].

[2] Zongyi Liu, "The Implications of Development of Interregionalism," World Economics and Politics, No. 4, 2008, pp. 43-45 [in Chinese].

[3] Zhimin Chen, "Interregionalism and Global Order: NATO, APEC and ASEM," Fudan International Studies Review, 2006, p. 8 [in Chinese].

[4] Bin Xiao, "Inter-regionalism in East Asia: Theory and Practice," Journal of Contemporary Asia-Pacific Studies, No. 6, 2010, pp. 36-38 [in Chinese].

[5] Christopher Dent, "From Inter-regionalism to Trans-regionalism? Future challenges of ASEM," Asia Europe Journal, No. 1, 2003, p. 224.

regional organizations into interregionalism and transregionalism. Interregionalism that was born in the process of dialogues and interactions between biregional organizations based on soft institutions can be deemed bilateral interregionalism, such as ASEAN – EU dialogue, while transregionalism is the process of institutionalized cooperation among organizations or countries from different regions, such as ASEM.① Ping He points out that, despite the lack of research on interregional cooperation from a global perspective, interregional links, by nature, constitute a component of regionalism. He also proposes that transregionalism is a further conceptual development based on interregionalism, and defines it as the process of deep integration of states or state groupings from two or more regions in cooperation, such as the Trans – Pacific Strategic Economic Partnership Agreement (TPSEP).②

In addition, the recent Russian research on transregionalism is stoking concern. Considering interregional spaces from a global perspective, their studies on transregionalism are often conceptually connected with "macro – regionalization" (макрорегионализация). According to Russian researchers, macro – regionalization refers to the aggregations of nation – grouped regions – integrations of a higher level of regions③, such as the EU – Latin America Free Trade Area. Kosolapov (Н. А. Косолапов) indicates that transregionalism is only tenable based on the concept of space that is beyond geographic limitations.④ Voskresenski (А. Д. Воскресенский) states that transregionalism refers not only to macro –

---

① Jürgen Rüland, "The EU as an Inter – and Transregional Actor: Lessons for Global Governance from Europe's Relations with Asia," 2002, p. 3.
② Ping He, "Transregionalism: Regulation Fusion Based on Coalition of The Willing," Fudan International Studies Review, No. 2, 2014, pp. 268 – 269 [in Chinese].
③ К. А. Ефремова, "От регионализма к трансрегионализму: теоретическое осмысление новой реальности," Сравнительная политик, Vol. 8, No. 2, 2017, p. 65.
④ Н. А. Косолапов, "Пространственно – организационный подход к анализу международных реалий," Международные процессы, Vol. 5, No. 3, 2007, p. 59.

regionalized process, but also to the relations between macro – regions. ① According to Kuznetsov (Д. А. Кузнецов), transregionalism is a form of globalization against the background of new regionalism—a phenomenon that regional groupings and countries seek partnership beyond geographic borders through transregional cooperations to establish new economic, political and social spaces with the aim to protect their own benefits and interests. ②It is further explained by Yevlemova (К. А. Ефремова) that the practices of transregionalism is logically different from countries' accession to regional organizations or conclusions of interregional agreements. Let's say regional and interregional groupings are established in pursuit of political, economic and secure cooperations, whereas transregional groupings are created to enable their member states to participate in global governance. The politics – based transregional cooperations call for compromise to share the same position, thereby bringing their stands on international affairs, including in the negotiations on international politics, trading and financial system reform, into close alignment with each other. ③ It shows that, despite being adept at the theory of space construction in the studies on transregionalism, Russian researchers often have the propensity for separation and isolation with protectionism and confrontation at the back of their minds.

These discussions on the theory of transregionalism, either from the perspective of interregionalism or transregionalism, all help us understand and interpret international relations by providing a transregional view between regional and global dimensions. Against the backdrop of diverse international actors today, their interactions are also flourishing. Transregionalism emerges as a theoretical response to such close and various forms of international cooperation. As a matter

---

① А. Д. Воскресенский, "Мировое комплексное регионоведение," Магистр: ИНФРА – М, 2014, p. 18.

② Д. А. Кузнецов, "Феномен трансрегионализма: проблемы терминологии и концептуализации," Сравнительная политика, 2016, Vol. 23, No. 2, p. 24.

③ К. А. Ефремова, " От регионализма к трансрегионализму: теоретическое осмысление новой реальности," Сравнительная политик, Vol. 8, No. 2, 2017, pp. 68 – 70.

of fact, multidimensional spaces involved in international relations keep changing and evolving, as does the theoretical research on transregionalism. In my opinion, transregionalism can be considered as institutionalized dialogues and cooperations between more than two international actors from different regions worldwide. As the Indian scholar Rajasree K. R proposed, transregionalism developed in two stages: the first began with the conclusion of the Yaoundé Convention between the European Economic Community (EEC) and 18 associated African states and Madagascar (AASM) in 1963, which was characterized by the establishment of EEC – centered interregional alliances; and the second stage started in the 1990s, when transregionalism was primarily linked to economic cooperation, energy, ecology and non – traditional security in the context of fast – track globalization, regionalization and trade liberalization. ① In fact, before 1963, the seeds of transregionalism had been sown in the international community. During the Cold War period, a variety of transregional alliances were established for the purpose of coordinating security and energy affairs sprang up, including NATO, Southeast Asia Treaty Organization (SEATO), Central Treaty Organization (CENTO) and Organization of Petroleum Exporting Countries (OPEC). After the threshold of the 21st century, the practices of transregionalism in the international community have become more frequent and diversified, such as the emergence of MIKTA (a grouping of Mexico, Indonesia, Republic of Korea, Turkey and Australia), BRICS (a grouping of Brazil, Russia, India, China, and South Africa), the Belt and Road Initiative (BRI), ASEAN Plus Three (APT), Regional Comprehensive Economic Partnership (RCEP), Trans – Pacific Partnership Agreement (TPP) and other transregional institutionalized processes.

---

① Rajasree K. R. , "The Evolution of Transregional Cooperation: A Case Study of Indian Ocean Rim Association for Regional Cooperation," Online International Interdisciplinary Research Journal, Vol. 5, No. 5, 2015, pp. 289 – 291.

## (2) The Internal Logic of Transregionalism

Based on the definition in this paper and the common grounds of the above – mentioned transregional practices, it is necessary to interpret transregionalism as follows:

The underlying logic behind transregionalism is regionalism. Regions are divided according to multi – factors such as geography, geopolitics and geo – economy. But as economic globalization is gaining momentum today, the so – called "regions" —a division increasingly subject to subjective decisions—even turns into the "communities in imagination"[①]. As Professor Richard Sakwa noted, Eurasia was not discovered, but narratively created.[②] Derived from international actions in created regions, transregionalism works to shape new regional spaces in turn. On the one hand, transregionalism highlights the fact that institutionalized processes between subjects and others are beyond their own regional borders, which is tinged with subjectivity. On the other hand, transregional links reinforce the tendency to cast off original regional cooperation and to construct new cross – border frameworks by reshuffling regional partnerships[③], thus intensifying new identities and affecting related regional governance. For example, the member states from Asia, Oceania, North America and South America in APEC all participate in institutionalized dialogues and cooperations in global economic governance, multilateral trading system, non – traditional security and people – to – people exchange beyond the boundaries, that is, they have "stepped out" of the traditional geographic limitations where the member states are located. At the same time, APEC has, in turn, strengthened the concept of "Asia – Pacific" and affected the economic governance in the region.

Transregionalism is developed by the logic of multilateralism and open-

---

① Ping He, "Transregionalism: Regulation Fusion Based on Coalition of The Willing," Fudan International Studies Review, No. 2, 2014, p. 266 [in Chinese].

② Richard Sakwa, "Challenges of Eurasian Integration," Russian Studies, No. 2, 2014, p. 15.

③ Tianxiang Zhu, "Research on Interregionalism: Achievements and Shortcomings," Journal of Contemporary Asia – Pacific Studies, No. 6, 2010, p. 27 [in Chinese].

ness. Some scholars, Xianwu Zheng for example, explicitly state that transregional practices should involve "more than two" participants when defining transregionalism. But other scholars describe participants in transregional arrangements as "countries or regional organizations from multiple regions worldwide". Despite the latter definition, an institutionalized cooperation between two countries from different regions—though it is studied from a perspective of transregionalism—should be interpreted as a bilateral cooperation rather than a transregional partnership. Therefore, when conceptually distinguishing transregionalism, it is necessary for us to preclude this misinterpretation and cling to the "more – than – two – participants" definition—the reason why transregionalism is established by the logic of multilateralism. Further, the openness of transregionalism is also pronounced with the more – than – two – participants scenario, since the uncapped number of partners can dynamically increase or decrease. For example, TPP was originally initiated by 4 countries, namely New Zealand, Singapore, Chile and Brunei, and then 12 countries including the U. S. , Australia, Vietnam, Japan and Mexico announced their involvements, but followed by the withdrawal of the U. S. in 2017. In view of that, we can say that the openness of transregionalism is a two – way street allowing both accession and withdrawal.

Transregionalism is practiced based on the logic of institutionalization. In existing research, transregionalism has been either loosely defined as "relationship" or explicitly perceived as "process of institutionalized cooperation" and "institutionalized dialogues and cooperations"[①]. It can be concluded that transregionalism is founded with the principle and the aim of dialogue, coordination

---

[①] According to Russian scholar Maria Lebedeva, transregionalism refers to the institutionalized cooperative process among countries and regional organizations from different regions worldwide. Meanwhile, as Tianxiang Zhu indicated, interregionalism is the institutionalized dialogues and cooperations carried out by nation – states and regional organizations from different regions or sub – regions worldwide, based on the original seperate or under a newly – established regional structure. See М. М. Лебедева, Д. А. Кузнецов, "Трансрегионализм – новый феномен мировой политики. Полис," Политические исследования, No. 5, 2019, p. 73; Tianxiang Zhu, "Research on Interregionalism: Achievements and Shortcomings," Journal of Contemporary Asia – Pacific Studies, No. 6, 2010, p. 12.

and cooperation, rather than confrontation. Despite varying degree of institutionalization in different transregional arrangements, all participants' recognition will invariably underlie the partnership. Transregional processes can be institutionalized in the forms of dialogue, forum and meeting with the aim to reach memorandum, statement, declaration and agreement. Subject to its nature, transregional cooperations are often faced with more conundrums than regional partnership, so transregionalism is often exercised in lowly institutionalized processes at the beginning, but with the possibility of improving. Lowly institutionalized transregionalism is more likely to be practiced in regions featuring low politics, but some transregional groupings opt for institutionalized cooperations in areas of high politics, such as G7 and NATO. It is worth noting that transregionalism, albeit as one form of integration, is possibly implemented without integration. For instance, in the BRI which spans multiple regions, the transregional cooperation between China and regional countries is not aimed at integration but in pursuit of achieving shared development and prosperity with win – win results. By the end of 2019, China had signed 200 BRI – based cooperative agreements with 168 countries and international organizations, and had established the working groups on promoting unimpeded trade with 8 countries, e – commerce cooperations with 22 countries and the cooperation in services trade with 14 countries[1]—a clear indication of institutionalized practices of transregionalism.

Transregionalism is also inclined to upgrade by the logic of globalization. The emergence and development of transregionalism are not determined by one country alone but objectivelyaccompany advancing globalization and regionalization. Compared to regionalism in which development is confined to regional boundaries, transregionalism is spared from such curbs and grows into a globalizing process to some extent. Transregional processes may grow global when partic-

---

[1] "Ministry of Commerce of the People's Republic of China. 2019 BRI Achievements in 6 Aspects," CINIC, Jan. 30, 2020, http://www.cinic.org.cn/xw/bwdt/715978.html? from = singlemessage [in Chinese].

ipants are able to involve in globalization to the extent and in the way that they accept, and when national and regional economic activities, experience models and even positions and envisions may be disseminated to other regions in transregional cooperation. Institutionalized cooperations of international actors in transregional spaces seems destined to split globalization but turns out to be a new pathway for growing global, that is, global interconnectivity will be more multi – layered and closely knit through transregional interactions.

Transregionalism is also logically connected with regional and global governance. In transregional schemes, international actors make efforts for multilateral institutionalized cooperation by crossing the boundaries—a cross – border international partnership that can be regarded as a positive action in pursuit of globalization and enhances the global significance. International cooperation may be implemented at national, regional and global levels which can be closely knitted in transregional spaces. Despite being traditionally present in the major forms of trade agreement, institutionalized meeting, dialogue and forum, transregionalism has been practiced through institutionalized cooperations of great diversity. Especially with the increasing chances to build partnership, more countries strive to make innovations and attempts in transregional cooperations. The BRI is a telltale example. First of all, China has gradually expanded the scope of transregional cooperations through lowly institutionalized projects, coupled with the establishment of financial institutions to provide reliable support and intensified by the joint efforts of China and Russia to actively connect the Silk Road Economic Belt and the Eurasian Economic Union (EAEU) —an innovation in transregional cooperative mechanisms and regional integrated organizations. Transregional partnership can essentially be perceived as international cooperations, and it may evolve into effective modes of regional and global governances as clinging to an open development. For a long time, global governance has been faced with difficulty in reaching coordinated consensus among different countries and regions. By contrast, a certain degree of unanimity about different issues in different fields may be achieved by international actors in transregional arrangements through collectively - recognized cooperative modes. In a word, transregional cooperative models are useful guidelines for regional and global governances, and the achievements of such cooperations can work as a new driving force to fuel the improvement of global governance.

Transregionalism can be regarded as a new institutionalized cooperative framework among specific international actors. As transregionalism is increasingly prevalent, multiple transregional processes may overlap in the same regions, and intricate transregional groupings established for cooperation or competition may inevitably be intertwined worldwide. Presumably, the looming spaghetti bowl effect would be on the horizon at regional and global levels if positive interactions were not formed between transregional schemes and between transregional and regional arrangements.

## III. The Analysis of BRICS Transregionalism

As a mechanism for multilateral dialogues and cooperations, BRICS remains the prominent feature of "crossing regions". The term "BRICS" was coined in 2001 by Jim O'Neil, a chief economist of Goldman Sachs, who claims that Brazil, Russia, India and China (BRIC) would be the fastest rising emerging economies in the world. 8 years later, under the impacts of the global financial crisis, the leaders of the four countries held their first official meeting in Yekaterinburg in June 2009, marking the establishment of the BRIC mechanism for multilateral dialogues and collaborations. As the Joint Statement of the BRIC Countries' Leaders, Yekaterinburg (2009) issued during the summit noted, "The dialogue and cooperation of the BRIC countries are conducive not only to serving the common interests of emerging market economies and developing countries, but also to building a harmonious world of lasting peace and common prosperity." BRIC had officially become BRICS, since South Africa's accession with the BRIC nations' unanimous approval through consultation in December, 2010. For a decade, the BRICS countries from Latin America, Europe, Asia and Africa have established a system of rotating presidency and a mechanism for multi - level dialogues. In addition to holding annual summits and ministerial meetings, BRICS has carried out various forms of cooperative dialogues in economy, trade, finance, agriculture and people - to - people exchange. BRICS, constituted by five countries from different regions of the world, is an archetype of transregional groupings. The transregional collaborations among BRICS nations not only align with the common nature of transregionalism but also exhibit their unique features:

(1) **BRICS has built transregional interactive spaces among emerging market countries and developing countries.**

As the American scholar Joseph Nye argued, there are twomajor power shifts occurring in international politics in the 21st century and one is among countries.[1] As a representative grouping of emerging countries, BRICS that emerged against the backdrop of profound transitioning and changing landscape worldwide has stoked great concerns from the international community. BRICS nations, the typical emerging market economies from different regions, all rank among the leading developing countries in terms of economy, industrialization and science and technology. The exemplary transregional partnership among BRICS in emerging markets has creatively paved the way for South - South cooperation. South - South cooperation is the mutually beneficial cooperation among developing countries in a number of fields, such as economy, technology and trade. Based on the respect of similar histories and the recognition of similar daunting challenges after national independences, it is an important way for developing countries to seek self - reliant and independent growth.[2] Having stood up to global financial crisis and other major challenges, the BRICS countries have pio-

---

[1] Joseph Nye, "The Future of power," Beijing: CITIC Press, 2012. p. 22 [in Chinese].

[2] Jingying Sun and Changqing Qiu, "South - South cooperation in the context of the BRI: Pathway and Future," Social Sciences in Guangxi, No. 2, 2016, p. 135 [in Chinese].

neered a new way for emerging market economies and developing countries in pursuit of solidarity, cooperation and mutually beneficial and win – win results.[①] The transregional dialogues and cooperation among the five countries have broken the traditional frameworks in the grip of geographical and cultural limitations. With the shared identity of emerging market economies, BRICS nations have set up transregional interactive spaces conducive to deeper mutual understanding, economic and trading collaborations and political communications among them. Meanwhile, since BRICS transregionalism, by the nature of openness, keeps developing and evolving, the established transregional spaces can attract and accommodate more emerging market economies and developing countries to join the dialogues and cooperation.

Subject to the underlying logic of regionalism, the transregional scheme of BRICS brings together major emerging market countries from four continents. As the BRICS institutionalized cooperation rolls out, increasing dialogues and collaborations are carried out between the grouping and other emerging market economies, developing countries in the transregional spaces, thereby making the location – specific cooperation effects carry over to other participants' soils. Because of the important role of emerging market economies and developing countries in global political and economic system, the BRICS – built spaces provide an opportunity for them to seek solidarity, cooperation and integration into the international system. It is expected that the transregional cooperation effects will have beneficial spillovers worldwide when the BRICS – led transregional partnership keeps developing to a certain degree. Therefore, in addition to regional significance, the transregional interactive spaces among emerging market economies and developing countries are present with global salience. It is worth noting that, instead of pursuing any integrated development at the cost of transferring partial sovereignty, BRICS has, by dint of these transregional practices, the aspiration

---

① Xi Jingping, "The address at the press conference of BRICS Summit in Xiamen," GOV, Sep. 5, 2017, http: //www.gov.cn/xinwen/2017 – 09/05/content_5222821.htm [in Chinese].

to build open, pluralistic and inclusive spaces instrumental in cross – border dialogues and cooperation. Its development will be beneficial to the building of a community with shared interests, responsibilities and destiny among emerging market economies and developing countries.

(2) "BRICS Plus" is an institutional innovation based on the open development in BRICS transregional scheme.

At the 2017 BRICS Summit in Xiamen, China, the term "BRIC Plus" was first officially used in the BRICS Leaders Xiamen Declaration. As ChinesePresident Xi Jinping pointed out at the opening ceremony of the BRICS Business Forum, BRICS is committed to the principle of open and inclusive cooperation, values the cooperations with other emerging market economies and developing countries, and has established an effective mechanism for dialogues, so it is necessary for us to seek extension of BRICS cooperations with the aim of making wide – ranging regions benefit from them, to promote BRICS Plus cooperative model, and to build an open and pluralistic network of partnership, thereby allowing more emerging market economies and developing countries to participate in the development featuring solidarity, cooperation and mutual benefit. [1] From the perspective of transregionalism, BRICS Plus is an institutional arrangement through which BRICS countries grouped as a whole to engage in dialogues and collaborations with international actors from other regions. Compared to the BRICS – built transregional spaces where emerging market economies and developing countries can interact with each other, BRICS Plus works as a channel for them to integrate into these spaces.

The emergence of BRICS Plus defers to the nature of BRICS transregionalism. At the Sanya Summit in 2011 right after South Africa was addedto the list to make BRIC become BRICS, the goal of BRICS transregional development was

---

[1] Xi Jingping, "Address at the Opening Ceremony of the BRICS Business Forum," Xinhua, Sep. 3, 2017, http://www.xinhuanet.com/politics/2017 – 09/03/c_1121596338.htm [in Chinese].

clearly identified: extending from "promoting reforms of international financial institutions" to "focusing on major contributions to advancing human society and to building a more equal and fair world"; and "strengthening global economic governance and intensifying democratic international relations on the basis of mutual respect and through collective decisions, and amplifying the voices of emerging and developing countries in international affairs"[1]. These principles will always underlie the BRICS' efforts in pursuing wide – reaching dialogues and cooperation. At the 2013 BRICS Summit in Durban, South Africa, the host country in presidency put the principle of open development in BRICS transregionalism into practice for the first time. Under the framework of BRICS cooperation, it held a BRICS – Africa dialogue meeting by inviting the leaders of African countries and organizations, including the presidents of Senegal, Chad, Angola, Cô te d' Ivoire, Benin, Congo, Mozambique, Uganda, Equatorial Guinea, Guinea, and Egypt, the Prime Minister of Ethiopia as well as the chairman of the African Union Commission. Brazil followed suit by involving 11 Latin American countries in a dialogue with BRICS at the Fortaleza Summit in 2014. In 2015, the BRICS Summit was held to coincide with the Shanghai Cooperation Organization (SCO) Summit in Ufa, Russia, at which the BRICS countries worked in concert with the member states of EAEU and SCO as well as the observer states to discuss the solidarity and collaborations with emerging market economies and developing countries for the purpose of improving people's well – being in these regions. In 2016, under the framework of the BRICS Goa Summit, a dialogue meeting was held between BRICS and the member states of the Bay of Bengal Initiative for Multi – Sectoral Technical and Economic Cooperation (BIMSTEC) in South Asia. In 2017, China, as the host country in presidency, formally proposed the mode of BRICS Plus and invited Egypt, Guinea, Mexico, Tajikistan and Thailand to participate in the BRICS Summit. Following the guidance of BRICS Plus,

---

[1] "Sanya Declaration of the Third BRICS Leaders Meeting (full text)," China News, Apr. 14, 2011, http://www.chinanews.com/gn/2011/04 – 14/2973144.shtml [in Chinese].

the Johannesburg BRICS Summit in 2018 invited not only African countries and regions, but also Argentina, Jamaica, Turkey, Indonesia and Egypt to discuss inclusive growth, common prosperity and other topics. Although BRICS Plus approach was not adopted during the 2019 Brasilia Summit in Brazil, BRICS summit was scheduled to take place concurrently with SCO summit in Russia in 2020. It is worth mentioning that, according to the 2020 priorities of BRICS development proposed by Russia as BRICS chair, the interactions with other BRICS partners should be strengthened by applying BRICS Plus and outreach approaches[1]. As some Russian diplomats and scholars stated, compared to BRICS Plus, the outreach activity refers to the efforts to outreach BRICS interactions with neighboring non-BRICS countries in the region where BRICS chair is located. As a matter of fact, the outreach approach was first adopted at the South Durban Summit in 2013[2]. The Russia-proposed outreach process is virtually a location-specific BRICS interaction.

So, it can be concluded that BRICS Plus has become an open institutional arrangement based on BRICS transregionalism. BRICS Plus is exercised by upholding the principle subject to geographic definition and developing countries identity, targeting either nations or regional organizations. Although the suspension at the 2019 Brasilia Summit seemed to put BRICS Plus in a tricky position according to some scholars[3], we have reason to believe that, based on the clear point of BRICS unanimity about "promoting cooperation with other emerging market economies and developing countries", BRICS collaborations in any form in future will virtually be the practices of BRICS Plus in good faith to allow more emerging market economies and developing countries to carry out dialogues and co-

---

[1] "Приоритеты председательства Российской Федерации в БРИКС," https://brics-russia2020.ru/russia_in_brics/20191226/1362/Prioritety-predsedatelstva-Rossiyskoy-Federatsii-v-BRIKS.html.

[2] "В МИД допустили возможность проведения саммита БРИКС в расширенном формате," РИА Новости, Nov. 11, 2019, https://ria.ru/20191111/1560805535.html.

[3] Letian Xie, "BRICS Plus Dilemma and Solution Based on The Brasilia Summit," Jul. 23, 2020, https://www.essra.org.cn/view-1000-896.aspx [in Chinese].

operations in BRICS - built transregional spaces. As the BRICS transregionalism is moving forward, the understandings and visions of BRICS Plus from different angles have been seen among the five members, since the scheme remains conceptually open and needs to be further improved and developed.

## (3) Balancing, governing and identity building are the major functions of BRICS transregionalism.

According to Jürgen Rüland, the functions of regionalism can be divided into seven: Balancing and bandwagoning, institution - building, rationalizing, agenda - setting, identity - building, stabilizing and development. [1] As to the BRICS regionalism, the transregional spaces built by the state grouping are not sealed off from outside world, but exert influence with joint efforts of the five countries for regional and global interactions. In summary, the functions of BRICS transregionalism are nationally, regionally and globally manifested in terms of balancing, governing and identity building.

The balancing function of BRICS transregionalism first is the power responsive to external balancers. Guided by BRICS transregionalism, the institutionalized cooperation of the five countries have been improved and a new state grouping of emerging market economies has been formed. BRICS hopes to throw off geographic shackles on growth by enhancing transregional relations in the global structure, to draw on collective resource advantages of emerging market economies and developing countries, and to strike a balance with developed countries, thereby dominating more favorable heights in the international system. The balancing function also plays a role within the grouping. Based on equal dialogues and a variety of cooperative mechanisms for mutually beneficial and win - win results, BRICS strives to constantly intensify links in various fields, balance internal interests and reach a consensus on development. By doing so, it has succeeded in

---

[1] Jürgen Rüland, "The EU as an Inter - and Transregional Actor: Lessons for Global Governance from Europe's Relations with Asia," 2002, p. 7.

balancing powers and stabilizing growth inside the grouping while providing channels and opportunities for the five countries to participate in global affairs, reinforce international status and sharpen competitive advantages.

The governing function of BRICS transregionalism is pronounced with its participation in regional and global governance. BRICS countries have the responsibilityto speak for emerging market economies and developing countries in the United Nations, the World Trade Organization, the International Monetary Fund, G20 and other major international arenas. The institutionalized cooperation based on BRICS transregionalism are exhibited in a variety of forms, span wide – ranging regions and involve a number of international cooperation, particularly exemplified by the BRICS Development Bank (NDB) which is an important breakthrough for the grouping to effectively join in regional and global governance. As the first entity resulting from BRICS – led transregional cooperation, the Shanghai – based NDB was founded by the five countries with an initial total of $10 billion in cash and was officially put into operation in 2015. Over the past five years, the New Development Bank has provided a slew of funding to BRICS countries, institutions and companies in the fields of energy, transportation, river management, environmental protection and public health. Brazil, for example, was loaned $1 billion to get a handle on the COVID – 19 pandemic.[①] In August 2017, the NDB launched the Africa Regional Center, which is emblematic of BRICS countries' commitment to unwavering support for funding sustainable infrastructure construction in Africa and helping African governments solve regional problems. The concept of openness, equality and win – win cooperation of NDB will make it a replicable exemplary model at the regional and global levels in efforts to change global financial order. At the same time, the NDB is also a necessary supplement to the current regional and global financial governance system. As the advantages of BRICS transregionalism are increasingly brought into

---

① "Approved – projects," New Development Bank, https://www.ndb.int/projects/list – of – all – projects/approved – projects/page/1/.

full play, its role in the areas of international finance, trade, energy, environmental protection and public health will continue in regional and global governance.

The function of BRICS transregionalism also rests on identity building. BRICS is not a naturally formed but an artificially honed geographical concept, and the BRICS identity should be relentlessly enriched and reinforced to associate the five nations as a collective in transregional cooperation one after another. Only when the five countries from different regions—albeit emerging economies withheterogeneity and uneven development—stand together continuously seeking transregional collaborative opportunities can BRICS scheme make the most of collective advantages. Through transregional cooperation, the mutual understanding among BRICS countries will be deepened, thus making them amenable to reaching a consensus on international and regional issues on the basis of expanding common grounds while shelving differences, and to joining a chorus for their interests in international arenas. By doing so, the collective cohesion inside the grouping will in turn be intensified. As the BRICS transregionalism is deeply going full steam ahead, BRICS has repeatedly stressed the importance of multilateralism in its annual summits, and has been devoted to the joint efforts to build an exemplary international political and economic order featuring fairness, equity, equality and democracy to cultivate the BRICS spirit of "mutual respecting and understanding, treating each other as equals, solidarity, mutual assistance, openness and inclusiveness for mutually beneficial results"[1]. The sense of connection among BRICS partners with shared appreciation is reinforced.

The next golden decade of BRICS is righton the horizon. To realize the aspiration of "amplifying the voices from emerging and developing countries in international affairs and building a more equal and just world", the BRICS – built interactive spaces based on transregionalism seem destined to have the advantage of

---

[1] "Xiamen Declaration of BRICS Leaders," Xinhua, Sep. 4, 2017, http://www.xinhuanet.com/world/2017-09/04/c_1121603652.htm [in Chinese].

connectivity among nations, regions and the world. It should be noted that, rather than the short - sighted partnership that is formed on a case - by - case basis, the transregionalism - based international cooperation of BRICS are rolled out strategically in pursuit of emerging market economies' underlying interests based on long - term development and prosperity. Despite some differences and conflicts among the five partners that cannot be solved at present, transregional cooperation of BRICS among emerging market economies and developing countries will steer the course unwaveringly as planned, in vivid contrast to the case - by - case partnership in general. It is found, by analyzing the functions of BRICS transregionalism, that BRICS is expected to play the dual roles as external and internal balancers and to find a practical pathway to growth through regional and global governance on a basis of identity building among the members. Meanwhile, since the three functions often work as an integrated whole, BRICS identity - building will be continuously strengthened as the governing and balancing functions are performed, resulting in the beneficial development of BRICS transregionalism. From the perspective of transregionalism, the gambit for BRICS institutionalization and identity - building has been a prospective one. So, it can be foreseen that whether the governing function is given into full play is the key to BRICS growth in next stage.

## Conclusion

As Chinese president Xi Jinping stressed at the closing ceremony of the China - France Global Governance Forum in 2019, four major deficits in global governance should be tackled by the China strategies. These deficits and strategies are: governance deficit which should be addressed through the commitment tofairness and equity; trust deficit, handled by seeking mutual consultation and compromise; peace deficit, solved by working in unison for common goals; and development deficit, delt with by pursing win - win benefits. At the same time, rising regional powers and increasingly intensive competition between regions both heighten the salience of regional governance, and the relationship between regional and global governance have come into focus. Living up to its responsibility as a super power in the world, China is able and willing to play an active role in global and regional governance. The BRICS spirit is in line with the China strategies for the four deficits in global governance. BRICS is not only an important platform for China to promote the reform of global governance system, but also a facilitator that provides various channels for the country to participate in regional governance. As a large country in Asia, China can make full use of the foundation and advantages of BRICS transregionalism and strive to hone the exemplary BRICS model instrumental for regional and global governance by fueling transregional growth of BRICS in the area. The transregional approach for BRICS development contributes to the connectivity both within and between regions, complementary to the BRI goal of improving world connectivity.

The concept of building a community with a sharedfuture for humanity is a vital component of China's diplomacy with Chinese characteristics. It is a Chinese vision that is present to shape a new international order. The envisaged community will subsist beyond geographic, cultural and political boundaries of regions and be guided by the logic of transregionalism. Since building a community with a shared destiny for humanity is a measured and phased process calling for bilateral, regional and transregional cooperation at multi-levels and in multi-dimensions, BRICS, as a transregional mechanism, can be regarded as a critical breakthrough. After the achievement of the "first golden decade", a community with shared interests has been actually formed among the BRICS countries. Particularly, under the impacts of COVID-19 pandemic and deglobalization, it is time to establish a BRICS community with shared responsibilities. Additionally, the BRICS-built transregional spaces for emerging market economies and developing countries, featuring equality and openness for mutual benefits, will provide opportunities to form a community with a shared destiny among the targeted participants in cross-border interactions based on BRICS interests and responsibilities. In this process, BRICS transregionalism should be exercised following the guidelines of strong national power. In view of this, it is necessary for China, with a clear – cut approach and careful plan, to bend energy to develop BRICS into a transregional platform for all – round mutually – beneficial cooperation between emerging market countries and developing countries, thereby carrying over the BRICS success to the next decade.

# The Evolution of Brazil's BRICS View and the Study of China – Brazil BRICS Cooperation

Xie Letian* Liu Mengru**

**Abstract**: Brazil, as one of the "Four Founding Countries" of BRICS, has experienced an evolution of its BRICS identity, from pursuing the status of a great power to attaching importance to economic benefits, then to downplaying its BRICS identity and readjusting its focus on the BRICS policy. This shift is related to the interest demands of the Brazilian government during different periods. Against the background of the new Brazilian government taking office, China, as an important member of BRICS country, should give full play to its unique advantages by starting from the "Three Pillars" of BRICS cooperation, focusing on strengthening Security Council reform and cooperation, expanding economic and trade exchanges, establishing a high – level people – to – people exchange mechanism, and promoting multilateral BRICS cooperation through bilat-

---

\* Xie Letian, PhD candidate in National Security, School of International Relations & Public Affairs, Fudan University.

\*\* Liu Mengru, Lecturer of Portuguese major in College of Western Language and Culture, Sichuan International Studies University, PhD in linguistics, University of Coimbra, Portugal, researcher of BRICs Research Institute, Sichuan International Studies University.

eral cooperation to help Brazil strengthen the recognition of BRICS identity and promote the continuous development of the BRICS mechanism.

**Keywords**: Brazil; Brazilian diplomacy; BRICS countries; China – Brazil Relations

The rise of the BRICS mechanism is largely due to the active efforts of Russia and Brazil. After more than a decade of development, BRICS cooperation mechanism has become an important force for emerging market countries and developing countries to participate in global governance. With the continuous maturation of the BRICS mechanism, in order to ensure that emerging market countries can play a greater role in global governance, a new round of expansion is necessary to allow more like – minded dialogue partners to join the BRICS mechanism. Brazil's initial recognition of the BRICS mechanism stems from its interest demands to expand its international influence. At the same time, it can be found that Brazil has certain similarities and differences in the fields of BRICS cooperation in different periods, and even shows its indifference and aversion to BRICS cooperation. So, what are the underlying reasons for the similarities and differences? How can China – Brazil cooperation be correctly positioned in the BRICS mechanism? These are the issues to be discussed in this paper.

# Ⅰ. The evolution of Brazilian government's "BRICS view"

## (1) Brazil's "BRICS view" inthe Lula period

The overall positioning of the BRICS mechanism

During the reign of Luiz Inácio Lula da Silva, Brazil actively participated in BRIC activities and hosted the second BRIC leaders' summit as the rotating presidency in 2010. Lula's government believes that South – South cooperation is the priority and core of Brazil's foreign policy. In view of this, it is one of the strategic priorities of Brazil's diplomacy to strengthen relations with emerging developing powers represented by BRIC countries. [1]

Based on this consideration, the Lula government's cognition and views on BRIC cooperation mechanism are generally positive. Under the BRIC mechanism, Brazil's ties with major developing countries make it possible for Brazil to achieve the goal of political power and enhance its international status. Specifically, on the one hand, during Brazil's hosting of the BRIC summit in 2010, Brazil made great efforts to institutionalize and regularize BRIC cooperation. Compared with the first Yekaterinburg Joint Statement, the second Brasilia Joint Statement is longer, covering more fields and covering a wider range of areas[2], and initially determines a dual – track – parallel mode for BRIC cooperation on political security, economy, trade and finance for the next stage. In addition, in terms of expanding cooperation mechanism, the Lula government also believes that BRIC countries should enhance their representation in emerging market countries and developing countries. For example, the 2010 summit not only made clear in the 2010 Joint Statement in which areas the BRIC countries will carry out cooperation in the future. [3] Meanwhile, the then president of South Africa, Jacob Zuma, also visited Brazil and held bilateral talks with the BRIC countries to discuss matters related to South Africa's entry into BRIC. With the joint efforts of BRICS member countries, South Africa officially joined the BRICS in 2011. [4]

Understanding of Brazil's BRICS demands

After Lula came to power in 2003, he clearly pointed out that Brazil should

---

[1] Wu Zhihua, "Brazil has worked hard to project an image as a great power," People's Daily, Dec. 29, 2010.

[2] See "Joint Statement of the BRIC Countries' Leaders," People's Daily, June 17, 2009; "2nd BRIC Summit of Heads of State and Government: Joint Statement," BRICS Information Centre, Apr. 15, 2010, http://www.brics.utoronto.ca/docs/100415 – leaders.html.

[3] See "2nd BRIC Summit of Heads of State and Government: Joint Statement," BRICS Information Centre, April 15, 2010, http://www.brics.utoronto.ca/docs/100415 – leaders.html.

[4] "Minister Nkoana – Mashabane on SA full membership of BRICS," Department of International Relations and Cooperation of Republic of South Africa, Dec. 23, 2010, http://www.dirco.gov.za/docs/2010/brics1224.html.

try to change the traditional diplomatic line of focusing only on the developed countries of the United States and Europe, and adopt a bolder and more sensible foreign policy, that is, striving to maintain a balance between the north and the south. ① Therefore, Lula actively promotes Brazil's domestic economic recovery and promotes all – round diplomacy, not only maintaining the relationship with traditional partners, but also giving priority to developing partnerships with South Africa, China and India. ② This positive action, to a great extent, foreshadows the establishment of the BRICS mechanism in the future. The reason why Lula's government chose to embrace the BRICS lies in the fact that the BRICS mechanism is in line with the interests of Brazil's great power diplomacy and strengthening its international influence. Under this mechanism, Brazil can effectively enhance its status as a political power and realize diplomatic transformation and breakthrough. Therefore, the core of the Lula government's appeal for BRICS lies in the idea that five countries are far more influential than an individual country in the international arena. ③

In addition, due to the outbreak of the world financial crisis in 2008, Brazil, which pursues an export – oriented economic policy, has been greatly affected. In order to deal with the crisis, it is necessary for the Brazilian government to take some active policies to expand the international market and hedge the crisis risk. At this time, the timely emergence of the G20 mechanism and BRICS cooperation mechanism provided an opportunity for Brazil's foreign trade to break through. During the first BRIC leaders' meeting in 2009, Lula stressed that the international financial crisis has made the international community aware of the importance of emerging countries. Strengthening cooperation among emerging

---

① Zhou Zhiwei, "Strategic consideration and effect analysis of Brazil's participation in BRICs cooperation," Latin American Studies, No. 4, 2017, p. 111.

② "Minister Nkoana – Mashabane on SA full membership of BRICS," Department of International Relations and Cooperation of Republic of South Africa, Dec. 23, 2010, http: //www. dirco. gov. za/docs/2010/brics1224. html.

③ Zhou Zhiwei, "Strategic consideration and effect analysis of Brazil's participation in BRICS cooperation," Latin American Studies, No. 4, 2017, p. 111.

countries will greatly affect international relations. BRIC cooperation has huge development space. It is necessary to expand bilateral trade and increase coordination and cooperation in financial and other fields, committed to building a better world. ①

The Lula government believes that BRICS cooperation is actually the only way for Brazil to become a political power. Therefore, Lula government tries its best to promote BRICS cooperation and is happy to see the BRICS influence expand day by day.

(2) **Brazil's "BRICS view" in Rousseff's period**
The overall positioning of the BRICS mechanism

As Lula's successor, Dilma Rousseff's foreign policy basically continues with the aggressive Pluralistic & Autonomous style of Lula's period, and still actively promotes the BRICS cooperation mechanism which stands at a new historical starting point after the BRICS Expansion. And in 2014, Dilma Rousseff hosted the summit of BRICS leaders in Fortaleza.

Duringher hosting of the Fortaleza summit, Rousseff proposed that BRICS countries should look to the future, unite and strengthen themselves, start to establish close and solid partnerships, improve global governance, and promote world multipolarization and democratization of international relations. ② Obviously, in the view of Rousseff government, the BRICS countries should continue to play the role of firm defenders of international order and reform practitioners. In view of this, the Brazilian government pushed the BRICS countries to strengthen the reform process in global economic governance, and finally pushed the BRICS countries to usher in an important milestone in the establishment of subordinate

---

① Cheng Zhijie, "The Origin of BRICS Cooperation Mechanism," International Research Reference, Issue 6, 2017, p. 6.

② He Shuangrong, "Cooperation Mechanism Between Brazil and BRICS Countries: Strategic Considerations, Results Evaluation and Possible Policy Adjustments," Contemporary World, No. 8, 2017, p. 26.

branches.① The developed countries, represented by the United States, began to change their attitude towards reform from positive stance to a delaying approach, and sought to regain the dominant position in the process②. At the same time, in the face of the severe controversy over the reform program of the 2010 International Monetary Fund (IMF), Brazil and other BRICS member countries, actively promoted cooperation in the field of financial security. Finally, they reached an important consensus on the statutory capital of the New Development Bank (NDB), the proportion of contributions and voting shares of each country, and the establishment of a Contingent Reserve Arrangement (CRA) with an initial capital scale of US $100 billion in order to help BRICS and other emerging markets and developing countries address infrastructure gaps, meet the needs of sustainable development, prevent systemic financial risks, and complement the existing international mechanisms. ③

In general, the Rousseff administration regards BRICS cooperation as an important channel to enhance its economic strength, promote Brazil's export - oriented economy to achieve greater achievements, and effectively enhance Brazil's ability to resist systemic financial risks and calmly cope with the economic crisis.

Understanding of Brazil's BRICS demands

Due to the weak self - growth ability of Brazil's economy, its economic structure is sensitive and fragile④, which in turn makes Brazil's economy face greater risks. Under Rousseff, this risk has been magnified by the economic downturn in the United States and the euro area, the fluctuation of international

---

① Ma Shuqiang and Han Xianyang: "BRIC Leaders' Meeting Held in Yekaterinburg," Guangming Daily, June 17, 2009.

② "Xi Jinping attended the sixth BRICS leaders' meeting and delivered an important speech," World Knowledge, 2014, No. 15, p. 6.

③ "End of the Brazilian BRICS Chairpersonship," Ministério das Relações Exteriores, Mar. 31, 2015, https://www.gov.br/mre/en/contact - us/press - area/press - releases/closing - of - the - brazilian - presidency - of - the - brics..

④ Zhang Jiaming, "IMF Reform and BRICS Emergency Reserve Arrangement," Theoretical Discussion, No. 6, 2014, p. 101.

commodity prices and other factors, as well as the already severe and complex economic situation in Brazil[1], which has led to the setback of Brazil's economic development. The pragmatic Rousseff government made appropriate adjustments at the diplomatic level according to the actual situation. The core reason is that economy is an important factor affecting Brazil's diplomacy. At the same time, Brazil's Accession to the Standing Committee to achieve the goals of regional leaders and world powers has not fundamentally changed. [2] This pragmatism adjustment is the reason why, as mentioned above, when developed countries refused to make concessions on the reform of global economic governance, Brazil chose to take the initiative to change and actively sought to achieve a breakthrough within BRICS during its term.

The Rousseff government believes that Brazil's participation in the BRICS cooperation mechanism and the smooth development of its work are still based on the basic consideration that Brazil's own interests will not be damaged. On the issue of the new development bank and the emergency reserve arrangement, the Brazilian government's vital interest is not to be satisfied with membership in the G20 to participate in global economic governance, but to further expand its voting power and voice. In response, Rousseff described it as a sign of the times, calling for reform of the International Monetary Fund. [3]Similarly, at the United Nations level, the Brazilian government still believes that BRICS cooperation can expand its political influence for Brazil, which is beneficial to seeking political power. After the outbreak of the Ukraine crisis in 2014, despite the enormous pressure from domestic opposition forces, the Rousseff government still believes that the consistent position of BRICS on Ukraine is in Brazil's own interests.

---

[1] "The 6th BRICS Summit: Fortaleza Declaration," BRICS Information Centre, Jul. 15, 2014, http://www.brics.utoronto.ca/docs/140715-leaders.html.

[2] Wang Yunping and Sheng Chaoxun, "Background, Path and Countermeasures of Manufacturing Recovery in Different Economies," China Economic and Trade Guide, No. 23, 2011, p. 28.

[3] Andrew F. Cooper and Asif B. Farooq, "Testing the Club Dynamics of the BRICS: The New Development Bank from Conception to Establishment," International Organisations Research Journal, Vol. 10, No. 2, 2015, p. 9.

Therefore, in March of the same year, Brazil, along with other BRICs countries, made a point of abstaining from the UN General Assembly resolution criticizing the Crimea referendum. ①

### (3) Brazil's "BRICS view" in Temer's period

The overall positioning of the BRICS mechanism

After a fierce domestic political struggle, Michel Temer succeeded Ms. Rousseff as acting president, and soon became president to complete her term. Temer is on the right of the political spectrum, and given the close link between domestic and foreign affairs, it is a question of concern whether the political changes in Brazil will lead to a shift or a tilt in a foreign policy that attaches importance to the BRICS mechanism and South – South cooperation.

In the face of the international community's query about the "Fading of the Gold Bricks", the Temer government has given the answer through practical actions. To be specific, Temer went to the G20 summit in Hangzhou at the beginning of his term, demonstrating to the outside world that the new Brazilian government will still promote global multilateral cooperation. More than that, when Temer attended the BRICS summit in Xiamen the following year, he also hit back at the "BRICS Fading Remarks", stressing that BRICS cooperation is strengthening rather than weakening. Moreover, the proposal of the "BRICS Plus" concept also means that the BRICS mechanism has been affirmed internationally. ② In addition, José Serra, the foreign minister of the Temer government, also said publicly at the inauguration ceremony that the new government's foreign policy will be committed to giving priority to the new partnership with Asi-

---

① Wu Guoping: From Lula to Rousseff, "Characteristics and Policy Adjustment of Brazilian Diplomacy," China International Strategic Review, 2011, p. 245.

② Chen Xiaowei, "The BRICS mechanism is constantly improving – an interview with Brazilian President Termel," People's Daily, Sept. 3, 2017.

an countries, especially China. ① Obviously, this also shows that the Temer government will continue to support BRICS cooperation as it has ever been.

On the whole, the Temer government does not change its cooperative attitude towards the BRICS mechanism as expected by the outside world, and still firmly supports the BRICS countries to play a greater role in global governance issues. On November 30$^{th}$, 2018, when BRICS leaders held an informal meeting during the G20 summit, Temer specially stressed that he had invited the new president, Jair Messias Bolsonaro, to attend the summit, but Bolsonaro failed to make the trip due to health problems. This move also further proves Temer government's positive attitude towards the BRICS mechanism and tries its best to leave a fortune of BRICS wealth for Brazil, which will take over the rotating presidency of the BRICS countries in 2019.

Understanding of Brazil's BRICS demands

Temer adopted a similar policy to the previous Labor Party government on the issue of cooperation between emerging market countries and developing countries. The reason is that in the late period of Rousseff's administration, the international financial crisis affected Brazil's economic growth significantly. However, the government failed to change the economic structure and development model in time, which led to the continuous decline of people's living standards and stirred public outrage. This factor eventually became one of the main reasons for Rousseff's impeachment and resignation. ② Moreover, Brazil's domestic "Left - right Party Rivalry" has also impacted the international environment of Brazil. After the impeachment case was concluded, a number of Latin American left - wing governments, represented by Venezuela, Bolivia and Ecuador, recalled their ambassadors in protest. In the serious domestic and foreign difficulties, the Temer government has to keep a low profile and be pragmatic.

---

① Yang Ling, "New Development of Brazil - Russia Relations under BRICS Mechanism," Latin American Studies, No. 3, 2015, p. 22.

② Chen Xiaowei, "The BRICS mechanism is constantly improving - an interview with Brazilian President Termel," People's Daily, Sept 3, 2017.

One of the solutions Temer government has chosen is to use multilateral venues to win more recognition of its ruling facts.① Based on this political consideration, increasing Brazil's presence in the BRICS cooperation mechanism is an important way to obtain diplomatic support from other countries. Under the BRICS mechanism, bilateral and multilateral cooperation in economy, trade and finance has brought the possibility for Brazil to accelerate its economic recovery. More than that, bilateral and multilateral cooperation also provides opportunities for Brazil to expand economic and trade cooperation with other developing countries, so as to expand commodity exports, promote Brazil's economic recovery, maintain social stability, and finally achieve the purpose of stabilizing domestic economic and social order through BRICS cooperation.

### (4) Brazil's "BRICS view" in Bolsonaro period

The overall positioning of the BRICS mechanism

The division between left and right politics is an unavoidable and stubborn disease in Brazil's political development.② In 2018, the rise of the right wing Bolsonaro has made Brazil's domestic and foreign affairs turn around almost 180 degrees. In view of Bolsonaro's many anti multilateralism remarks, Brazil's new government's attitude towards BRICS cooperation is not ideal.③

In terms of BRICS cooperation, although Bolsonaro still presided over the BRICS summit in Brasilia, he did not hold the "BRICS Plus" dialogue, which to a large extent weakened the enthusiasm of BRICS member countries. In addition, during the special BRICS Foreign Ministers' Meeting on the COVID-19 in 2020, Brazil was clearly at odds with other BRICS member countries on "po-

---

① Wang Fei, "China-Pakistan Economic Cooperation in the Post-Rousseff Era," World Knowledge, No. 20, 2016, p. 59.

② Xu Shicheng, "The Process and Causes of Brazilian President Rousseff's Impeachment by Congress," China National People's Congress, No. 14, 2016, p. 54.

③ Zhou Zhiwei, "The Political Ecology and Diplomatic Trend of Brazil after the Impeachment of the President," Contemporary World, No. 10, 2016, p. 69.

liticizing and stigmatizing the pandemic".

With the increasingly severe domestic epidemic situation in Brazil, the urgent needs of economic recovery, vaccine research and development and vaccination, Bolsonaro's unfriendly attitude has also changed. In addition to the economic, trade and financial fields, Brazil has gradually attached importance to cooperation with other BRICS member countries in the field of health and medical care. During the BRICS summit in 2020, Bolsonaro explicitly condemned the "politicization of the epidemic" and stressed that overcoming the adverse effects of the epidemic requires the joint efforts of all partners in the world, including BRICS countries. Brazil also believes that BRICS cooperation will not be destroyed by the epidemic because it is forced to switch online. On the contrary, cooperation among BRICS member countries will become closer.[1] In February 2022, Bolsonaro defied US pressure from the United States,[2] and visited Moscow amid escalating tensions in Ukraine to discuss cooperation with Vladimir Vladimirovich Putin on the issues of multilateral platforms such as the UN Security Council, the BRICS and the G20.[3]

On the whole, Bolsonaro's attitude towards BRICS cooperation has changed from negative to positive, which not only means that the cooperation between BRICS countries has played an obvious positive role in improving Brazil's current economic problems of people's livelihood, but also shows the resilience of BRICS cooperation mechanism.

Understanding of Brazil's BRICS demands

A country's foreign policy shift is usually triggered by the change of leader-

---

[1] Fang Xufei, "The Division, Changes and Prospects of the Left and Right Political Parties in Brazil," Latin American Studies, No. 5, 2020, p. 49.

[2] See "No reason for 'Tropical Trump' to disrupt relations with China: China Daily editorial," China Daily, Oct. 29, 2018, https://www.chinadaily.com.cn/a/201810/29/WS5bd702e9a310eff303285424.html.

[3] "Discurso do Presidente da República, Jair Bolsonaro, na Cerimônia de Cúpula de Líderes do BRICS," Fundação Alexandre de Gusmão, Nov. 09, 2021, https://www.gov.br/funag/pt-br/centrais-de-conteudo/politica-externa-brasileira/discurso-do-presidente-da-republica-jair-bolsonaro-na-cerimonia-de-cupula-de-lideres-do-brics.

ship, and often occurs in the early days of a new leader's administration.[①] After Donald Trump, known for his anti establishment and unpredictability style of governance, took office, a series of black swan incidents followed.[②] Taking Trump's success as a representative, in countries and regions deeply affected by globalization, the phenomenon of political polarization has also become increasingly prominent, with conservatism, populism and anti globalization thoughts emerging one after another.[③] In Brazil's 2018 presidential election, Bolsonaro, a popular far-right politician, was dubbed the "Tropical Trump" during his election campaign. In the early days of his administration, he even reconsidered Brazil's diplomatic priorities, goals and objectives, and made no secret that the main goal was to further promote the relations between Brazil and the United States.[④]

Nevertheless, Brazil-US relations have not made a major breakthrough despite Bolsonaro's enthusiasm. Facing the increasingly severe domestic epidemic situation, Brazil's foreign trade has been unprecedentedly affected, and the domestic social order has also been confronted with unstable factors. Under some left-wing political parties and a large number of social movements, large-scale demonstrations broke out not only in the capital Brasilia, but also in the state capitals of Sao Paulo and Rio de Janeiro, as well as in more than 200 cities across the country, protesting against the government's unfavorable response to the COVID-19 pandemic and demanding the impeachment of President Bol-

---

① See in Jonny Tickle, "US trying to prevent Brazilian president visiting Russia," Russia Today, Feb. 01, 2022, https://www.rt.com/russia/547909-us-pressuring-brazils-bolsonaro/.

② Bentley, Michelle and Maxine David, "Unpredictability as doctrine: Reconceptualising foreign policy strategy in the Trump era," Cambridge Review of International Affairs, Vol. 34, No. 3, 2021, pp. 383-406.

③ Broz, J. Lawrence. et al, "Populism in Place: The Economic Geography of the Globalization Backlash," International Organization, Vol. 75, No. 2, 2021, p. 465.

④ Dmitry Razumovsky, "BRICS-How Will the Organisation Get a 'Second Wind'?" Valdai Discussion Club, Jul. 14, 2022, https://valdaiclub.com/a/highlights/brics-how-will-the-organisation-get-a-second-wind-/?sphrase_id=139361.

sonaro. ① In view of this, there are many crises in Bolsonaro's diplomatic layout, which proposes to be close to the United States and its far right allies, to show no interest in South South cooperation and global governance, to handle relations with regional countries through ideological closeness, and not to have intention of leading regional integration. ② He had to pay attention to the diplomatic efforts of other BRICS countries, and began to rethink the BRICS strategic choice of the government, hoping to ease the tension by properly promoting the BRICS cooperation foreign policy. Therefore, the primary reason why Bolsonaro's foreign policy and its attitude towards BRICS cooperation fluctuated greatly lies in his consideration of his own political ambition and his self – interest.

## II. Progress and future of China – Brazil cooperation within the BRICS mechanism

### (1) China – Brazil Security Council Affairs Cooperation under the pillar of political security

As early as 2009, during the first BRIC leaders' meeting, it was agreed to "support the United Nations to play a central role in addressing global threats and challenges"③ Strengthening BRICS cooperation at the Security Council level within the framework of the United Nations is an important part of deep cooperation in the field of political security.

At present, there are organizations in the international community that promote the reform of the Security Council, such as the Group of Four, the African

---

① Sun Yanfeng, "Bolsonaro Government Encounters the Biggest Ruling Dilemma," World Knowledge, No. 13, 2021, p. 48.

② Dmitry Razumovsky, "BRICS – How Will the Organisation Get a 'Second Wind'?" Valdai Discussion Club, Jul. 14, 2022, https://valdaiclub.com/a/highlights/brics – how – will – the – organisation – get – a – second – wind – /? sphrase_id = 139361.

③ Sun Yanfeng, "Bolsonaro Government Encounters the Biggest Ruling Dilemma," World Knowledge, No. 13, 2021, p. 48.

Union, the Caribbean Community, L69 and the Uniting for Consensus, but their role in promoting the reform of the Security Council is not obvious. On the one hand, because of the severe competitiveness among them, they are easy to be pulled apart and dealt with separately. On the other hand, it is difficult for the five permanent members to reach a consensus on which countries should be admitted to the UN Security Council as permanent members, which has also considerably increased the difficulty of the reform group's work. In addition, although it is feasible to increase the number of its members, it will lead to a significant reduction in the share of the permanent members of the Security Council in the capacity of global powers, which will directly challenge the "Yalta Formula" which is the core of the United Nations.[1] Therefore, the reform of the Security Council is relatively slow.

Nevertheless, in order to show the "global vision" of BRICS cooperation and their willingness to participate in global governance under the framework of the United Nations, BRICS cooperation will inevitably involve the issue of Security Council reform. However, the issue of reform concerns the gains and losses of the core interests of all countries, which makes it difficult for the BRICS to make a substantive breakthrough on this issue. There is a clear division of interests between China and Russia and India, Brazil and South Africa, which will inevitably damage the willingness and determination of the BRICS countries to carry out all-round cooperation. This is the reason why by so far no BRICS declaration has explicitly made a unanimous commitment to the "accession" of Brazil, India and South Africa.[2] In addition, although both China and Russia support the reform of the Security Council, there are obvious differences between the two countries in terms of which countries they support. This is also a microcosm of the continu-

---

[1] Matthew D. Stephen. "Legitimacy Deficits of International Organizations design drift and decoupling at the UN Security Council," Cambridge Review of International Affairs, 2018, Vol. 31, No. 1, p. 115.

[2] Zhu Tianxiang and Xie Letian, "Connotation and Challenges of BRICS Political Security Cooperation," Latin American Studies, No. 6, 2020, p. 41.

ous differences among BRICS countries on the issue of Security Council reform. This difference and divergence also makes BRICS countries " shout slogans and no real action" on the issue of UN Security Council reform.

At this stage, the best way for China and Brazil to carry out cooperation related to Security Council reform is to carry out cooperation in the mode of "permanent members + non permanent members". This cooperation approach has been verified in 2011 when BRICS cooperation started.

In 2011, all BRICS countries were members of the Security Council. Throughout 2011, the Security Council held 235 meetings[1], a total of 66 resolutions were adopted. [2] Among them were two draft resolutions on the situation in the Middle East (S / 2011 / 24) and (S / 2011 / 612)[3] respectively which failed to be adopted because of the "one vote veto" of the United States and China and Russia. In addition, Resolution 1973 on the situation in Libya and Resolution 2023 on peace and security in Africa were adopted with 10 votes in favour, 0 against and 5 abstentions, and 13 in favour, 0 against and 2 abstentions respectively. [4] As these four resolutions are closely related to the interests and disputes of the member states of the Security Council, the draft resolution S / 2011 / 612 is taken as an example to make the following analysis. The 6627th meeting of the UN Security Council on October 4, 2011 to discuss the situation in the Middle East was held at 6 p. m. During the voting process of the meeting, China and Russia voted against the draft resolution, resulting in the failure of the draft resolution. At the same time, India, Brazil and South Korea abstained. After the

---

[1] Zhu Tianxiang, ed. "BRICS and Global Governance," Current Affairs Press, 2019, p. 185.

[2] Zhu Tianxiang and Xie Letian, "Connotation and Challenges of BRICS Political Security Cooperation," Latin American Studies, No. 6, 2020, p. 41.

[3] See "2011 United Nations Security Council Minutes," United Nations Security Council, https: //www. un. org/securitycommittee/zh/content/meetings – records – 2011.

[4] See "the resolutions adopted by the Security Council in 2011," United Nations Security Council, https: //www. un. org/securitycommittee/zh/content/resolutions – adopted – security – council – 2011.

vote, the BRICS applied to speak. ① Among them, Chinese representative Li Baodong then pointed out that China, like many members of the Security Council, believes that under the current situation, sanctions or the threat of sanctions will not help solve the Syrian issue, rather it may further complicate the situation. ② Brazil's representative, Maria Luiza Ribeiro Viotti, stressed that the only way out of the crisis in Syria is to engage in meaningful and inclusive dialogue and effective political reform. To this end, Brazil will continue to do what it can to help peacefully resolve the Syrian crisis. ③ More importantly, Russian representative Vitaly Ivanovich Churkin also affirmed the highly consistent position of BRICS countries in the voting on this draft resolution. ④ The united stance of BRICS countries effectively constrained the western countries' attempts to overthrow the Syrian government through the "Arab Spring", and played a positive role in maintaining the overall stability of the Middle East situation.

In 2022, Brazil was reelected as a non-permanent member of the UN Security Council. When it is difficult to make substantial progress in the reform of the Security Council, China and Brazil, as well as the BRICS countries in a larger scope, and even the whole southern world can cooperate through the mode of "permanent + non permanent members" to make the voice of developing countries and represent their fundamental interests and demands at as many Security Council meetings as possible.

---

① "The veto cast by the permanent members of the Security Council in public meetings," United Nations Security Council, https://www.un.org/securitycommittee/zh/content/veto-90-present.
② "The veto cast by the permanent members of the Security Council in public meetings," United Nations Security Council, https://www.un.org/securitycommittee/zh/content/veto-90-present.
③ "The veto cast by the permanent members of the Security Council in public meetings," United Nations Security Council, https://www.un.org/securitycommittee/zh/content/veto-90-present.
④ "The veto cast by the permanent members of the Security Council in public meetings," United Nations Security Council, https://www.un.org/securitycommittee/zh/content/veto-90-present.

## (2) Economic and trade cooperation between China and Brazil under the pillar of economic and trade finance

Brazil is China's largest trade partner in Latin America. Since 2009, China has been the largest trade partner of Brazil. ① In the first quarter of 2022, China's total exports to Brazil were about 19 billion US dollars, accounting for 23% of Brazil's total imports; China's total imports from Brazil were about 19.7 billion US dollars, accounting for 29% of Brazil's total exports. ②

In May 2022, the China – Brazil high – level coordination and cooperation committee held its sixth meeting, reaching consensus on matters including promoting bilateral cooperation in agricultural trade development, low – carbon and clean technology investment and other areas, and agreed to actively carry out a series of substantive cooperation in the fields of digital economy. ③

Bulk commodities are the ballast stone of economic and trade exchanges between China and Brazil. According to the data released by the Ministry of Commerce of China, the most important commodities Brazil exports to China are mineral products represented by iron ore and plant products represented by soybeans. In 2019, for example, the above two categories of products accounted for 79.7% of Brazil's major exports to China. ④

Since Brazil is mainly an exporter of primary products and this export commodity structure perfectly matches China's demand for imported raw materials in its economic development, so the trade between China and Brazil is obviously

---

① See "Total Import and Export Volume between China and Latin America (USD 10,000)," https://data.stats.gov.cn/easyquery.htm, National Bureau of Statistics.cn = C01.

② Li Ning, "New Opportunities for China – Brazil Economic and Trade Cooperation," China Business News Network, June 8, 2022, https://www.comnews.cn/content/2022 – 06/08/content _ 10031.html.

③ See, "Total Import and Export Volume between China and Latin America (USD 10,000)," https://data.stats.gov.cn/easyquery.htm, National Bureau of Statistics.cn = C01.

④ Li Ning, "New Opportunities for China – Brazil Economic and Trade Cooperation," China Business News Network, June 8, 2022, https://www.comnews.cn/content/2022 – 06/08/content _ 10031.html.

complementary.① However, the uncertainty of geopolitics, the global economic imbalance caused by polarization, and the reduction of coordination and cooperation mechanisms make the future of trade between China and Brazil full of uncertainty. At the same time, in Brazil, the trade structure is excessively dependent on primary agricultural products, which is neither sustainable nor able to provide greater international benefits for Brazil.② The structural pressure of this "resource curse" has also made successive Brazilian governments face the difficulty of how to adjust the structure of import and export trade.

In the economic and trade exchanges between China and Brazil, the lack of high value – added product trade between the two sides makes it difficult to substantially improve economic and trade cooperation. For example, between January and November 2017, high value – added goods accounted for only 3.76% of Brazil's total exports to China. However, in Brazil's exports to the United States in the same period, the proportion of industrial processing products in the export volume was up to 56%, reaching 13.71 billion US dollars. Embraer's aircraft, the second largest category, accounted for 8.1% of total exports to the United States.③ What's more, in 2018, Embraer cooperated with Boeing to establish a joint venture to develop the KC – 390 military transport aircraft.④ On this basis, in September 2022, Embraer, together with L3 Harris of the United States, announced that they would equip the KC – 390 transport aircraft with hard – tube refueling equipment and modern communications equipment, and make it a multi –

---

① "List of outcomes of the sixth meeting of the China Brazil high tech Commission," Ministry of Commerce of the people's Republic of China, May 24, 2022, http://www.mofcom.gov.cn/article/syxwfb/202205/20220503313636.shtml.

② See "Brazil's trade in goods and bilateral trade between China and Brazil in 2019," Ministry of Commerce of the people's Republic of China, https://countryreport.mofcom.gov.cn/record/view110209.asp?news_id=67262.

③ Chen Huaqiao, "Research on bilateral trade relations under the framework of China Brazil development strategy, doctoral dissertation," Central China Normal University, 2012, .

④ Shen Yanzhi, Liu Houjun, "sustainable development of resource dependent economies: a case study of Brazil," Modern Management Science, 2013, No. 8, p. 7.

purpose transport / refueling aircraft and try to sell it to the US Air Force. ①

The close trade exchanges between Brazil and the United States in high value – added products reflect that Brazil should not be regarded only as a raw material exporting country. In the future, China – Brazil economic and trade cooperation should seek new paths and breakthroughs, to further consolidate and deepen the trade partnership between China and Brazil.

In the field of aviation, Embraer is the world's leading commercial jet aircraft market with 130 seats and below. Its products are widely exported to worldwide. Several major airlines in mainland China, including China Southern Airlines and China Eastern Airlines, have Embraer regional jets in their fleets. At present, COMAC and the Russia United Aviation Manufacturing Group Co. Ltd. are jointly developing the C929 large long – range wide – body passenger aircraft. This kind of cooperation in the field of sophisticated manufacturing industry has strengthened the industrial innovation capacity of China and Russia to some extent. In the future, we should be committed to whether China can carry out aviation cooperation with Brazil similar to China and Russia, and jointly develop regional airliners or carry out "aircraft diplomacy", and increase aircraft orders to promote economic and trade cooperation between China and Brazil.

Similarly, in the space sector, since 1988, China and Brazil have jointly developed a series of China – Brazil Earth Resources Satellites (CBERS). By 2019, the two sides had cooperated in the development of six satellites, and upgraded satellite data receiving stations in South Africa and Singapore to expand satellite application capacity. In addition, China and Brazil also jointly established the China – Brazil Joint Space Weather Laboratory in 2014, aiming to take advantage of the natural geographical advantages of both countries to explore and examine the near – Earth space environment in low latitude regions. The existing

---

① "China is Brazil's largest commodity export destination," South American overseas Chinese daily, December 13, 2017, http: //epms. br – cn. com/static/content/news/qs _ news/2017 – 12 – 13/887318451058638849. html.

cooperation in this field has even nurtured multilateral space cooperation at the BRICS level. In 2015, the China National Space Administration launched the BRICS Remote Sensing Satellite Constellation Cooperation Initiative. In 2021, the five countries formally signed an agreement on cooperation among the BRICS Remote Sensing Satellite Constellation , which explicitly stated that cooperation will rely on existing satellites, including the China – Brazil Earth Resources Satellite. Obviously, how to effectively integrate the existing China – Brazil space cooperation into the BRICS space cooperation and enhance the overall competitiveness of BRICS space cooperation should also be regarded as an important breakthrough in the future China – Brazil cooperation in cutting – edge fields.

In addition, China has already extended an invitation to Brazil to join "the Belt and Road" Initiative as soon as possible.[1] However, Brazil has not yet signed the "Belt and Road" Initiative cooperation document with China. Nevertheless, Argentina, which has important influence in Latin America and is applying to join the BRICS countries, is ahead of Brazil. During Argentine President Fernandez's visit to China in 2022, the two sides reached a series of outcome documents, such as Joint Statement on Deepening China – Argentina Comprehensive Strategic Partnership and the Memorandum of Understanding on Jointly Advancing the Construction of the Silk Road Economic Belt and the 21st Century Maritime Silk Road, marking that the two sides will work together to formulate a framework conducive to sustainable development and inclusive economic cooperation. To promote the deepening, innovation and diversification of economic relations between the two countries and enhance regional connectivity.[2] Building on the foundation of other Latin American countries having signed cooperation plans

---

[1] Valerie Insinna, "Boeing, Embraer agree to KC – 390 joint venture," Defense News, Dec. 17, 2018, https://www.defensenews.com/air/2018/12/17/boeing – embraer – agree – to – kc – 390 – joint – venture/.

[2] Stephen Losey, "L3Harris, Embraer team up on KC – 390 tanker, eye US Air Force sales," Defense News, Sept. 19, 2018, https://www.defensenews.com/air/2022/09/19/l3harris – embraer – team – up – on – kc – 390 – tanker – eye – us – air – force – sales/.

with China on the joint construction of the Belt and Road, and in light of the practical development needs of China – Brazil cooperation, in November 2024, China and Brazil signed the "Cooperation Plan between the Government of the People's Republic of China and the Government of the Federative Republic of Brazil on the Alignment of the Belt and Road Initiative with the 'Accelerated Growth Plan' the 'New Industrial Plan of Brazil' the 'Ecological Transition Plan' and the 'South American Integration Roadmap.'". The signing of this document serves as an exemplary role, promoting other BRICS countries and BRICS Plus partners to sign Belt and Road cooperation plans with China at an early stage.

### (3) China – Brazil bilateral people – to – people exchanges under the pillar of people – to – people exchanges

Since the establishment of diplomatic relations between China and Brazil in 1974, from the "cautious diplomacy" at the beginning of the establishment of diplomatic ties, the two countries have developed into a strategic partnership featuring extensive cooperation in various fields. Especially since the beginning of the 21st century, the cooperation in politics, economy, trade and culture between the two countries has entered a period of rapid development.[①] In May 2009, Brazilian President Lula paid a state visit to China. During this visit, the two sides jointly formulated the 2010 – 2014 Joint Action Plan, which was officially implemented in 2010. The final release of this outcome document indicates that China – Brazil relations are moving towards consolidating the political foundation of strategic partnership, broadening and deepening bilateral relations in various fields and promoting multi – directional and comprehensive development in areas

---

[①] Yang Wanming, "Ambassador to Brazil, received an exclusive interview with Sao Paulo, Brazil," Embassy of the people's Republic of China in the Federal Republic of Brazil, March 06, 2022, http://br. china – embassy. gov. cn/dsxx/dshd/202203/t20220306_10648380. htm.

of common concern to the two countries.① In addition, the two sides signed a 10 - year cooperation plan between the two governments in 2012. In 2013, the two countries decided to establish the China - Brazil Business Forum and determined the annual meeting mechanism of the foreign ministers of the two countries, basically realizing the establishment of a high - level exchange framework. In July 2014, President Xi Jinping paid a state visit to Brazil after the sixth BRICS summit. The two sides issued the Joint Statement on Further Deepening China - Brazil Comprehensive Strategic Partnership, covering culture, education, sports, tourism and other fields of people - to - people exchanges and cooperation. This is not only a continuation of the previous China - Brazil Joint Action Plan, but also indicates that there is a consensus at the top level of China and Brazil to strengthen people - to - people exchanges and make it a substantial leap forward.

Judging from the achievements of people - to - people exchanges, China and Brazil have carried out a series of exchange activities in the fields of music, drama, acrobatics, plastic arts, radio, film, television, books and publishing. In recent years, China has successfully held large - scale cultural activities in Brazil, such asthe Chinese Cultural Festival, cultural relics exhibition, art works exhibition and commercial tour. In the same way, Brazil has also held "Approaching China - Brazil National Exhibition" and "Brazil's Amazon" photo exhibition and other exchange activities in China. In 2013, the two countries held "Culture Month" activities in each other's countries. The Ministry of Education has set up Chinese teaching centers in the University of Brasilia and the University of Sao Paulo. The Sino - Foreign Language Exchange and Cooperation Center under the Ministry of Education has set up 11 Confucius Institutes and 6 Confucius schools in Brazil. There are more than 40 research centers related to Chinese studies. The number of Chinese research institutions ranks first in Latin

---

① "Joint statement of the people's Republic of China and the Argentine Republic on Deepening China Argentina comprehensive strategic partnership," People's Daily, Feb. 06, 2022.

America. Communication University of China and Asian Cultural Center of Sao Paulo in Brazil have Portuguese proficiency tests and Chinese proficiency test respectively. The Latin American Institute of Chinese Academy of Social Sciences and Peking University have a Center for Brazilian studies and a Center for Brazilian culture respectively. China Central Television (CCTV) and China Radio International have a Latin American central station and a Latin American regional terminal in Brazil respectively. ① Although these humanities exchanges and cooperation basically cover the main fields of humanities exchanges, the achievements of these humanities exchanges are scattered, separated from each other and lack of coordination and coherence.

It should be noted that although China established a strategic partnership with Brazil as early as 1993 starting a new chapter of China – Brazil strategic partnership②, unfortunately, due to the geographical distance between the two countries and the language barriers, the people of both sides know little about each other and there is a great communication bottleneck. ③As a result, the people – to – people exchanges between the two countries is difficult, which in turn affects the establishment of a high – level foreign exchange mechanism between China and Brazil. It is worth emphasizing that factors such as language barrier, inconvenient communication and geographical distance, hinder the concrete practice of people – to – people exchange, affect the establishment of a high – level exchange mechanism for other people's languages, fail to realize the genuine com-

---

① Zhou Zhiwei, "Sino Brazilian relations: historical review and Prospect – Commemorating the 35th anniversary of the establishment of diplomatic relations between China and Brazil," Contemporary World, No. 8, 2009, p. 55.

② See "The joint action plan of the government of the people's Republic of China and the government of the Federal Republic of Brazil for 2010 – 2014," Ministry of foreign affairs, Apr. 22, 2010, https://www.mfa.gov.cn/web/zyxw/201004/t20100422_307566.shtml.

③ See "China Brazil relations," Ministry of Foreign Affairs, https://www.mfa.gov.cn/web/gjhdq_676201/gj_676203/nmz_680924/1206_680974/sbgx_680978/.; "Investigation report on Brazilian Chinese Studies in 2022 was released," Surging News, Sept. 16, 2022, https://www.thepaper.cn/newsDetail_forward_19927150.

munion among the people, and may inhibit deep cooperation and exchanges in other fields.

Faced with the obvious shortcomings of China – Brazil relations in the field of people – to – people exchanges and cooperation, and the global ravages of the COVID – 19 pandemic, governments all over the world have chosen to tighten the entry and exit permits to varying degrees, which has made the people – to – people exchanges and cooperation between China and Brazil more difficult. Therefore, it is particularly important to find a suitable way to relieve the dilemma.

On the one hand, regarding the issue of further expanding the existing cooperation achievements, China and Brazil have held many experience exchanges on epidemic prevention and control, and have also carried out many cooperation on joint research and development of vaccines under the BRICS framework. In the future, we can start with the prevention and treatment of coronavirus, and further strengthen the professional people – to – people exchanges among medical and health sectors, related scientific research workers and medical staff in the joint research and development of vaccines and sharing of medical prevention and treatment experience, so as to create a new model of people – to – people and cultural exchanges between China and Brazil, which can be used as a reference for the smooth development of exchanges in other fields. On the other hand, to fill in the gaps in cultural exchanges, VR and other new technologies can be used to set up online people – to – people and cultural exchange pavilions and launch online cultural exchange years, so as to provide more people with a platform to know each other's customs and folk styles. Confucius Institutes can also be established to strengthen language training or to create book – translating projects to enhance mutual understanding of each other's traditional culture and national spirit. In addition, at the BRICS level, China and Brazil can also strengthen cooperation. In 2019, when President Xi Jinping attended the summit of BRICS leaders in Brasilia, he made it clear that "BRICS countries provide the best practical experience for the exchange of world civilizations". [1] As far as the current development of people – to – people and cultural exchanges and cooperation among BRICS countries is concerned, BRICS countries have carried out a series of cooperation in fields such as science, education, culture and sports, etc., and have successively held diversified activities including BRICS Games, BRICS Vocational Skills Competition, BRICS Women's Innovation Competition, and online training courses for media in five countries. However, since most of these activities are conducted under the leadership of the government and concentrated in first – tier cities, focus on adopting in a "down – to – earth and people – benefiting" way and strengthen local cooperation is the future direction of BRICS efforts. In this process, non – official actors are encouraged to engage in relevant cooperation, and certain policy guidance and support are given to these actors, so that they can participate in BRICS cooperation more extensively and deeply, helping tell the "BRICS story" and "BRICS Plus" story well, to promote the transformation of BRICS people – to – people and cultural exchange mode to "people – oriented" mode, and make contributions to the deepening of BRICS cooperation and its going deep in people's hearts.

## III. Conclusion

Brazil's "BRICS view" has different forms of expression and interest demand in different periods, which is closely related to the political orientation of Brazil's ruling party and politicians, Brazil's pursuit of political power status, and Brazil's domestic economic and social conditions. Brazil's current BRICS strategy has shown signs of recovery, which requires the current Brazilian government, the future new government and other BRICS countries to work together. In this process, China, as a key member of BRICS and the rotating presidency in

---

[1] Men Honghua and Liu Xiaoyang, "Strategic Assessment and Prospect of China's partnership," World Economy and Politics, 2015, Issue 2, p. 65.

2022, should take advantage of the important opportunities for the positive development of the existing China – Brazil bilateral relations and strive for change. At the 14th meeting of BRICS leaders, President Xi Jinping made it clear that "as a representative of emerging market countries and developing countries, China has made correct choices and taken responsible actions at the critical juncture of the development, which is very important for the world". [1] 2022 is a year that embraces multilateralism. Lula, who pursued multilateralism and emphasized BRICS cooperation, was re – elected as the president of Brazil in 2022. We have every reason to believe that China – Brazil relations and BRICS cooperation mechanism at a new historical starting point should take a more active attitude to carry out more valuable dialogues and cooperation under the "three pillars" of political security, economy, trade, finance and people – to – people exchanges. Relying on the existing "three – wheel – driven" cooperation framework, BRICS countries will to strive to embark on a new historic starting point of membership expansion.

---

[1] Wang We and Wang Junliang, "Experience and Improvement of BRICS People to People Exchange Mechanism," edited by Zhu Tianxiang, Research on BRICS Countries and Cooperation (Volume 1), Current Affairs Press, 2019 edition, p. 55.

# A Study on the Mainstream Indian Newspapers and Media and Their China Related Reports

Duan Mengjie[*]

**Abstract**: India is one of the countries with the most complicated language situation in the world. At the same time, India's media industry is very developed. This combination contributes to the multilingual nature of Indian media. Currently, the primary means of understanding Indian media's perception of China is through English – language sources. In view of this situation, this paper aims to provide an accurate portrayal of China in Indian media, specifically focusing on the Hindi media perspective. Examine the current language composition in Indian media, and analyze the historical and social factors influencing this language distribution.

**Keywords**: Indian media; Chinese image; Hindi media

---

[*] Duan Mengjie, Lecturer of School of Oriental Language and Culture, Sichuan International Studies University, doctoral candidate of School of International Communication. This paper is a phased achievement of the Chongqing Postgraduate Research Innovation Project "Text Travel and Cross cultural Communication" (CYB21227) and the Sichuan International Studies University Research Project "Image of China in Hindi Newspapers and Periodicals Mirror" (sisu202034).

India has complex national conditions and manyethnic groups. It is known as the "Ethnicity Museum", and its linguistic situation is equally complex. There are 461 languages in India. According to the 1950 Indian Constitution, the official languages of India are Hindi and English. In addition, 21 other regional official languages are recognized. The complexity of language in India has directly contributed to the multilingual nature of its media. In addition, India has a large population base, and the media industry is "highly developed, even to an advanced level". The circulation of newspapers and magazines in the country is nearly 10,000, ranking first in the world "[1]. This complexity poses challenges to comprehensively and objectively understanding how Indian media shapes the image of China. Currently, the understanding of Indian media in China is mainly limited to English – language sources, which are used to assess Indian media's coverage of China. Tang Lu, the former chief reporter of Xinhua News Agency in India, also pointed this out clearly in the article "Indian Media Market – Not as Simple as Imagine", "The audience of Indian media varies significantly by language. In fact, Chinese media often introduce only the reports of English – language media. However, the number of Hindi media and readers is the largest, and the share of English media in the Indian media market is very small"[2]. The use of multiple languages in Indian media presents a significant challenge in comprehending the portrayal of China in Indian media. From the following data analysis, we can see that it is not comprehensive or even accurate to study and analyze the image of China in the minds of Indian people from Indian English – language media alone. During a period of both turbulence and positive developments in China – India relations, it is essential to have a comprehensive understanding of India's news reports on China, recognizing their significant role.

---

[1] Li Kun, "Study on India's Media Coverage of China and Its Influence," Fudan University, 2012, p. 2.

[2] Tang Lu, "The Indian Media Market: Not as Simple as Imagined," Journal of International Communication, 2010, Vol. 3, p. 58.

# Ⅰ. Each Performs Its Own Role—Two Ecology of Indian Media

The two hundred years of British colonial rule in India left many indelible marks on Indian people. These include the adoption of English and the habit of newspaper reading. Up to now, English remains a powerful tool for the Indian upper class to demonstrate their education level. Additionally, it is widely used as a medium of instruction in higher education. Due to the large number of Indian languages and thelinguistic differences between the northern and southern regions, English also plays a role as a bridge for communication between these regions to a certain extent. However, in the daily lives of Indian people, the Indian languages of various places are still the main languages. India can be divided into 14 linguistic regions. ① Hindi, the official language of India, is mainly used in the north. The region includes nine states, including Uttar Pradesh, Rajasthan, Bihar, Haryana and Madhya Pradesh. Hindi is also the official language actively promoted by the Indian government. ② The core language in addition, the Punjabi language is mainly used in the Punjabi state in the northwest of India; Bengali is mainly spoken in six states in the northeast, including West Bengal and Tripland; Gujarati is mainly spoken in the western state of Gujarat. ③ In the central and western regions of India, Maharashtra State predominantly uses Marathi language; Oriya is mainly spoken in Orissa in the east; Telugu is mainly spoken in the central and eastern states of Trengana and Andhra Pradesh; Kannadu is mainly used in Karnataka in the southwest, and Malayalam is mainly used in Kerala; Tamil is mainly spoken in Tamil Nadu in the southeast, so Indian media

---

① 14 of these languages have been lost, and the data are from: https://www.mapsofindia.com/culture/indian-languages.html.

② This division is based on the language map of the official website of the National Map of India, and the data is from: https://www.mapsofindia.com/culture/indian-languages.html.

③ Liao Bo, "Language Dilemma in India," Southeast Asian and South Asian Studies, Vol. 3, 2015, p. 78.

has a strong regional character. According to my understanding when I was in India, due to the national conditions and policies[①], Indian people have strong language skills. Generally, everyone can master at least two languages: Hindi and the local mother tongue. Indian people with high education or diverse family composition can even master four to five languages. This special multilingual state has created "two ecosystems" in which Indian English media and Indian language media perform their respective rolespattern. [②]

India is a federal democracy. States have a high degree of autonomy and people have the right to vote. Indian language media in various regions have become propaganda battlefields for politicians, who aim to secure votes from the majority of voters. It is evident that the audience of Indian language media primarily consists of grassroots individuals who are interested in national policies, leadership elections, sports, entertainment, and local news. The audience of English media primarily comprises the educated middle and upper classes. They care about the financial stock market, foreign policy, overseas study information and other information related to themselvesas the elite class. The people of this class are mainly engaged in the business industry. Simultaneously, due to their educational background, they pay significant attention to national foreign policy decisions.

Although Indian language media and English media operate within different circles, styles, and concerns, they both play a crucial role in the decision-making process of Indian policies. Ignoring either of them may lead to irreparable mistakes. According to publisher Narendra Mohan, renowned for his contribution to Indian newspapers, "People residing in Delhi are greatly influenced by English newspapers. This is why Nehru misjudged India and made a tragic mistake. It is also the reason why British Gandhi misread India and lost the election. To truly

---

① In 1963, the Indian government issued the Official Language Act, which stipulated that Indian schools must teach three languages: Hindi, English and the native language in non Hindi areas; Teach Hindi, English and an Indian language in Hindi speaking areas.

② Refers specifically to the "trilingual programme" mentioned above, ibid.

understand India, one must rely on local language newspapers."①

**Table 1   2017 Daily Newspaper Readership Questionnaire issued by the Indian Media Users Committee (in all languages)**

| RANKING | NEWSPAPER NAME | TOTAL READERSHIP | LANGUAGE |
| --- | --- | --- | --- |
| 1 | Dainik Jagran | 70377 | Hindi |
| 2 | Hindustan | 52397 | Hindi |
| 3 | Amar Ujala | 46094 | Hindi |
| 4 | Dainik Bhaskar | 45105 | Hindi |
| 5 | Daily Thanthi | 23149 | Regional Indian Language |
| 6 | Lokmat | 18066 | Regional Indian Language |
| 7 | Rajasthan Patrika | 16326 | Hindi |
| 8 | Malayala Manorama (D) | 15999 | Regional Indian Language |
| 9 | Eenadu | 15848 | Regional Indian Language |
| 10 | Prabhat Khabar | 13492 | Hindi |
| 11 | The Times Of India | 13047 | English |
| 12 | Ananda Bazar Patrika | 12763 | Regional Indian Language |
| 13 | Punjab Kesari | 12232 | Hindi |
| 14 | Dinakaran | 12083 | Regional Indian Language |
| 15 | Mathrubhumi | 11848 | Regional Indian Language |
| 16 | Gujarat Samachar | 11784 | Regional Indian Language |
| 17 | Dinamalar | 11659 | Regional Indian Language |
| 18 | Daily Sakal | 10498 | Regional Indian Language |
| 19 | Sandesh | 10352 | Regional Indian Language |
| 20 | Patrika | 9823 | Hindi |

① Tang Lu," The Indian Media Market: Not as Simple as Imagined," Journal of International Communication, 2010, Vol. 3, p. 58.

Taking Indian paper media as an example, from the report published by the Media User Research Council of India (MURC) in 2017. [①]For the period from 2014 to 2017, the number of readers of Indian paper media had increased rather than decreased, mainly in rural areas, while in urban areas, the number of readers had increased, and the reading mode has become electronic. In addition, the number of Hindi audiences has always maintained a leading position. From the comparison of Table 1, it is evident that the top four daily newspapers among the top 20 in terms of the number of readers in 2017 are Hindi daily newspapers, followed by *Awakening Daily*, *Hindustan Daily*, *Eternal Light Daily* and *Sun Daily*, a total of 8 Hindi language daily newspapers entered the top 20 daily newspapers; In addition, there are 11 other Indian language daily newspapers in the top 20, although their combined readership is lower than that of Hindi language dailies; Only the Times of India, an English language daily, ranked 11th among the top 20 daily newspapers. It can be said that in terms of the number of daily readers, Indian language daily newspapers represented by Hindi occupy the dominant position.

Table 2  2017 Magazine Readership Questionnaire issued by the Indian Media Users Committee (in all languages)

| MAGAZINES | IRS 2017 |
| --- | --- |
| India Today (English) | 7992 |
| India Today (Hindi) | 7159 |
| Samanya Gyan Darpan (Hindi) | 6882 |

---

① The statement of "two kinds of ecology" was first mentioned by Tang Lu in the article "Indian media market – not as simple as imagined": "Generally speaking, if the outside world wants to understand the Indian people's views on diplomatic issues, it should study and judge the views of Indian English newspapers, and if you want to truly understand Indian politics, you need to read the Indian language newspaper. This phenomenon actually reflects two kinds of ecology of Indian media, namely English media and Indian language media, including local languages. The readers influenced by these two types of media are entirely distinct, as are the topics covered and the editorial styles adopted."

续表

| MAGAZINES | IRS 2017 |
| --- | --- |
| Vanitha (Malayalam) | 6126 |
| Pratiyogita Darpan (Hindi) | 5924 |
| Meri Saheli (Hindi) | 4623 |
| Saras Salil (Hindi) | 4318 |
| Bal Bhaskar (Hindi) | 3598 |
| General Knowlege Today (Eng) | 3493 |
| Champak (Hindi) | 3336 |
| Sarita (Hindi) | 2958 |
| The Sportstar (Eng) | 2937 |
| Cricket Samrat (Hindi) | 2920 |
| Diamond Cricket Today (Hindi) | 2809 |
| Grish Shobha (Hindi) | 2759 |
| Anada Vikatan (Tamil) | 2708 |
| Diamond Cricket Today (English) | 2549 |
| Grehlakshmi (Hindi) | 2469 |
| Jagran Josh Plus | 2423 |
| Filmfare (Fortnightly) | 2333 |

According to the survey on the number of readers of Indian magazines conducted by the Media User Research Council of India. Committee (see Table 2), English magazines account for a larger proportion than daily newspapers. Among the top 20 Indian magazines, 5 are English magazines, and Indian magazines still comprise the largest portion, with a total of 13 magazines. This also shows that magazine subscription is closely related to people's consumption habits. Magazines typically target subscribers with higher purchasing power. It also shows that Hindi media plays an important role in Indian media. In terms of audience numbers, Hindi media holds the largest share. It is the Indian language media that can best reflect the concerns of ordinary Indian people and some middle and upper class people, and it is also an indispensable part of our summary of how Indian media influences the perception of China.

## Ⅱ. Watching the Moon in the Water — Chinese Image in Hindi Media

India and China are both major developingand populous countries, as well as emerging economies in Asia. They have a long history of exchanges since ancient times. However, compared with Chinese media, Indian media tend to focus more on China – related news. However, India is still inferior in economic development and infrastructure construction. It is understandable that the media regard China as the "benchmark" for India's development[1]. China related reports in mainstream Indian English media have long been studied and classified. According to the scholar's analysis: "As English media in India do not have a large number of natural readers like local language media, their survival mainly depends on advertising, which makes the market competition between English print media and television stations for readers (audience) fiercer"[2], this suggests that Indian English media, heavily influenced by commercial considerations, tend to report more on China. And it can be seen that Indian English – language media are deeply influenced by business factors, so they report more about China. At the same time, the views of the English mainstream media also reflect the perspectives of the Indian middle class and some young students on current politics and diplomacy, especially the views of some retired government officials, relevant elite scholars and non – governmental scholars who often participate in TV debate programs. Consequently, the commentary on China by the

---

[1] Yan Yining,' India's "Great Power Dream" and the Media Representation of China: A Case Study of Hindustan Times 'Coverage of China', Journal of South Asian Studies Quarterly, Vol. 3, 2012, p. 33.

[2] Tang Lu," The Responsibility of Chinese and Indian Media in Eliminating Misunderstandings," Journal of International Communication, No. 5, 2010, p. 6.

mainstream Indian English media is generally described as "neutral and negative".

So what is the attitude of the Hindi language media, which has the largest readers in India but is not well – known in China, in reporting on China? Subsequently, this article will present a list of mainstream Hindi print media and their coverage of China – related news in 2018. This analysis aims to outline the recent portrayal of China in the Hindi media, analyzing the language used in reports about China in the mainstream Hindi media, with the aim of capturing the recent perception of China within the Hindi media landscape.

Although the circulation of Hindustan Daily is less than that of Awakening Daily, ranking the second among Indian Daily newspapers, it can be counted as one of the old Indian newspapers. It was founded by Mahatma Gandhi and commenced publication in 1932. It has a wide popularity in India. However, in 1942, during the "Quit India" movement[1], it stopped publishing for six months. However, it played a significant role in advancing the Indian independence movement. The newspaper frequently featured novels by the celebrated writer and revolutionary fighter Yeshebar, which garnered strong support from Mahatma Gandhi and the Congress Party.

According to the Hindustan Daily's report on the informal meeting between Chinese President and Indian Prime Minister Modi in Wuhan on April 28, 2018[2], which was released one day later than the relevant Chinese news, making it less timely; From the content of the report, the photo report "Prime Minister Modi's Tour of China" mainly reported that the President and Prime Minister Modi had discussed and reached an agreement on border issues and terrorism,

---

[1] The translated names of newspapers are unofficial, which are all translated by the author himself. In order to prevent mistranslation, the original names in Hindi are written together.

[2] On August 8, 1942, Gandhi made a speech in Mumbai. In order to let India gain independence as soon as possible, he launched the Exit from India. But less than 24 hours after the speech was delivered, it was suppressed by the British Indian authorities. The main leaders of the Congress Party, including Gandhi, were sent abroad to be imprisoned. The Congress Party was banned from activities and the movement was transferred underground.

and would work together to combat terrorism, work towards reducing border conflicts, establishing a mutual trust mechanism, strengthening cooperation in areas such as economy, education, entertainment, and increasing collaboration in film exchange. However, it did not directly mention China's Belt and Road Initiative. The concluding paragraph of the news highlights the positive nature of the conversation between Indian Prime Minister Modi and the President, suggesting its potential to strengthen China – India relations. The basic attitude of Hindustan Daily is objective and positive. The newspaper places significant emphasis on Prime Minister Modi's visit to China and offers substantial affirmation. Of course, to some extent, this can be attributed to the close relationship between Hindustan Daily and the Congress Party. Therefore, the views of the newspaper also represent the views of the current Congress Party to a certain extent, which makes it a valuable reference for understanding the Congress Party's stance. According to the author's understanding during his study in Agra, Uttar Pradesh, India, the newspaper has always held a positive attitude towards relevant reports on China. It once conducted an exclusive interview with Chinese students and was reported on the front page of the local edition of Hindustan Daily.

The Awakening Daily was founded in 1942, a crucial year in India's struggle for independence. It is currently the most popular daily newspaper in northern India and has the highest circulation among all newspapers in India. At the same time, it was recognized by the World Association of Newspapers as the newspaper with the highest number of readers worldwide. It has great influence in India.

The Awakening Daily focusesprimarily on China's investment, military and entertainment news. The Awakening Daily has recently paid more attention to the news about recent development in China – US relations, the Chinese aircraft carrier going to sea, the Indian film "Bahubali" being released in China, and the Chinese Wanda Group's investment in Haryana. From the release time, it is evident that the news lacks timeliness, and because the newspaper itself has a wide range of readers, it focuses more on entertainment and other pages. Of course, there are also some editorial reviews on it. On Prime Minister Modi's visit to China, the Awakening Daily published an editorial on May 11, "Analysis: China should recognize the importance of India and improve the geopolitical environment". [1] The main point of the editorial is to call on China to acknowledge the importance of India and treat it as an equal and cooperative partner. In addition, regarding the failure of China Wanda Group's investment in Haryana, the analysis argues that the government of Haryana failed to appreciate the importance of attracting Chinese investment.

In addition to the above two mainstream Hindi newspapers, there are many Hindi - language media with a large number of readers (audience), each of which has its own specific interests and similarities, so we will not list them here. The Hindi language media has a great influence on Indian people, especially the people of northern India. It serves as the primary source for them to acquire external information and shape their perception of China. In the process of browsing the China related news reports of major Indian newspapers, the author is glad to discover that the Indian media are "moderately positive" in the overall construction of China's image, but there is also a feeling of "watching the moon in the water", due to some Indian media reports that do not accurately portray the reality of China, and by catering to the curiosity of Indian readers about China.

## Ⅲ. On the Top Floor: Comprehensively and Objectively Grasp the Image of China in Indian Media

With the increasein high - level visits and non - governmental exchanges between China and India in recent years, the significance of China - India relations has become increasingly prominent. China - India exchanges date back to the Western Han Dynasty, and with the spread of Buddhism and the popularity of Legalism, these exchanges reached a golden age in the Tang Dynasty. After the

---

[1] Retrieved from the official website of Awakening Daily, screenshot from: https://www.jagran.com/search.

founding of the People's Republic of China, India was the first non-socialist country to establish diplomatic relations with China. China-India relations have experienced fluctuations and complexities, twists and turns. The towering Himalayas have long posed a barrier to the mutual understanding between China and India. However, with the respective development of China and India, peaceful and friendly coexistence is an inevitable trend, and also the basis for mutual benefit and win-win cooperation between the two countries. Both China and India are ancient cultural nations and powerful cultural countries. However, people in both countries know little about each other and news reports are mostly stereotyped. Therefore, cultural exchanges have a long way to go. The media in China and India need to enhance understanding and mutual trust.

The multi-language composition of Indian media determines that we must "engage on multiple fronts" or even "use a multi-pronged approach". If we want to understand the image of China in Indian media, it is impossible to "gain acomprehensive understanding". We must understand and analyze it from the perspective of multi language, and must "go up again" to observe Indian media from a higher and more comprehensive perspective. English media and Hindi media are like two pillars of Indian information landscape. Without either the information available is incomplete. "Generally speaking, if the outside world wants to understand the Indian people's views on diplomatic issues, it should study and judge the views of Indian English newspapers, and if you want to truly understand Indian politics, you need to read Indian language newspapers."[1] These two ecosystems of Indian media are prominent features of Indian media. It is also the key point that we cannot get around when studying Indian media's reports on China.

At present, with the exchanges between Chinese and Indian enterprises, many Chinese Internet enterprises have expanded into the Indian market. For ex-

---

[1] Tang Lu, "The Indian Media Market: Not as Simple as Imagined," Journal of International Communication, 2010, Vol. 3, p. 58.

ample, UC Headlines and Today Headlines have begun to build an integrated platform for mobile news in English and Indian languages in India, which provides a good platform for us to better understand China's image in India. The transition from a single English language to Indian English bilingual language is the objective requirement to comprehensively grasp the image of China in the Indian media. By gaining proficiency in Bengali, Tamil, and other major Indian languages, one can have a morenuanced understanding of India's reports related to China.

# The Status Quo, Measures and Prospects of Poverty Governance in Russia[*]

Wang Zifan[**], You Han[***]

**Abstract**: At present, poverty has become one of the important challenges in the world. Many factors, such as insufficient "pro – poor" promotion, social inequality, controversial poverty line setting standards, rising unemployment rate, and external sanctions, constitute Russia's unique poverty situation and restrict the development potential of poverty governance in Russia. Since taking office, Putin has developed poverty governance through a series of measures such as fostering economic development, promoting fair distribution, optimizing poverty indicators, promoting employment, and participating in international poverty reduction cooperation. Driven by the Russian government's policies, poverty governance has made remarkable progress in the areas of reducing the number of

---

[*] This paper is a phased achievement of the National Social Science Fund Youth Project "Comparative Study on Global Governance Strategies between China and Russia" (19CGJ021).

[**] Wang Zifan, Graduate student of Comparative Institutional Studies, Sichuan International Studies University, Grade 2021.

[***] You Han, Associate Professor, School of International Studies, Sichuan International Studies University.

people in poverty, improving the livelihood of poor people, and enhancing the ability of risk prevention. However, weak economy, exclusion of special social groups, imbalance between environmental protection and economic development, recurrence of the COVID – 19 pandemic and Western sanctions will continue to restrict the effectiveness of Russian poverty alleviation.

**Keywords**: poverty in Russia; poverty alleviation; poverty governance

Poverty is one of the important challenges facing the world today. International factors such as the Great Power Game, the COVID – 19 pandemic, the Russian – Ukrainian conflict, etc. have caused various countries to fall into different degrees of recession, resulting in a series of social problems. Poverty reduction has become the core content of promoting global sustainable development, and it is also an important measure for countries to participate in global governance and make the global governance system more just and equitable. As an emerging economy and one of the most influential countries in Europe and Asia, poverty problems in Russia are unique in their own way. On the one hand, it directly or indirectly originates from the political and economic transformation of the country after the disintegration of the Soviet Union; on the other hand, the poverty problem in Russia is also influenced by its own economic development and international environment. Therefore, anti – poverty is of great practical significance for Russia to achieve sustainable development, maintain political stability, solve a series of social problems to provide residents with a good quality of life, and participate in the reform of the global governance system. Although Russia claims to have overcome extreme poverty, according to the data of the Federal Service for State Statistics (Rosstat), there are still quite a few people living below the poverty line in Russia today, and it is still very urgent to solve and eliminate the poverty problem.

Since 2018, Russian President Vladimir Putin has repeatedly emphasized the importance of poverty alleviation in hisannual State of the Union Address, proposing the goal of reducing poverty in Russia by at least half by 2024, expanding the implementation of poverty reduction policies in pilot areas, and pointing out that poverty eradication will be used to evaluate the performance of local officials.① Moreover, Putin has repeatedly stressed that Russia needs to be more keenly aware of poverty, high unemployment rate and other issues, and strengthen social security, support large, pregnant and single-parent families, and implement the growth assistance policy for children and adolescents, and ask the government to make progress in restoring the labor market, increasing people's income and eradicating poverty.② From the information conveyed by Russia for several years, it can be seen that poverty remains a problem that Russian society needs to face and solve. This paper focuses on the problem of poverty in Russia, analyzing the status quo of poverty in Russia from both domestic and international aspects, evaluating the effectiveness of poverty governance, and studying the challenges it faces.

# Ⅰ. The Status Quo of Poverty in Russia

Poverty exists in Russian society and evolves with the times. In the long run, poverty is not a concept that only exists in therealms of economics. The exploration of poverty problem that Russia is facing today must be based on the perspective of development.

### (1) Russia's insufficient "pro-poor" promotion

The theory of pro-poor growth holds thata combination of economic growth

---

① Bolin Liu, "Poverty in Russia: Current situation, characteristics and governance," Russian, Eastern European, Central Asian Studies, No. 6, 2022, pp. 27-28.

② "Владимир Путин принял участие в XVIII Ежегодном заседании Международного дискуссионного клуба 《Валдай》. Стенограмма пленарной сессии," Valdaiclub, сентября 11, 2022, https: //ru. valdaiclub. com/events/posts/articles/vladimir - putin - xviii - ezhegodnoe - zasedanie - mezhdunarodnogo - diskussionnogo - kluba - valday - stenogramma/? sphrase_id = 538647#masha_0 = 1: 1, 1: 1.

and a fairer income distribution system can realize the rapid reduction of the poverty level[1], and it is not true otherwise. Russia's economy has been characterized by a single industrial structure for a long time, and it has been affected by the world pandemic situation, western sanctions, war conflicts and other external impacts, resulting in unstable economic development and insufficient economic growth. In the second quarter of 2022, Russia's GDP was only 3466.6 billion rubles. Compared with the same period in 2021, the real GDP decreased by 4.1%, and the deflator increased by 17.0%. Domestic final demand fell by 6.4% as final consumption expenditure fell by 4.1% and aggregate accumulation fell by 13.8%. The reason for the decrease in consumption is that people's purchasing power has declined[2]. The direct result is that the domestic economic development slows down, the population problem deepens and the poverty problem intensifies.[3] According to Rosstat, in the first quarter of 2022, the poverty line in Russia was 12916 rubles and the incomes of 20.9 million people, or 14.3% of the population, were below the poverty line, an increase of 100,000 people year – on – year. The main reason for the increase in the poverty rate is that inflation exceeds the growth of per capita income.[4] According to the Ministry of Economic Development of the Russian Federation, the real disposable income of Russian people will drop by 6.8% in 2022, and the real wage income will drop by 3.8%.[5]

---

[1] Qinghong Zhang, "The connotation and realization path of poverty – friendly growth: a literature review," Journal of Xinjiang University of Finance and Economics, No. 3, 2014, pp. 5 – 12.

[2] "Комментарий к оценке ВВП методом использования доходов и методом формирования по источникам доходов за II квартал 2022 Года," Rosstat, сентября 28, 2022, https://rosstat.gov.ru/folder/313/document/182915.

[3] Снимщикова И. В., Шамраи К. Е, "Некоторые аспекты обеспечения эконо – мическои безопасности России скои Федерации//Институциональные тренды транс – формации социально – экономической системы в условиях глобальнои нестабильности," Краснодар, 2021, pp. 432 – 438.

[4] "Росстат представляет информацию о границе бедности в I квартале 2022 года," Rosstat, сентября 28, 2022, https://rosstat.gov.ru/folder/313/document/168756.

[5] "The Russian Ministry of Economic Development forecasts the real disposable income of Russian residents," Ministry of Commerce People's Republic of China, September 03, 2022, http://ru.mofcom.gov.cn/article/jmxw/202205/20220503313035.shtml.

Besides, Russia switched individual income tax from a progressive rate to a flat rate of 13% in 2001, resulting in the poor actually paying a higher tax burden than the rich and high – income differentiation.[①] Therefore, the instability of economic development and the imperfection of its income distribution system lead to insufficient pro – poor growth and a persistent feature of poverty.

### (2) A huge social inequality in Russia

Firstly, there is a huge gap between the rich and the poor. Russia's income inequality first intensified during its transition period, peaking after the outbreak of the economic crisis in 1998, and then gradually decreased from 1998 to 2015.[②] However, the reduction of this gap does not fully realize social equality. A 2022 study by Fin Expertiza, an international audit and consulting firm, based on data from the Rosstat, divided people into five groups in order of their lowest to highest monthly income in 2021. According to the study, the average monthly income for all Russians in 2021 will be 40000 rubles. Among them, the average monthly income of the least affluent Russians (group 1) in 2021 is 10800 rubles, that of the second group is 20300 rubles, the third group is 30300 rubles, the fourth group 45400 rubles, and the average monthly income of the wealthiest Russian citizens (group 5) is 93500 rubles. The income gap between the richest and the poorest groups was 8.6 times, and the income of group 5 accounted for 46.7% of the total income of the Russian people. However, the income of group 1 is only 5.4% of the total income of all groups.[③] At the same

---

① Liancheng Guo, "An analysis of income distribution in Russia," Research on Financial and Economic Issues, No. 1, 2021, pp. 114 – 122.

② Lisina A, Van Kerm P, "Understanding Twenty Years of Inequality and Poverty Trends in Russia," Review of Income and Wealth, Vol. 68, No. 1, 2022, pp. 108 – 130.

③ "Will the 8.6 times income Gap between rich and poor in Russia improve in 2022?" Dragonnewsru, September 01, 2022, http://www.dragonnewsru.com/static/content/home/headlines_home/2022 – 06 – 01/981635395177820160.html.

time, only 7% of Russians are middle class① showing the huge gap between the rich and the poor in Russian society. Moreover, public opinion also shows dissatisfaction with the income gap in Russia. In May 2022, the Russian Public Opinion Research Center surveyed 1600 Russians over 18 years old. According to the survey results, more than half of the Russians (55%) think that the country should narrow the income gap among residents. ②

Secondly, the main causes of poverty are the wage difference between industries and the low wages in some economic activities. ③ In Russian society, "the employed poor" is also an acute problem. Low wages cannot lift a considerable number of Russian workers out of poverty, especially for single - parent families and families with many children. Although many people in Russia are working, their income is very low, even below the minimum living standard. ④ Based on the data of the Rosstat, RIA Novosti calculated the median income of various industries in Russia and found that for some industries, the monthly salary of middle - level employees could reach 50000 or even 60000 rubles, but for industries with lower income, the median is less than 25000 rubles. The median income of the highest industry (65000 rubles for the mining industry) is three times that of the lowest industry (20500 rubles for the light industry). ⑤

Thirdly, there is a significant age difference among the poor. By January 12022, according to the data from the Rosstat, the minimum subsistence per ca-

---

① Снимщикова И. В., Шамраи К. Е., "Некоторые аспекты обеспечения эконо - мической безопасности РоссийскойФедерации // Институциональные тренды транс - формации социально - экономической системы в условиях глобальной нестабильности," Краснодар, 2021, pp. 432 - 438.

② "Poll: 55% of Russians are in favor of the state narrowing the income gap between residents," Sputniknews, October 12, 2022, https: //sputniknews. cn/20220621/1042059249. html.

③ Chunyu Li, "On the Structural Premise of Poverty in the Process of Modernization - Taking Russia as an Example," Theory and Modernization, No. 02, 2017, pp. 24 - 30.

④ Xiuhua Diao, "The Problem of the Polarization between the Rich and the Poor in Russia," Journal of Russian Studies, No. 6, 2021, pp. 59 - 72.

⑤ "Survey: The average Russian earns 35, 000 rubles a month," Sputniknews, October 20, 2022, https: //sputniknews. cn/20200803/1031887957. html.

pita in Russia was 12654 rubles, 13793 rubles for able-bodied people, 10882 rubles for pensioners and 12274 rubles for children.[①] It can be seen that the pensioners and children in Russia do not reach per capita minimum subsistence. In the poor groups, the proportion of children is more than 1.5 times higher than the proportion of children in the total Russian population. The growth of low-income groups is mainly due to the large number of children.[②] From 2013 to 2018, due to the serious aging problem in Russia, the deficit of pension funds rose from 1791 billion rubles to 2479.1 billion rubles, with a cumulative increase of 38.4%, and its proportion in Russia's GDP increased from 2.45% to 2.99%.[③] It can be seen that children and pensioners constitute the main part of the poor in Russia.

Fourthly, the poor are unevenly distributed in different regions. Due to the uneven distribution of Russia's natural resources such as oil and gas, the regions with rich oil and gas resources develop well, enjoying a high economic aggregate and a relatively high living standard. At the same time, there is also a gap between the rich and the poor between urban and rural areas. For example, there is a huge gap between the income of urban residents in Moscow and St. Petersburg and that of poor rural people. RIA Novosti calculated the median household income using the data from the Rosstat and found that the average ratio of the median monthly income per capita to the cost of fixed goods and services in all of Russia in 2019 was 1.65, with 65 regions below the average level and 20 regions above the average level. Among them, Yamalo-Nenets Autonomous District ranks first, followed by another oil and gas region in the north, namely Nenets Autonomous Region, while Moscow, which ranks third, is nearly 30% behind the

---

① "Кабмин внес в Думу проект об увеличении прожиточного минимума в 2023 году до 14 375 рублей," Tass, октябр. 02, 2022, https://tass.ru/obschestvo/15897239?.

② K. Goulin, Juck Zhang, K. "Inequality and Poverty of Russian Residents," Jiangxi Social Sciences, No. 9, 2012, pp. 247-248.

③ Yaqiong Tian, "Research on raising funds for old-age security in Russia under the background of aging, PhD Thesis, Central University of Finance and Economics, 2020, pp. 113-115.

first in this indicator. In the Republic of Tuva, which ranks last (85th), the index is only 0.97, and the index of four other regions is in the range of 1.0 – 1.1. In all 15 regions of Russia, the index is no higher than 1.3. [1]

### (3) Disputes about the standard of the poverty line

The poverty line in Russia is generally referred to as "minimum subsistence" or "minimum consumption basket". The total value of the consumption basket is based on the consumer price level of food, non-food goods and services released by the Rosstat. The minimum subsistence and poverty rate are the core elements of the government's poverty reduction policy. However, the poverty line in Russia faces many criticisms. First, the minimum living standard is too low, which does not reflect the actual cost of daily life[2]; Second, poverty indicators have not been fully considered, such as rent, service consumption, etc. If these indicators are taken into consideration, the number of poor people in Russia will increase significantly. [3] Dittmann and Goebel believe that the reason why the poverty line in Russia is set this way is that when poverty is defined as an absolute threshold, the problems of social inequality or uneven distribution of income and wealth in Russia can be masked to some extent. [4]

### (4) The rising unemployment rate leading to family poverty

Aganbegyan, a member of the Russian Academy of Sciences and economic adviser to the first president after the dissolution, told Russia's Business Online in August 2022 that the unemployment rate in Russia would double, including

---

[1] "Названы российские регионы с самым высоким уровнем бедности," Ria, октябр. 23, 2022, https://ria.ru/20200706/1573926441.html.

[2] Martin Brand, "The OECD poverty rate: Lessons from the Russian case", Global Social Policy, Vol. 21, No. 1, 2021, pp. 144 – 147.

[3] Weiyun Ma, "Poverty line in Russia: Basic concepts and methods of measurement," Russian, Central Asian and Eastern European Studies, No. 05, 2008, pp. 26 – 32.

[4] Martin Brand, "The OECD poverty rate: Lessons from the Russian case", Global Social Policy, Vol. 21, No. 1, 2021, pp. 144 – 147.

hidden unemployment. From the social perspective, on the one hand, due to various forms of social exclusion, blue - collar workers who lack employment stability and families with children, including single - parent families, are at a higher risk of falling into extreme and permanent poverty.[1] On the other hand, in recent years, due to their respective socio - demographic factors, some Russian people are at risk of low - income poverty and deprivation poverty. Gender factors, marital status, dependency burden, health status, and residence type all indicate that the socio - demographic characteristics of the poor groups in Russia are related to the position of individuals in the labor market.[2] Besides, in recent years, in addition to external factors, Russia's scientific and technological potential development is insufficient, and the traditional energy industry is facing challenges and the loss of elites leads to the deterioration of the quality of human resources.[3] Although the current unemployment rate is estimated at 3.8%, Russian media said that the actual number of unemployed people in Russia at least doubled the official figure.[4] At the same time, the Ministry of Economic Development of the Russian Federation predicted that the unemployment rate in Russia would rise to 6.7% by the end of 2022, and would not return to the level of 2021 (4.8%) until 2025.[5]

**(5) The squeeze of sanctions aggravating the poverty problem**

From the Ukrainian crisis in 2014 to the outbreak of the Russian - Ukrainian

---

[1] Yaroshenko, S, "'New' Poverty in Russia After Socialism," Laboratorium: Russian Review of Social Research, Vol. 2, No. 2, 2012, pp. 221 - 251.

[2] Chunyi Liu, "Characteristics and Distribution of the Poor Class in Russia," People's Forum, No. 11, 2017, pp. 110 - 111.

[3] Yujun Feng, "The Political and Social Roots of Russian Economy and the Prospect of National Development," Eurasian Economy, No. 1, 2022, pp. 1 - 11.

[4] "Russia's unemployment rate may reach 12%," Sputniknews, October 16, 2022, https://sputniknews.cn/20201001/1032239907.html.

[5] "Russia's unemployment rate will be 6.7% in 2022," Ministry of Commerce People's Republic of China, October 06, 2022, http://ru.mofcom.gov.cn/article/jmxw/202205/20220503313033.shtml.

conflict in 2022, western countries imposed a series of economic sanctions on Russia, ranging from industrial and agricultural products to energy strategic sectors such as oil and gas, to daily necessities such as infant milk powder and toiletries①, even closing the airspace② and the blockade of science and technology leading to a decrease of tens of billions of rubles in Russia's economic income and a corresponding increase in job unemployment, which inevitably leads to a downturn in economic development. ③ Raudales, the head of *Independiente*, pointed out in an interview that Western sanctions against Russia can be felt all over the world, and the rising prices of fuel and raw materials will lead to the aggravation of global poverty. Many families will lose the ability to buy food and become poorer and hungrier. ④

Faced with the long-term Western sanctions against Russia's economy and military and the persistence of the Russia-Ukraine conflict, Russia has obviously invested too much resources in the military and diplomatic fields, which impede poverty reduction. According to official Russian data, its defense budget increased by approximately 9.2% in 2022, reaching $86.4 billion. However, the Stockholm International Peace Research Institute (SIPRI) believes that this figure accounts for only 78% of Russia's estimated annual defense spending. In particular, the special allocation for "mobilization and additional troop training" amounted to as much as $245 million, a year-on-year increase of about 119% compared to 2021. ⑤ Faced with the risk of a huge fiscal deficit, the pace

---

① Poling Xu, "Resilience, Roots and Future Direction of Russian Economy under the Pressure of American and European Sanctions," Journal of Russian Studies, No. 4, 2022, pp. 22 – 47.

② "Russian Travel Agency Association: Russia's tourism industry lost tens of billions of rubles due to the closure of western airspace," Sputniknews, October 15, 2022, https://sputniknews.cn/20220722/1042644623.html.

③ Zhenjun Jiang, "Analysis of Russia's Economic Development under the Impact of Western Sanctions and Epidemic," Siberian Studies, No. 4, 2022, pp. 21 – 32.

④ "El Salvador leftist leader: Sanctions against Russia lead to increased poverty in the world," Sputniknews, August 05, 2022, https://sputniknews.cn/20220402/1040446422.html.

⑤ "Trends in World Military Expenditure, 2022," Stockholm International Peace Research Institute, April, 2023, p. 5.

of poverty reduction has been slowed down.

Looking back at the evolution of poverty in Russia, itcan be found that after Russia entered the social transition period, the inflation of ruble was aggravated due to the aggravation of inequality, the decline of the economy, the increase of the unemployment rate, and the decline of gross domestic product. During Putin's two terms in office, the poverty problem in Russia was somewhat alleviated. However, in recent years, due to the dual influence of international and domestic factors and some problems left over from history, there is a new poverty phenomenon in Russia today.

## Ⅱ. Russia's Poverty Governance Measures

Faced with poverty, the Russian government has taken a series of measures such as promote economic development, promote the fair distribution, optimize poverty indicators, promote employment, and actively participated in international poverty reduction cooperation.

### (1) Promoting the pro – poor growth

Russia improved the insufficient pro – poor promotion by stimulating economic development and adjusting the income distribution system. The poverty problem in Russia lies in the slow development of the national economy, so it is necessary to alleviate the burden of economic development and tackle corruption in the country. Russia has continuously formulated and improved the National Anti – Corruption Plan to address the problems rooted in the Russian economic operation and development model from the legislative level. [1] It is also necessary to strengthen the resilience of economic development. In recent years, Russia has attached great importance to the development of the digital economy and adjusted

---

[1] Sun Qi, "New Trends of Anti – Corruption in Russia," Prosecutorial Storm, No. 10, 2021, pp. 58 – 59.

its economic structure and mode of economic growth. Since 2016, Russia has put forward the task of formulating the digital economy plan through documents such as the Russian Information Society Development Strategy (2017 – 2030) and On the National Goals and Strategic Objectives of the Development of the Russian Federation for the period up to 2024. [1] In addition, the Russian authorities have also carried out a large number of talent introduction policies, such as the Federal Special Plan for Innovating Russian Scientific, Technological and Educational Talents (2009 – 2013)[2], and the Support Measures for Young Talents in the Russian Federation (2009). [3] To a certain extent, these laws and regulations have played a role in cultivating young people in science and technology innovation, attracting overseas students to return home, and then promoting the innovative development of the national economy, so as to realize sustainable economic development. As for the adjustment of the income distribution mechanism, two scholars, Lisina and Kerm, have studied the significant changes in Russia's income distribution from 1994 to 2015 and found that the main reasons for the changes in Russia were the decrease of income in the private sector, the increase of pension and the income level in the public sector. [4] In addition, Russia has taken the adjustment of personal income tax as an important step in the reform of residents' income distribution system, and implemented a tax policy that can narrow the income gap of residents. [5] To some extent, these measures have helped the poor indirectly benefit from economic growth, which in turn has promoted the

---

[1] Qingxin Lan, Chunyu Wang, Nikolai, "The Development of Russian Digital Economy and the New Challenges Faced by Sino – Russian Digital Economy Cooperation," Northeast Asia Forum, No. 5, 2022, pp. 111 – 126.

[2] Sijia Li, "The Russian government's science and technology talent policy," China Science and Technology Information, No. 6, 2013, p. 118.

[3] "О мерах государственной поддержки талантливой молодёжи," Normativ Kontur, октябр. 07, 2022, https://normativ.kontur.ru/document?moduleId=1&documentId=235515.

[4] Lisina A, Van Kerm P, "Understanding Twenty Years of Inequality and Poverty Trends in Russia", Review of Income and Wealth, Vol. 68, No. 1, 2022, pp. 108 – 130.

[5] Liancheng Guo, Shi Yuan, "An analysis of income distribution in Russia," Research on Financial and Economic Issues, No. 1, 2021, pp. 114 – 122.

decline of the poverty rate.

(2) **Adjusting the gap between the rich and the poor**

First, to solve the problem of the large wage difference among industries, Russia has adopted the legal guarantee to alleviate social income inequality. According to the Russian Constitution and Labor Law, a number of laws have been issued to raise the minimum wage standard. For example, the Labor Code of the Russian Federation stipulates that employees' labor remuneration shall not be lower than the national minimum wage standard.[①] Minimum Wage Law of the Russian Federation has been promulgated one after another. In 2020, Putin also signed the federal law (No. 473 - FZ, December 29th, 2020) on the revision of the minimum living expenses, stipulating that the statutory minimum wage in 2021 will be 12792 rubles (about 1115.21 yuan) per month, an increase of 5.5% over the previous year.

Second, as for the obvious age difference among the poor, Russia focuses on improving welfare security by helping the elderly and children, two major groups of poor people. Against the background of increasing aging, Russia has gradually formed a Three - Pillar new old - age security system, which is divided into three different levels of security modes: state pension, compulsory old - age insurance and individual voluntary old - age insurance.[②] And from June 1st, 2022, Russia's minimum wage standard, minimum living standard and pension for the unemployed elderly will be raised by 10%. Therefore, the average pension of unemployed pensioners will increase to 19360 rubles.[③] On the issue of tackling child poverty, Putin emphasized in his 2020 State of the Union Address

---

[①] "Трудовой Кодекс Российской Федерации," Normativ Kontur, декабр. 31, 2001, https://normativ.kontur.ru/document?moduleId=1&documentId=454527.

[②] Yaqiong Tian, "Research on raising funds for old - age security in Russia under the background of aging," PhD Thesis, Central University of Finance and Economics, 2020, p. 57.

[③] "Правительство проиндексировало пенсии, прожиточный минимум и минимальный размер оплаты труда на 10%," Government, октябр. 02, 2022, http://government.ru/news/45559/.

that the state support for families with children would be strengthened. It is stipulated that the state will pay monthly allowance for the first child and the second child for low-income families according to the minimum living standard of children in specific areas①, and will further revise the government resolution in 2022, to provide monthly subsidies to children aged 3 to 8, distribute monthly benefits to children aged 8 to 17②, and provide more support to families with many children highlighting the necessity of reducing children poverty.

Thirdly, as to the uneven distribution of poor people in different regions, Russia develops the economy of poor areas by allocating funds, promoting vocational education of rural youth and providing legal and medical assistance.③ For example, Order No. 1435-r of June 4, 2022, requires that more than 5.6 billion rubles be allocated to some regions such as Khanty-Mansiky, Yamalo-Nenets Autonomous District and Republic of Dagestan④ to promote local economic development, provide vocational training for local unemployed youth, provide soft loans, legal and medical assistance and support programs for small businesses in rural areas.⑤ To some extent, it has alleviated the problem of regional inequality between the rich and the poor.

## (3) Optimizing poverty indicators

Since 2005, the poverty line in Russia has been determined independently

---

① "Колесник А. П. Информационная система для мониторинга и управления материальным положением семей в Российской Федерации, предотвращения попадания их в состояние бедности и контроля за выведением из бедности (экосистема семья)," Стратегии Бизнеса, No. 7, 2020, pp. 11–13.

② "Правительство расширило доступ к социальной поддержке для семей с детьми," Government, сентября 30, 2022, http: //government. ru/news/45303/.

③ Chunyu Li, "On the structural premise of poverty in the process of modernization: A case study of Russia," Theory and Modernization, No. 2, 2017, pp. 24–30.

④ "Правительство направит ещё более 5, 6 млрд рублей для выплат на детей от 3 до 7 лет," Government, октябр. 02, 2022, http: //government. ru/news/45625/.

⑤ Ржаницына Л. С., "Москва Как снизить бедность в России," Журнал Новой Экономической Ассоциации, Vol. 2, No. 18, 2013, pp. 180–183.

by each federal entity. In 2006, the State Duma passed the government bill of Russia Consumption Basket Plan, which stipulated to increase in the monthly per capita food consumption expenditure and cultural service consumer goods in Russia[1], to improve the formulation of the poverty line. In addition, according to Decree No. 2049 of the government of the Russian Federation on November 26th, 2021, the Rosstat introduced the initial value of the basic poverty line, the poverty rate calculated by Russian per capita monetary income, the poverty line calculated by being compared with household income, and other indicators, and stipulated that the overall poverty data of the Russian Federation must be updated quarterly, and each federal entity should determine it once a year, which made the evaluation of poverty indicators more refined and accurate.[2]

### (4) Policy guarantees to increase the employment rate

In order to stabilize the labor market, Russia promulgated the Employment Act of the Russian Federation as early as April 19th, 1991, which has undergone 55 amendments so far to realize the full employment of the people who are least protected by employment, including youth, disabled people and women.[3] To fully stimulate employment, Russia has launched a number of programs to create jobs. Mikhail Mishustin, Prime Minister of the Russian Federation, said that in March 2021, the implementation of the National Plan for the Social and Econom-

---

[1] Weiyun Ma, "Poverty line in Russia: Basic concepts and methods of measurement," Russian, Central Asian and Eastern European Studies, No. 5, 2008, pp. 26 – 32.

[2] "Об утверждении Правил определения границ бедности в целом по Российской Федерации и по субъектам Российской Федерации, используемых в оценках показателя" Уровень бедности " в целом по Российской Федерации и по субъектам Российской Федерации, и о внесении изменений в Федеральный план статистических работ," Publication Pravo, октябр. 22, 2022, http://publication.pravo.gov.ru/Document/View/0001202111270008.

[3] Jinshun Park, "Translation Practice Report of Employment Law of Russian Federation (the first four chapters)," Yanbian University Master's Thesis, 2021, p. 1.

ic Development of the Arctic Region① created tens of thousands of new employment opportunities and increased people's income. At the same time, the Russian Prime Minister also said at the government meeting that in 2022, the Russian government will allocate about 40 billion rubles (about 380 million US dollars) to implement a series of employment protection measures, of which more than 25.5 billion rubles (about 240 million US dollars) will be used to create temporary jobs for citizens facing unemployment risks and provide public service jobs for job seekers who have registered in employment centers. It is estimated that 400,000 people can get the above support. ②

### (5) Strengthening international cooperation

As a common challenge facing the world, poverty has been brought into the research field of global governance in recent years and gradually became the core topic of the global agenda. Russia actively participates in promoting the Global Development Initiative put forward by China, including participating in the activities of the Group of Friends of Global Development Initiative on the United Nations. Together with China, Russia has called for poverty reduction to be the priority area of cooperation for the international community and supported poverty governance cooperation as the core agenda of BRICS, the Shanghai Cooperation Organization and the Eurasian Economic Union. Therefore, Russia has become an important participant and promoter of global poverty governance and played an important role in revitalizing multilateralism. In the face of Western sanctions, Russia has taken the initiative to expand its interaction with countries in Asia, Africa and Latin America to improve its own economy, which will also promote the economic development of countries in Asia, Africa and Latin America. For

---

① "Russian government approves the national plan for social and economic development of arctic region," China Marine Development Research Center, October 05, 2022, http: //aoc. ouc. edu. cn/2021/0415/c9829a319182/pagem. htm.

② "Russian government to allocate 40 billion Lubbock jobs," Ministry of Commerce People's Republic of China, October 03, 2022, http: //ru. mofcom. gov. cn/article/jmxw/202203/20220303289282. shtml.

example, the South African Minister of Defence and Military Veterans Modise said that Russia has the potential to invest in development and become a partner. Cooperation with African countries will reduce poverty and promote development in Africa. ①

## Ⅲ. Prospects of Poverty Governance in Russia

Under the efforts of the government, the poverty problem in Russia has been greatlyalleviated and a series of constructive achievements have been made. First of all, the number of poor people has been greatly reduced. From 2019 to the end of 2021, the number of poor people in Russia has decreased from 18.1 million to 16.1 million, with an average annual decrease of 1 million, and the poverty rate has dropped from 12.3% to 11%. Secondly, the lives of poor people have been improved. On the one hand, welfare policies such as reforming the tax system, increasing people's income, adjusting the minimum subsistence, raising pensions, and supporting families with children have ensured the lives of the poor groups. ② On the other hand, the government's employment assistance policy has improved poverty alleviation. In the first quarter of 2022, the employed population reached 71.5 million, a year – on – year increase of 1%, and the average nominal accrued salary was 60, 101 rubles, a year – on – year increase of 15.0%. ③ Third, the ability to prevent poverty risks has been improved. For example, under the influence of the COVID – 19 pandemic in 2020, experts from the World Bank held that the support measures of the Russian government have

---

① "Kirill Kallinikov, South African Ministry of Defence: Russia plays an important role in the development of African countries," Sputniknews, September 20, 2022, https: //sputniknews.cn/20220817/1043120859.html.

② "Russian Statistical Office: The poverty rate in Russia has decreased," Sputniknews, October 03, 2022, https: //sputniknews.cn/20210415/1033488230.html.

③ "Росстат представляет информацию о границе бедности в I квартале 2022 года," Rosstat, сентября 03, 2022, https: //rosstat.gov.ru/folder/313/document/168756.

kept the poverty rate from rebounding on a large scale. Seligman pointed out that according to the forecast that GDP will decrease by 4% in 2020, 14.2% of the population will be below the official poverty line in 2020, and the authorities' remedial measures will reduce this figure to 11.6%. The poverty rate in 2020 is equal to or slightly lower than the level predicted before the outbreak of the epidemic, which shows that the measures of poverty governance in Russia have achieved its goal. Russia's support measures are comparable to that of comparable economies, and the combination of social security measures has been effective, without increasing poverty due to the crisis. [1]

Despite a series of constructive achievements, a series of poverty problems caused by Russia's weak economy, social problems and the imbalance between environmental protection and economic development have not subsided. In addition, in recent years, the spread of COVID-19, the intensification of Western sanctions against Russia and the outbreak of the Russia-Ukraine conflict have had a huge impact on Russia's economy, posing a certain threat to poverty reduction in Russia, and thus Russia's poverty reduction still faces many challenges.

First, Russia's economy is weak. Russia's economic development mode has been fixed, and it has long been faced with problems such as single industry, low competitiveness of the manufacturing industry, low labor productivity, weak organization and insufficient scientific and technological development. However, in recent years, it has been subjected to Western technical blockade and sanctions, which may restrict Russia's economic development for a long time. [2] Olga Belenkaya, the head of the macroeconomic analysis department of Finam, a Russian financial institution, said that the challenge of poverty governance may be related to the insufficient development of the economic potential of the poor ar-

---

[1] "World Bank: The Russian government's support measures have prevented the poverty rate from rebounding due to the pandemic," Sputniknews, September 29, 2022, https://sputniknews.cn/20201216/1032728783.html.

[2] Богданова В. П., Родионова С. Д., "Факторы российской бедности," Современные Проблемы Науки и Образования, Vol. 1, No. 1, 2015, p. 1494.

eas. She pointed out that from a strategic point of view, it is important to develop the productive potential of these poor areas and build the necessary infrastructure to make better use of their natural resources and logistical advantages. ①

Second, social problems pose the challenge of anti - poverty. First of all, Russia's socialexclusion makes it difficult for foreign workers to integrate. To some extent, migrant workers have solved Russia's population problem and brought a large number of working - age workers. However, many Russians still believe that migrant workers will lead to negative effects such as rising crime rate, intensified corruption and increasingly fierce competition in the labor market. ② Secondly, the social exclusion of poor rural areas in northern Russia has caused the dilemma of regional poverty governance. Many factors, such as the harsh natural environment, remote geographical location and insufficient public investment, have caused the economic, social and spatial isolation of poor rural areas in northern Russia, resulting in regional poverty syndrome. Thirdly, there is a problem of female exclusion in Russian society. Many women are not only responsible for family support, but also for housework, so they are mostly engaged in low - income jobs. Women often find it difficult to find jobs because of gender and social exclusion. ③ Finally, as the outflow of a large number of elites to Western developed countries is accelerating, the labor market will become worse. Foreign labor, poor rural areas in the north, social exclusion of women and outflow of elites all hinder the development of the Russian labor market, aggravate social contradictions, and make it more difficult to fight against poverty. ④

---

① "Will the 8.6 times income Gap between rich and poor in Russia improve in 2022?" Dragonnewsru, September 01, 2022, http://www.dragonnewsru.com/static/content/home/headlines_home/2022 - 06 - 01/981635395177820160.html.

② Zhiqin Song, Chenchen Pu, "Current situation and influence of foreign labor migration in Russia," Eurasian Humanities Studies, No. 3, 2022, pp. 21 - 32.

③ Ярошенко, Светлана Владимировна, "Женская занятость в условиях гендерного и социального исключения," Социологический Журнал, No. 3, 2002, pp. 137 - 150.

④ Ярошенко, Светлана Владимировна, "Женская занятость в условиях гендерного и социального исключения," Социологический Журнал, No. 3, 2002, pp. 137 - 150.

Third, the imbalance between environmental protection and economic development also poses new challenges to poverty reduction in Russia. The frequent occurrence of natural disasters such as drought, floods and forest fires caused by global climate change has caused great damage to Russian society and economy, which has shaken Russia's position on energy transformation. Low – carbon transformation will be one of the key directions of Russia's future development. However, due to thefact that the Russian economy relies too much on fossil energy at present, achieving carbon neutrality will lead Russia's economic development into difficulties, and then affect poverty governance. [1] According to Sputnik News Agency of Russia, Russian experts pointed out in the report of Impact of Various Forms of Carbon Pricing on Reducing Greenhouse Gas Emissions and Social and Economic Development that the carbon price in Russia will reach 10 dollars per ton in 2030 and increase to 50 dollars per ton in 2050, which will reduce the average annual GDP growth rate by 1.5 percentage points. Therefore, Russia's carbon regulation may lead to an economic slowdown, increased inflation and unemployment rate, reduced investment, and may eventually be accompanied by an increase in the poverty rate. [2]

Fourth, the uncertainty of global poverty alleviation has increased during the pandemic. Since the outbreak of the COVID – 19 pandemic, the economic development of various countries has been severely hindered, the gap between the rich and the poor has further widened, and the number of people living in absolute poverty has soared globally. At the same time, the blockade of the COVID – 19 pandemic has disrupted international trade. In its trade forecast, the WTO indicated that the growth forecast of commodity trade in 2022 was lowered from 4.7%

---

[1] Liu Gan, "Challenges of Russian Energy Industry under the Background of Low – carbon Transformation," Eurasian Economy, No.1, 2022, pp. 12 – 26.

[2] "Russian Experts: Russia's carbon regulatory policy may lead to poverty and price increase, but giving up will be worse," Sputniknews, September 20, 2022, https://sputniknews.cn/20220715/1042512623.html.

to 3%.① Therefore, the COVID – 19 pandemic has caused a bleak prospect of international trade, which may lead to a shortage of raw materials and higher inflation in the world. The pandemic has brought a serious negative impact on Russia's unstable economic development. Not only has Russia's breakthrough growth and new cycle of investment plans been laid aside, but the long – term development of the epidemic has also changed the propensity of residents to consume and save, and the energy market has remained sluggish.②

Finally, sanctions aggravate the poverty problem in Russia. After the Russian – Ukrainian conflict, the United States and Europe launched a series of broader and larger sanctions against Russia.③ A large number of multinational companies have withdrawn from Russia with their products and services. As a result, a large number of jobs have been cut, the unemployment rate has increased, and because of the devaluation of the ruble, the purchasing power and livelihood of Russian citizens have dropped sharply. Russia will face the difficulties caused by its rapid and extensive decoupling from the international financial system. In the long run, all these measures will have an important impact on Russia's economy, thus affecting Russia's anti – poverty development.

On the whole, the instability of Russia's economic development has affected the effect of poverty reduction, and a series of problems such as social exclusion, the imbalance between environmental protection and economic development are the important challengesRussia faces in poverty reduction, while the epidemic situation and the sanctions in the western world have increased the uncertainty of poverty reduction. Russia still has a long way to go to get rid of poverty. Russia needs to adjust its development strategy to maximize the effect of poverty reduction.

---

① "The latest forecast of WTO: Global trade growth of 3.0% in 2022," The National Development and Reform Commission, October 05, 2022, https://www.ndrc.gov.cn/fggz/lywzjw/jwtz/202204/t20220428_1323609.html? code = &state = 123.

② Poling Xu, "The Impact of COVID – 19 Epidemic on Russian Economy: Anti – epidemic and Anti – crisis Measures, Economic Operation and Growth Prospects," Xinjiang Finance and Economics, No.4, 2020, pp.57 – 68.

③ Wenlin Chen, Yunmou Lv, Hongtu Zhao, "Characteristics, influence and enlightenment of Western energy sanctions on Russia," International Petroleum Economy, No.9, 2022, pp.1 – 10.

# Thoughts on the Approaches of Deepening People – to – People Exchanges Between China and BRICS in the New Era

You Yupin[*]

**Abstract**: People – to – people exchanges have become a critical part of the BRICS "Three – Wheel Drive" mechanism of political, economic and cultural cooperation, so consolidating and deepening BRICS cooperation in the field of people – to – people exchanges is of great significance to building a lasting and stable BRICS partnership. The theory and practice of people – to – people exchange between China and other countries have been discussed much in existing literature. Therefore, this paper mainly focuses on deepening the subject and field, which are two major elements of people – to – people exchanges between China and BRICS, and puts forward new paths and measures that will help deepen people – to – people exchanges between BRICS on the basis of describing the status quo and shortcomings.

**Keywords**: BRICS; people – to – people exchanges; path

---

[*] You Yupin, Portuguese teacher of the College of Western Languages and Cultures, Sichuan International Studies University. Her research interests include Portuguese – Chinese translation and area studies of Portuguese – speaking countries.

# I. Introduction

On September 9, 2021, President Xi Jinping attended the 13th BRICS Summit and delivered a speech entitled "Advanced BRICS Cooperation to Meet Common Challenges Together". In his speech, President Xi proposed that the BRICS strengthen people – to – people exchanges in the spirit of mutual learning and further enhance the quality of practical cooperation.[1] Since attending the Fifth BRICS Summit in March 2013 as president of the People's Republic of China, President Xi has always attached great importance and high expectations to promoting people – to – people exchanges among the five BRICS countries. This is not only because people – to – people exchanges have become a critical part of the BRICS "Three – Wheel Drive" mechanism of political, economic and cultural cooperation[2], but also because "the friendship between peoples holds the key to building sound state – state relations", as consolidating and deepening BRICS cooperation in the field of people – to – people exchanges is of great significance to building and developing a lasting and stable BRICS partnership.

The current international situation is marked by complex changes. The regional situation witnesses turmoil and transformation. The major changes unseen in a century and the once – in – a – century pandemic are intertwined with each other, resulting in various contradictions. And various comments and opinions against the BRICS are also heard from time to time.[3] 2021 marks the 20th anniversary of the concept of BRICS that the political identity and common interests of BRICS determine the consensus that these countries will deepen practical cooperation invariably, and the value and potential of BRICS cannot be questioned.

---

[1] "Xi Jinping's Speech at the 13th BRICS Summit," State Council of the People's Republic of China, September 10, 2021, http://www.gov.cn/xinwen/2021-09/10/content_5636527.htm.

[2] Wu Bing, Liu Hongyu: "Progress, Challenges, and Pathways in Cultural Exchanges Among BRICS Countries," Contemporary World, No. 12, 2019, pp. 26-32.

[3] "Twenty years on, the Brics have disappointed," Financial Times, Nov. 29, 2021, https://www.ft.com/content/034ba0e7-7518-437e-854c-7c0dd5d74e34.

However, there is no denying that compared with political connections and economic and trade exchanges, people – to – people exchanges are still a weak link of current BRICS cooperation, facing many problems and challenges such as unstable foundation, slow progress, unbalanced participation of countries, and imperfect mechanism building. Therefore, we must fully understand the indispensable role of deepening BRICS people – to – people exchanges and cooperation in promoting high – quality and practical cooperation among BRICS countries in the current international environment. In 2022, China will take over the rotating chairmanship of BRICS from India. The question we need to consider carefully and answer seriously in the new era and a new situation is how can China lead by example to propose China's approaches to promoting institutional innovation, method innovation and content innovation of people – to – people exchanges between China and BRICS, and contribute Chinese wisdom to enhance the breadth, thickness and depth of BRICS people – to – people exchanges, while injecting Chinese vitality into BRICS people – to – people exchanges and cooperation under the influence of major changes and the pandemic.

The theory and practice of cultural exchange between China and foreign countries have been adequately discussed in the existing research.[1] It is also common to discuss the construction of people – to – people exchange and cooperation mechanisms in BRICS countries from a macro level.[2] There is also a special chapter in this book devoted to discussing the current difficulties and obstacles facing people – to – people exchanges among BRICS. In view of this, this article will mainly focus on the two major elements of deepening people – to – people exchanges and cooperation between China and BRICS, the subject and field, to

---

[1] Recent discussions on the theory and practice of Sino – foreign people – to – people exchanges can be found in Zhang Ji and Xing Liju, eds. , "The Great Changes and Sino – Foreign People – to – People Exchanges Unprecedented in a Century," World Knowledge Press, 2021.

[2] Representative studies such as Pu Gongying: "Analysis of BRICS People – to – People Exchange and Cooperation Mechanism", Russian Eastern Europe and Central Asia Studies, No. 4, 2017, pp. 46 – 56; Xu Xiujun, "Building the BRICS People – to – People Exchange Mechanism: Roles, Challenges and Countermeasures," Contemporary World, No. 8, 2018, pp. 26 – 29.

propose some new approaches and measures that will help China deepen people – to – people exchanges with BRICS members on the basis of describing the current situation and shortcomings.

## II. Promote the Diversification of BRICS People – to – People Exchanges

As China continues to expanding opening up, it is obvious that the traditional single mode of cultural and people – to – people exchanges, which is "the government setting the stage and playing the lead role", can no longer fully meet the requirements of the new situation. Since China's opening up is all – round, the subjects of cultural and people – to – people exchanges in China should also be diversified. Therefore, to achieve the "quality and efficiency" of people – to – people exchanges between China and BRICS in the new era, we must unswervingly promote the diversification of the main bodies of people – to – people exchanges, and we must give full play to the exemplary role of high – level leadership and make good use of the guiding role of top – level design, while truly shifting the focus of people – to – people exchanges, and guide and encourage more subjects to participate in and invest in people – to – people exchanges between China and BRICS by fully mobilizing all mobilizable forces such as local forces, non – governmental forces, and overseas forces, so as to form an all – round and whole – of – society synergy. In this process, we should focus on selecting subjects with great potential for people – to – people exchanges, and explore new ideas, new models and new actions for China to deepen people – to – people exchanges with BRICS countries. Governments at all levels need to strengthen policy guidance, platform building and resource integration for multi – subjects to participate in BRICS people – to – people exchanges, so as to create conditions, to provide support and security for promoting the diversification of BRICS people –

to – people exchange subjects.

Specifically, in the new era, the subjects willing to play and capable of playing a "leading role" in the process of deepening people – to – people exchanges with BRICS countries mainly include: overseas Chinese enterprises, overseas Chinese in BRICS countries, Chinese scholars engaged in international academic exchanges, Chinese cities that have established sister – city relationships with BRICS countries, and the Chinese youth generation.

### (1) The role of Chinese enterprises in people – to – people exchanges

According to the Guide for Countries and Regions on Overseas Investment and Cooperation compiled by the Chinese Academy of International Trade and Economic Cooperation, the Department of Foreign Investment and Economic Cooperation of the Ministry of Commerce and other relevant institutions, the bilateral trade volume between China and Brazil in 2020 has reached 119.04 billion US dollars, and the scale of Chinese enterprises' investment in Brazil has continuously extended, involving oil, electricity, new energy, infrastructure, agriculture, manufacturing, communications, e – commerce and many other fields. Chinese enterprises signed 77 new project contracts in Brazil in the same year. The new contracts amounted to 3.250 billion US dollars, and the completed turnover reached 1.637 billion US dollars. [1] The bilateral trade volume between China and South Africa in 2020 is close to 36 billion US dollars. The stock of China's direct investment in South Africa now ranks first in Africa, and South Africa has become the first choice for the regional headquarters of Chinese – funded enterprises in Africa, and well – known Chinese enterprises such as SF Express and Didi Taxi have built in South Africa. [2] According to statistics from the Ministry of Commerce, in 2019, Chinese enterprises signed 209 new project contracts

---

[1] "Country (Region) Guide for Outbound Investment Cooperation: Brazil (2021 Edition)," MOFCOM website, http://www.mofcom.gov.cn/dl/gbdqzn/upload/baxi.pdf.

[2] "Country (Region) Guide for Outbound Investment Cooperation: South Africa (2021 Edition)," MOFCOM website, http://www.mofcom.gov.cn/dl/gbdqzn/upload/nanfei.pdf.

in India, with a new contract value of 5.173 billion US dollars, a turnover of 2.539 billion US dollars, a total of 1,419 labor service personnel of various types, and 2,073 labor service personnel in India at the end of the year. [1] The trade volume between China and Russia in 2019 reached 110.79 billion US dollars. Chinese enterprises signed 160 new project contracts in Russia, and the amount of newly signed contracts was 16.918 billion US dollars, the turnover was 2.767 billion US dollars, and the total number of labor personnel was 3,486 and there are 6,694 labor workers in the Russian Federation at the end of the year. [2]

There is no doubt that in the process of transnational investment and operation in the BRICS countries, Chinese enterprises have actually become international organizations representing China, not only undertaking the task of promoting the BRICS economic and trade connectivity, but also undertaking the responsibility of promoting people-to-people exchanges between Chinese and the people of the BRICS countries. The thriving growth and gratifying achievements of Chinese enterprises in BRICS countries are important material for the China Story. However, the road of Chinese enterprises going global is by no means smooth. Their projects in BRICS countries often involve highly sensitive fields such as infrastructure construction, energy and information technology, so their normal economic activities often become the focus of negative attention and false reports on China by some Western media, even being dubbed "neocolonialism", seriously affecting the normal development of Chinese enterprises' overseas business. Therefore, Chinese enterprises actively participate in people-to-people exchanges and tell their own "China's stories", which is also an internal need for their own development. In other words, by playing the principal role in people-to-people exchanges, Chinese enterprises operating and investing in BRICS

---

[1] "Country (Region) Guide for Outbound Investment Cooperation: India (2020 Edition)," MOFCOM website, http://www.mofcom.gov.cn/dl/gbdqzn/upload/yindu.pdf.

[2] "Country (Region) Guide for Outbound Investment Cooperation: Russia (2020 Edition)," MOFCOM website, http://www.mofcom.gov.cn/dl/gbdqzn/upload/eluosi.pdf.

countries are not only conducive to enhancing the corporate image and China's international image, but also helping enhance mutual recognition and understanding between Chinese enterprises and the people of BRICS, to reduce or eliminate misunderstandings and prejudices, and shape regional cultural identity and value identity while ensuring the smooth implementation of engineering projects, and ultimately enhance the legitimacy and support of Chinese enterprises' economic activities in BRICS countries.

Therefore, to deepen people – to – people exchanges between China and BRICS, we must explore the potential of Chinese enterprises in people – to – people exchanges and awaken the subjective consciousness of Chinese enterprises to tell China's stories well and participate in people – to – people exchanges. In this process, relevant government departments should consciously carry out diversified and all – round training for Chinese enterprises in BRICS countries. In the process of going overseas, Chinese enterprises will gradually grow into the most powerful international force for China's cultural and people – to – people exchanges with other countries through the formation of a complete enterprise training mechanism.[①] At present, China still faces problems such as low enthusiasm and participation in people – to – people exchanges in BRICS countries, insufficient investment by enterprises, misalignment of exchange partners, and lack of a regular people – to – people exchange mechanism and interaction model. Therefore, it is recommended that Chinese enterprises and relevant non – governmental organizations in BRICS countries play an active role in people – to – people exchanges under the condition that the government participates in the coordination provides certain support, and takes the initiative to find or independently build an exchange platform with local people as the main body based on the actual needs of their own operations, and actively participate in various local social welfare

---

[①] Wang Wen: "Sino – foreign People – to – People Exchanges in the Post – epidemic Era: Opportunities and Challenges," in Zhang Ji and Xing Liju, eds., "The Great Changes Unprecedented in a Century and Sino – Foreign People – to – People Exchanges," World Knowledge Publishing House, 2021, p. 62.

activities, and explore a new model for Chinese enterprises to participate in people – to – people exchanges in BRICS countries through the establishment of the BRICS People – to – People Exchange Enterprise Foundation or other forms.

### (2) The role of overseas Chinese in people – to – people exchanges

In 2018, then – Brazilian President Temer signed a decree officially setting August 15 as Brazil's Chinese Immigration Day which not only reflects that more than 200 years of hard work and dedication of overseas Chinese get recognition from all sectors of Brazil and that Brazil attaches great importance to the development of China – Brazil relations, and reflects the deep friendship between the Chinese and Brazilian people, and reflects the improvement of the social status of overseas Chinese in Brazil. [①] According to relevant statistics and estimates, the number of overseas Chinese in Brazil is about 300, 000. [②] Brazil has become the second largest settlement of the Chinese in South America after Peru. According to the latest Report on Overseas Chinese (2021) published by the Institute of Chinese and Overseas Chinese, there are currently about 150, 000 Chinese citizens in Russia, more than 3, 600 Chinese citizens with long – term residence permits, and about 27, 000 international students. [③] The total number of overseas Chinese in Russia is about 350, 000. According to relevant statistics, the total number of overseas Chinese in South Africa is about 300, 000. [④] South Africa is

---

[①] "East – West Question Ⅰ Former Chinese diplomat Liu Zhengqin: Why did Brazil set up Chinese Immigration Day?" China News Network, October 15, 2021, https: //www. chinanews. com. cn/gn/2021/10 – 15/9587365. shtml.

[②] Shu Changsheng, "Review of Literature and Demography of Overseas Chinese Studies in Brazil," Overseas Chinese Historical Research, No. 1, 2018, p. 36. It should be pointed out that the accurate statistics of the population of the Chinese diaspora in Brazil have always been a problem that has plagued researchers, so the relevant data in this paper are reasonable estimates based on existing research.

[③] Wang Yi, "Analysis of Overseas Chinese in Russia in 2020," in Zhang Chunwang et al., "Blue Book of World Overseas Chinese (2021)," Social Sciences Academic Press, 2022, p. 167.

[④] Lv Ting, "Analysis of Education Needs and Exploration of Supply Patterns of New Immigrants to Overseas Chinese," in Jia Yimin et al., "Research Report on Overseas Chinese and Chinese (2016)," Social Sciences Academic Press, 2017, p. 260.

also the African country with the largest overseas Chinese community. Due to various reasons, the number of overseas Chinese in India has always been small, and according to incomplete statistics, the total number of overseas Chinese in India is less than 10, 000. This shows that there are a considerable number of overseas Chinese in the BRICS countries, and they can play a more active role in promoting people – to – people exchanges and enhancing people – to – people connectivity among BRICS.

The development of people – to – people exchanges among countries requires a broad social base. The BRICS countries have their own social civilization patterns and cultural habits, so the complexity and differences in people's livelihood and conditions in various countries become obstacles to deepening people – to – people exchanges. With the growing number of overseas Chinese in BRICS countries and the continuous improvement of their economic strength and social status, they have irreplaceable advantages in promoting people – to – people exchanges between China and BRICS. The overseas Chinese are not only the carriers of Chinese culture, but also the spokespersons and shapers of China's image in the BRICS countries. They have great potential for spreading Chinese culture and telling China's stories in the BRICS countries, and promoting people – to – people exchanges and people – to – people diplomacy. Therefore, to deepen cultural and people – to – people exchanges between China and BRICS, we must give full play to the role and influence of overseas Chinese, and guide and encourage them to take advantage of their special local subject identity to actively participate in and shape the cultural and people – to – people exchanges between China and BRICS.

In view of this, relevant departments and governments should actively promote the role of overseas Chinese in BRICS countries as a link between people and encourage them to play their unique role as a bridge across different civilizations to actively integrate the subjective consciousness of people – to – people exchanges into their local life and work, and communicate with local people and governments in the languages of their countries and regions, telling China's stories with the cultural customs and thinking habits of local people so that the people of BRICS countries can understand. In this process, people – to – people communication should become the main path, and local overseas Chinese groups should be the main carriers of such exchanges, so as to enrich the connotation of BRICS people – to – people exchanges and foster bilateral relations through non – government contacts. In the process of exploring the potential of overseas Chinese to participate in people – to – people exchanges, we should pay attention to maintaining their connections with the motherland, especially to enhance their actual contact with China in the new era and increase their perceptual understanding of the development achievements of China in the new era, so as to truly enhance the willingness of overseas Chinese in the BRICS countries to actively participate in people – to – people exchanges.

### (3) The role of Chinese scholars in people – to – people exchanges

Academic research is regarded as the most profound and mission – oriented means of people – to – people exchanges and dialogue among civilizations.[1] Therefore, scholars engaged in academic research also play an important role in people – to – people exchange activities. In terms of enhancing the BRICS understanding of China and telling the story of China's development scientifically and systematically to the people of the BRICS countries in the new era, Chinese scholars are not only the front – line participants in the people – to – people exchanges with foreign countries, but also an important breakthrough for deepening people – to – people exchanges with BRICS countries in the new era.[2] On the other hand, by conducting BRICS studies, Chinese scholars can provide knowl-

---

[1] Zhang Fan et al., "China and Latin America: People – to – People Exchange from the Perspective of Soft Power," Chaohua Press, 2020, p. 162.

[2] Huang Hao et al., "Research on Model Construction in the Mechanism of High – level People – to – People Exchange in Academic Fields and Abroad," in Zhang Ji and Xing Liju, eds., "The Great Changes Unprecedented in a Century and Sino – Foreign People – to – People Exchanges," World Knowledge Press, 2021, p. 121.

edge supply and theoretical support for extensive exchanges and cooperation in politics, economy, trade, culture and other fields through knowledge production. It will also play an important role in enhancing mutual understanding and strengthening the foundation for people – to – people exchanges among BRICS.

China attaches great importance to BRICS research, and at present, there are a number of rapidly developing BRICS research institutions with their own characteristics, distributed in relevant universities and government departments. However, the degree of internationalization of China's BRICS research needs to be improved, and the speed and intensity of the dissemination of Chinese scholars' voices and achievements in BRICS countries are far from enough. Due to differences in language and academic research models, the frequency and degree of academic exchanges between scholars from BRICS countries and their Chinese counterparts are still insufficient, especially in information sharing, experience exchange and cooperative research. The global spread of the COVID – 19 pandemic has further blocked the actual academic exchanges among BRICS, which has greatly increased the difficulty for Chinese scholars to visit BRICS countries for field research and fieldwork. How can Chinese scholars give full play to their role as the main subject of people – to – people exchanges under the new situation and improve the quality and quantity of BRICS people – to – people exchanges at the academic level is an issue that China must seriously consider in the process of deepening people – to – people exchanges with BRICS.

In order to effectively promote the academic exchanges of BRICS countries, fully mobilize and give full play to the main role of Chinese scholars in participating in BRICS people – to – people exchanges, and enhance the academic interaction and exchanges between Chinese scholars and their BRICS counterparts, it is proposed to build a "BRICS Academic Community" to promote the integration of China's BRICS research with China research in Russia, India, South Africa and Brazil. The establishment of the BRICS Academic Community can not only effectively expand the connotation and extension of China's BRICS research, but also rapidly enhance the internationalization of BRICS research by Chinese scholars. Once a regular communication mechanism is established within the BRICS Academic Community, the exchange and sharing of research resources within BRICS countries is expected to be realized. On the other hand, the establishment of the BRICS Academic Community is actually to explore the substantive cooperative relations between China and the BRICS countries in academic exchanges, which is conducive to improving the overall academic discourse power of BRICS countries and breaking the hegemony of Western academic discourse. Therefore, to encourage Chinese scholars to actively participate in BRICS people – to – people exchanges, it is suggested to increase the weight of indicators related to internationalization in terms of academic assessment and reward mechanism, so as to encourage Chinese scholars to go global, attend academic seminars, publish articles and talk to the media in BRICS countries, and make China's voice heard and tell China's story well as a more convincing and authoritative subject of people – to – people exchanges. At the same time, the BRICS Academic Community should attract more scholars from BRICS countries to carry out research in China, and relevant institutions and universities should set up special projects and grants for this purpose to encourage them to take root in China and conduct field research.

It must be pointed out that, in recent years, China has paid more and more attention to the establishment and communication of think tanks in BRICS, because giving full play to the professional advantages and collaborative effects of think tanks is conducive to the development of decision – making and cooperation among BRICS. Therefore, think tanks, mainly composed of scholars and researchers, who provide policy advice to government departments, should also be regarded as a special and important subject of people – to – people exchanges. In fact, with the comprehensive deepening of BRICS cooperation, the mechanism of exchange and cooperation between BRICS think tanks is also constantly developing and evolving.[①] In the process of deepening people – to – people exchanges with BRICS countries, we should attach importance to the intellectual support of think tanks for BRICS cooperation, especially the suggestions and measures on improving the BRICS people – to – people exchange mechanism and enhancing BRICS strategic mutual trust.

**(4) The role of sister cities in people – to – people exchanges**

In the new era of China's opening up, the status and role of cities as diplomatic subjects are becoming increasingly important, and the rise of city diplomacy is reshaping the path and channel of people – to – people exchanges between countries. As a unique diplomatic subject, city diplomacy is an institutionalized communication activity between a city government with legal identity and representative ability and the official and unofficial institutions of other countries around non – sovereign affairs under the authorization and guidance of the central government, for the safety, prosperity and value of the city.[②] In other words, because of their inherently sub – government nature, cities as diplomacy subjects are more likely to play the role of bridges and links in foreign exchanges. In practice, cities as important subjects of people – to – people exchanges have received more and more attention. In May 2014, President Xi Jinping first used the term "city diplomacy" at Events Marking the 60th Anniversary of the Chinese People's Association for Friendship with Foreign Countries. According to incomplete statistics, China has established more than 2,600 pairs of sister city and state relations with nearly 140 countries in the world. As a supporting activity of the BRICS Summit, the BRICS Friendship Cities and Local Government Cooperation Forum was first held in Sanya, Hainan Province, in 2011. Since then, it has become an important stage for BRICS members to strengthen cooperation among cities and

---

① Pu Gongying, "Analysis of the BRICS People – to – People Exchange and Cooperation Mechanism," Russian Eastern Europe and Central Asian Studies, No. 4, 2017, p. 49.
② Zhao Kejin, "Urban Diplomacy: Exploring the Diplomatic Role of Global Cities," Foreign Affairs Review, No. 6, 2013, p. 69.

promote people – to – people exchanges. Since 2011, China has established sister cities relations with the BRIC countries at a rate of more than 10 pairs per year.[①] It can be seen that sister cities, as special subjects of people – to – people exchanges among BRICS, are not only a useful supplement to the existing BRICS people – to – people exchange mechanism, but also provide strong support for promoting the profound development of BRICS people – to – people exchanges.

In the process of continuously deepening the cooperation and exchanges between China and BRICS sister cities, it is not only necessary to maintain the enthusiasm for city – to – city and people – to – people exchanges in various ways and activities, but also to explore the potential of sister – city exchanges among BRICS. Particularly, we need to enhance the vitality of Chinese cities that have established sister – city relations with BRICS countries as the main body of people – to – people exchanges and effectively improve the quality of such exchanges. The New Delhi Declaration of the 13th BRICS Summit in 2021 commended the progress of BRICS countries in tackling new challenges in urban areas and noted the contribution of the BRICS Smart City Workshop, the Urbanization Forum, and the Friendship Cities and Local Government Cooperation Forum in deepening BRICS people – to – people exchanges.[②] In addition to continuing to carry out regular exchanges and cooperation between BRICS friendship cities, it is necessary to make full use of city diplomacy, explore the commonalities and complementarities between China and BRICS friendship cities in local cultural characteristics and carry out cooperation in key areas and blank areas, especially in the context of the COVID – 19 pandemic, focusing on the development of "cloud exchanges" and digital cooperation between sister cities. On the basis of exchanges between sister cities, it is necessary to make better use of the interoperability and complementarity of type, scale and resources among BRICS cities, expand the

---

[①] "BRICS Sister Cities and Local Governments jointly release the Chengdu Initiative," Reference News Network, July 13, 2017, http://www.cankaoxiaoxi.com/china/20170713/2186134.shtml.

[②] "New Delhi Declaration of the 13th BRICS Summit," State Council website, September 10, 2021, http://www.gov.cn/xinwen/2021 – 09/10/content_5636528.htm.

"circle of friends" among BRICS friendship cities, and gradually form a "people – to – people exchange group" among BRICS friendship cities, so as to achieve large – scale and shared growth of people – to – people exchanges. In this process, local governments at all levels in China should be encouraged to enhance their sense of subjectivity, and continuously improve the contact and dialogue mechanism between BRICS friendship cities. To strengthen transnational communication between our sister cities, we should establish offices and agencies, and establish an interactive mechanism for people – to – people and cultural exchanges between our sister cities, so as to enhance the quality of BRICS sister – city relations from the perspective of institutional guarantees. At the same time, we should contribute city strength and wisdom to BRICS people – to – people exchanges through practical cooperation between our sister cities.

### (5) The role of Chinese young generation in people – to – people exchanges

The world will prosper only when young people thrive. The young generation is not only a new force for BRICS countries to participate in global governance and solve global problems, but also the main force for promoting mutual learning and cultural exchanges among civilizations of all countries. As the most energetic and creative group in the new era, the young generation can provide new ideas for BRICS countries to explore new paths for people – to – people exchanges, and make new contributions to deepening BRICS people – to – people exchanges, and at the same time benefit from this process and improve themselves. At present, BRICS youth exchanges have formed a normalization mechanism represented by the BRICS Young Diplomats Forum, the BRICS Youth Summit, the Meeting of BRICS Youth Ministers, the BRICS Youth Innovation and Entrepreneurship Partnership, and the BRICS Young Scientists Forum, which undoubtedly helps the young generation play the key role in shaping the development prospects of BRICS from the perspective of cultivating future leaders. However, on the whole, the young generation still plays a relatively minor role in participating in and promoting people – to – people and cultural exchanges between China and BRICS countries, and their influence is still weak. With the deepening of people – to – people exchanges among the five BRICS countries, BRICS youth will certainly have a stronger demand for participation and leadership in people – to – people exchanges. In view of this, it is necessary to attach great importance to the main role of the young generation in the process of deepening BRICS people – to – people exchanges. While helping the majority of young people to establish a sense of "ownership", we should innovate the paths of BRICS youth people – to – people exchanges, and give full play to the role of the young generation as a bridge and link in the mutual learning of civilizations and people – to – people exchanges among BRICS countries.

In order to give full play to the main role of young people in participating in and promoting people – to – people exchanges between China and BRICS countries, it is necessary to increase mutual recognition and understanding between BRICS youth, especially the objective and true exchanges between BRICS youth on China's development in the new era, which requires effectively enhancing substantive contacts and exchanges between young people in China and BRICS. Therefore, it is necessary to invest more resources to support the BRICS youth study abroad and exchange program, and attract more BRICS youth to study and visit China and experience China's development and culture in person by cultivating BRICS Youth See China, BRICS Youth China Tours, BRICS Culture Carnival Youth, Workshop for BRICS Youth, summer camps and other people – to – people exchange programs. On the other hand, we should encourage the young generation of China to continuously broaden their global vision, and participate in the dialogue and mutual learning among BRICS civilizations. We should also increase our efforts to cultivate international young talents who are proficient in the BRICS language and familiar with BRICS culture and customs to promote Chinese youth to go to the BRICS countries and spread the voice of Chinese youth in their language and methods. It should be noted that youth innovation and entrepreneurship have become an important way for young people in BRICS countries to pursue their ideals and aspirations and realize the meaning of life, so we should take advantage of the development opportunities of young people from all countries to start businesses in China, creatively give full play to the positive guiding role of youth innovation and entrepreneurship in deepening people – to – people exchanges between China and BRICS, and integrate people – to – people exchanges into youth innovation and entrepreneurship activities in a gentle and silent way, so as to help young people in BRICS countries grasp China's development opportunities in the new era while enhancing mutual exchanges and mutual understanding.

## III. Expand the New Connotation of BRICS People – to – People Exchanges

As the status and role of people – to – people and cultural exchanges in BRICS cooperation have been significantly enhanced, the areas of people – to – people and cultural exchanges among BRICS countries have also been on the rise, and member states have new expectations for the effectiveness and harvest of people – to – people and cultural exchanges in different areas. This section will combine the latest development trend of BRICS people – to – people exchanges, starting from the development status of the four major fields of people – to – people exchanges, including education, science and technology, culture and sports, and discuss new ideas and measures to promote the connotative development of the above fields in the process of deepening BRICS people – to – people exchanges.

(1) **People – to – people exchanges in the field of education**

The field of education has always been a key area for BRICS countries to carry out people – to – people exchanges and cooperation, not only because BRICS cooperation in the field of education started early and in a complementary way, but also because educational exchanges and cooperation have rich connotations and broad prospects. So far, the BRICS countries have successfully established a senior and high - level people - to - people exchange mechanism represented by the Meeting of BRICS Ministers of Education, reached a consensus among the BRICS countries on deepening education cooperation through a series of ministerial declarations such as the Beijing Declaration on Education, and also created multilateral cooperation mechanisms in higher education such as the BRICS University Alliance and the BRICS Network University, as well as permanent mechanisms in the field of education such as the BRICS - ESCO. It can be said that BRICS countries have achieved fruitful cooperation results in people - to - people exchanges in the field of education. Both the form and content of our cooperation are impressive. Education cooperation has become the flagship of BRICS people - to - people exchanges. Under the special situation of the COVID - 19 pandemic, to deepen people - to - people exchanges between China and BRICS in the field of education, we must improve mechanism construction, adhere to contribution and shared benefits, deeply explore the potential of cooperation, and enrich the connotation of cooperation. In fact, whether we can effectively expand the connotation of people - to - people exchanges in the field of education will become the key to the BRICS countries building a second "golden decade".

In his speech at the 13th BRICS Summit, President Xi Jinping proposed to set up a BRICS alliance for vocational education to organize vocational skills competitions, and create a platform of exchanges and cooperation for the vocational colleges and businesses in the five countries. [1] This shows that BRICS people - to - people exchanges in the field of education are extending from higher education to vocational education, and vocational education and related skills training will become a new direction and hot spot for BRICS education cooperation in the post - pandemic period. In response to President Xi's proposal to effectively promote the connotative development of vocational education and skills in BRICS countries, it

---

[1] "Xi Jinping's Speech at the 13th BRICS Summit," State Council website, September 10, 2021, http://www.gov.cn/xinwen/2021 - 09/10/content_5636527.htm.

is necessary to strengthen the exchange of teachers and students in BRICS vocational schools and the construction of internship training bases, and improve the international level and international core competitiveness of BRICS vocational colleges by building an open and inclusive platform for vocational education and exchange.[1] In addition, we should focus on the advantages of vocational education in BRICS countries, carry out multilateral and pragmatic cooperation under the guidance of the principles of joint contribution, shared benefits, complementarity and mutual benefit, we should carry out multilateral practical cooperation, promote cooperation between China and BRICS to cultivate more high-level and highly skilled professionals, and encourage BRICS countries to share the achievements and valuable experience of vocational education development. In the process of expanding the connotation of vocational education cooperation, BRICS countries can draw on the successful experience of representative international vocational education brands and platforms such as Luban Workshop, and focus on creating a BRICS brand of vocational education cooperation, so as to promote overseas vocational education practice and innovation in BRICS countries, and to cultivate more skilled professionals for BRICS member countries to serve their respective industrial development and production capacity cooperation.[2]

At the same time, BRICS people-to-people and cultural exchanges in the field of education should adhere to openness, inclusiveness and transcending cultural differences, and focus on promoting global education governance, achieving education equity, and improving the quality and internationalization of education. BRICS countries should make use of existing mechanisms and platforms to carry out more extensive and profound cooperation in education. While focusing

---

[1] "2021 China-India Vocational Education Cooperation Seminar Successfully Held," website of China Education Association for International Exchange, December 29, 2021 http://www.ceaie.edu.cn/newslist/2826.html.

[2] "Jin Yongwei, member of the National Committee of the Chinese People's Political Consultative Conference: Building an international brand of vocational education," Luban Workshop website, March 9, 2022, http://www.lubanworkshop.cn/html/2022/rmgf-lb_0309/426.html.

our efforts on addressing global educational challenges, BRICS countries should also focus their efforts on strengthening mutual recognition and coordination among BRICS members to realize true people – to – people connectivity.

As the backbone of promoting BRICS people – to – people exchanges, China should actively create a policy environment conducive to deepening BRICS education cooperation, encourage relevant domestic universities to participate in the BRICS education alliance, upgrade the level of existing educational cooperation with BRICS countries, promote multilateral cooperation in talent training in BRICS countries, and promote innovative cooperation among BRICS in various fields such as personnel visits, academic exchanges and scientific research cooperation, especially pay attention to cultivating compound talents of international organizations and foreign – related compound talents who master the languages of BRICS countries, enabling teachers, students and education leaders of BRICS countries to enhance mutual understanding and cognition through frequent and regular communication.

**(2) People – to – people exchanges in the field of science and technology**

The main purpose of people – to – people and cultural exchanges in the field of science and technology is to expand the basis for friendly public opinion between countries through a series of activities, such as personnel interaction, academic cooperation, research and policy coordination, and to enhance mutual political trust while improving the level of science and technology, and thus exert a positive impact on the overall relations between countries.[1] It can be seen that people – to – people exchanges in science and technology are an indispensable and important part of people – to – people exchanges among BRICS. As pointed out by BRICS leaders in the New Delhi Declaration, it is very important for

---

[1] Mao Ruipeng, "Sino – US Science and Technology People – to – People Exchanges in the Construction of a New Type of Major Country Relations," in Zhang Ji and Xing Liju, eds., "The Great Changes Unprecedented in a Century and Sino – foreign People – to – People Exchanges," World Knowledge Publishing House, 2021, p. 181.

BRICS researchers to carry out cooperation in science, technology and innovation and to tackle new and emerging challenges, creating favorable conditions for promoting scientific and technological progress and promoting mutual trust among BRICS members. [1] After more than a decade, BRICS science, technology and people – to – people exchanges have initially formed an exchange framework with the BRICS Ministerial Conference on Science and Technology Innovation as the main mechanism and the BRICS Science, Technology and Innovation Work Plan as the action plan. Fruitful results have been achieved in such areas as science and technology and people – to – people exchanges. For example, the BRICS Science Popularization Forum held by the China Science and Technology Exchanges in October 2021 aims to implement the specific measures of the BRICS Science, Technology and Innovation Work Plan (2020 – 2021) adopted at the 8th BRICS Ministerial Conference on Science, Technology and Innovation in 2020. [2] The latest BRICS Action Plan on Innovation Cooperation (2021 – 2024) was adopted at the 9th BRICS Ministerial Conference on Science, Technology and Innovation in November 2021. [3] In the long run, scientific and technological cooperation, which is mainly characterized by openness, innovation and mutual benefit, has great potential, and will certainly play a stronger supporting and leading role in the process of deepening people – to – people exchanges between China and BRICS, so that scientific and technological innovation achievements can benefit BRICS countries and people through people – to – people exchanges.

In 2022, China will take over the rotating chairship of the BRICS countries. Strengthening cooperation in science, technology and innovation not only

---

[1] "New Delhi Declaration of the 13th BRICS Summit," State Council website, September 10, 2021, http://www.gov.cn/xinwen/2021 – 09/10/content_5636528.htm.

[2] "30 Chinese Representatives Participate in the BRICS Science Popularization Forum," Ministry of Science and Technology website, October 22, 2021, http://www.most.gov.cn/kjbgz/202110/t20211022_177433.html.

[3] "Vice Minister of Science and Technology Zhang Guangjun Attends the 9th BRICS Ministerial Meeting on Science, Technology and Innovation," Ministry of Science and Technology website, November 30, 2021, http://www.most.gov.cn/kjbgz/202111/t20211130_178263.html.

reflects the common will of BRICS members to jointly tackle global challenges, but also points out the direction for China to enrich the connotation of people – to – people exchanges with BRICS countries. Under the guidance of the concept of consultation, joint contribution and shared benefit, China should focus on the driving force and demand of scientific and technological innovation under global challenges, promote the improvement of the BRICS science and technology partnership network, help build a multi – dimensional BRICS science and technology exchange system, and also focus on the priority areas of science and technology development of the BRICS countries, and deepen exchanges and cooperation with the BRICS countries in science communication, science popularization and science and technology services. In addition, BRICS countries should be more fully integrated into the global science and technology governance system. The cooperation and exchanges between China and major international science and technology organizations should be strengthened, especially through non – governmental science and technology exchange channels to serve the global multilateral governance system with the United Nations at its core. China should strengthen exchanges and cooperation with BRICS countries in frontier areas such as medicine and health, clean energy, aviation and aerospace, and promote the establishment of a BRICS cooperation network on science and technology transfer. China should also promote the exchange and mutual visits of BRICS scientific and technological talents through a series of pragmatic measures such as setting up the BRICS scientific and technological personnel exchange program, holding the BRICS Young Scientists Forum and building the BRICS Scientific and Technological Innovation Incubation Platform. At the same time, China will organize related activities such as the BRICS Scientific and Technological Personnel China Tour", so as to build a service platform for the exchange and research of outstanding scientific and technological personnel from BRICS countries in China.

(3) **People – to – people exchanges in the field of culture**

Exchanges and cooperation in the field of culture have always been the top priority of people-to-people exchanges among BRICS, not only because understanding and respect between countries and between people come first from curiosity and mutual appreciation of different cultures, but also because cultural exchanges and dialogues are most compatible with people-to-people exchanges themselves. Under the guidance of senior and high-level mechanisms such as the Meeting of BRICS Culture Ministers, BRICS people-to-people exchanges have flourished in the fields of culture, literature and art. Under the guidance of the Agreement between the Governments of the BRICS states on Cooperation in the Field of Culture and relevant action plans, China and the BRICS countries have focused on cultural heritage protection, folk art exchanges and the development of the creative economy, and through the BRICS Alliance of museums, art galleries, libraries and other professional institutions, as well as the BRICS Film Festival and other cultural events, and carried out all-round, multi-level and wide-ranging practical cooperation in the cultural field, and forged a bond of friendship between peoples through cultural exchanges.[1] In fact, in the context of the COVID-19 pandemic and the uncertain global situation, the role and importance of deepening people-to-people exchanges between China and BRICS through the cultural field are becoming increasingly prominent. As André Heller-Lopez, a professor at the Federal University of Rio de Janeiro, pointed out "In the current situation, culture is our only way out, because only culture and art can permanently awaken our humanity. We must continue to consolidate the cultural ties between the BRICS countries and work together to help each other."[2] Therefore, to deepen people-to-people and cultural exchanges with BRICS countries in the new era, China must fully explore the huge potential in the cultural field, in particular, enrich the forms and connotations of cultural cooperation, and

---

[1] "BRICS Holds Sixth Video Conference of Ministers of Culture," Ministry of Culture and Tourism website, July 6, 2021, https://www.mct.gov.cn/whzx/whyw/202107/t20210706_926239.htm.

[2] "BRICS em perspectiva: intercâmbios culturais e interpessoais, o estado da Arte," Coordenadoria de Estudos da Ásia da Universidade Federal de Pernambuco, 22 de junho de 2021, https://ceasiaufpe.com.br/?p=2648.

consolidate the popular support for people – to – people and cultural exchanges among BRICS countries through colorful and fascinating cultural exchanges.

In order to promote people – to – people exchanges between BRICS countries in culture and other related fields, it is not only necessary to continue to hold various regular and normalized people – to – people exchange activities, but also to creatively enrich the connotation of BRICS cultural exchanges. Specifically, China should make full use of cultural products and art forms that the people of BRICS countries like, such as film, TV, literature, music and new media, and explore the content and expression forms of cultural exchanges from different themes and dimensions, and take advantage of the empathy of literary and artistic works to inspire cultural empathy among BRICS people. New media such as the Internet and social platforms should be used to shorten the sense of distance between the people of BRICS countries to experience each other's culture, so that culture can reach the hearts of the people. BRICS member countries should be encouraged to cooperate and share resources in the field of media and communication to accelerate the circulation of cultural products among countries, and support cross – border cooperation among cultural and creative personnel to produce more cultural works such as Where Has the Time Gone and Half the Sky. China should also further promote traditional cultural cooperation and world heritage tourism cooperation among BRICS countries, develop BRICS characteristic tourism routes, and promote BRICS cultural and tourism cooperation to a new level. In addition, it is necessary to set up more cultural centers like the Russian Cultural Center in Beijing within the BRICS countries as an important platform for carrying out and promoting people – to – people exchanges among member states and effectively promoting their own culture, so as to establish a good image of their own countries in the target countries and consolidate the foundation for spiritual communication between the two peoples.

### (4) People – to – people exchanges in the field of sports

The BRICS countries led by China are no strangers to hosting world sports events, especially the two Beijing Olympic Games, which have greatly promoted people – to – people exchanges between China and other countries in the world. Sports have always been an important area for BRICS countries to carry out people – to – people exchanges. Since the first BRICS Games were held in Guangzhou in June 2017, the friendly cooperation in the field of sports among BRICS countries represented by the BRICS Games has achieved fruitful results. Sports exchanges among BRICS countries have extended from bilateral to multilateral and from single games to comprehensive events. The competition and mutual learning in the arena not only embodies the spirit of BRICS partnership featuring openness, inclusiveness, and win – win cooperation, but also enhances the friendship and closeness among the BRICS people and plays a positive and unique role in promoting BRICS people – to – people exchanges. In the process of deepening people – to – people exchanges between China and BRICS, BRICS member countries should be encouraged to carry out more extensive and richer cooperation in the field of sports. As we all know, football is the eternal pain of Chinese sports, and Brazil, which has won the most World Cup football championships, is known as the Kingdom of Football. The potential for cooperation and people – to – people exchanges between the two countries in the field of football is huge. As Lana, a former women's football world champion and now vice president of Brazil's China – Brazil Football Exchange Center, observed: China is currently vigorously developing football, especially youth football and school football. As a world football power, Brazil can help China cultivate high – level coaches and introduce Brazil's leading youth training system to China. China has a huge football market and has made massive investments in football, and cooperation with China can help Brazilian football get more international financial support. [1] It can be seen that China, Brazil and other BRICS countries are highly complementary in carry-

---

[1] "Tightening People – to – People Ties and Building the Third Pillar of BRICS Cooperation: Voices from the BRICS Forum on People – to – People Exchanges," Guangming Daily, December 3, 2019, https://epaper.gmw.cn/gmrb/html/2019 – 12/03/nw.D110000gmrb_20191203_1 – 07.htm.

ing out people – to – people exchanges in the field of sports with great potential.

In August 2020, BRICS countries held their first ministerial meeting and adopted a memorandum of understanding on cooperation. In the process of deepening people – to – people exchanges and cooperation among BRICS, China will strengthen sports cooperation with BRICS countries under the framework of the memorandum of understanding, implement the important consensus reached by BRICS leaders on strengthening sports exchanges, and promote people – to – people connectivity among BRICS. [1] In the future, it is necessary for China and BRICS to strengthen institutionalized cooperation and exchanges in the field of sports, carry out broader and deeper cooperation in key sports fields such as football, rugby, hockey, synchronized swimming, rhythmic gymnastics and ice and snow sports, and increase support for exchanges and visits between athletes from BRICS countries, and promote the dissemination and development of traditional Chinese sports such as Wushu in BRICS countries.

## Ⅳ. Conclusion

Today, the world is facing major changes unseen in a century and a pandemic that has not been encountered in a century, and the relationship between countries around the world is also undergoing major changes. A wise man changes his way as circumstances change; a knowledgeable person alters his means as times evolve. At a time when there are growing obstacles to cooperation between countries and when exchanges are facing difficulties, it is all the more necessary for us to strengthen people – to – people exchanges and to strengthen communication between different cultures, broaden communication channels, and constant-

---

[1] "BRICS Sports Ministers Adopt Memorandum of Understanding on Cooperation," website of the General Administration of Sports, August 26, 2020, https://www.sport.gov.cn/n20001099/n20001302/n20067050/n20067068/c20151214/content.html.

ly strengthen consensus and build identity.[1] BRICS people – to – people exchanges are carried out in different cultures, languages and regions, and the systems and mechanisms for organizing people – to – people exchanges among member states are inevitably different, and different countries have their own expectations for the effects and impacts of people – to – people exchanges. However, no matter what difficulties and challenges they face, as long as BRICS member countries can change with the times and follow the trend, and unremittingly promote the deepening and progress of BRICS people – to – people exchanges, and promote the building of a Community with a Shared Future for Mankind, BRICS people – to – people exchanges will certainly continue to go steadily and bring new vitality to BRICS in the new era, brightening the future of win – win cooperation.

---

[1] Qin Yaqing, "A Century of Changes and the Relationship between New Cultures," in Zhang Ji and Xing Liju, eds. , "The Great Changes Unprecedented in a Century and Sino – foreign People – to – People Exchanges," World Knowledge Publishing House, 2021, p. 7.

# The Building of a Community of Shared Future for BRICS: Based on the Perspective of Crisis Management Theory

Zhang Qing[*], Chen Guo[**], Sun Haoyang[***]

**Abstract**: The theory of crisis management provides an original perspective for the building of a community of shared future for BRICS. Since crisis management can be divided into the pre – crisis prevention, crisis management and post – crisis outcomes stages, efforts should be made in different stages accordingly. In the pre – crisis prevention stage, efforts must be directed toward the coordination between internal preparedness and external positions. In the crisis management stage, internal thinking and actions should be synchronized by strong leadership and cohesion, and external endeavors need to focus on support from other stakeholders. The post – crisis efforts include enhancing internal learning by reviewing of crisis and building positive social evaluations in the external environment

---

[*] Zhang Qing, Professor and Doctor at Sichuan International Studies University, Director of the Institute for Humanistic Exchange Studies, BRICS Institute.

[**] Chen Guo, Master of Comparative Institutional Studies from the School of International Relations, Sichuan International Studies University, Senior Registered Engineer in Architectural Structure.

[***] Sun Haoyang, Master's candidate in Comparative Institutional Studies at the School of International Relations, Sichuan International Studies University.

to reach a consensus of higher level and greater range. In this light, the requirements of crisis management's three stages coincide with and offer referential significance for various missions of building a community of shared future for BRICS.

**Keywords**: community of shared future; BRICS; crisis management theory

# I. Introduction

With the advent of the 21st century, human society is confronted with three global challenges—peace, development and governance. In an era defined by continually upgraded interdependence, no country can manage these challenges alone. The international community needs to be guided by lasting peace and prosperity and to map out the blueprint and implementation scheme. Xi Jinping, the Chinese President, proposed the idea of "a Community of Shared Future for Mankind", which has been studied from such perspectives as connotation, features and ideological origin. As a rudimentary framework, this article attempts to view the building of a community of shared future for BRICS from the perspective of crisis management theory, to enrich research methods and implementation strategies.

# II. Crisis and Crisis Management

Crisis is any event that is going or is predicted to lead to an unstable and dangerous situation affecting an individual, group, community, or whole society. Crises are deemed to be negative changes in security, economic, political, societal, or environmental affairs, especially when they occur abruptly, with little or no warning.

Charles Hermann[1] believed that a foreign policy crisis is the most important and major factor threatening the political unit, and limits the time for thinking, planning, and responding to change the probable outcome. Hermann's emphasis is that a crisis is a situation perceived by the units of a government. Rosenthal considered this definition to be too narrow since it only concerns the units of a government. Instead, he'd rather take crisis as a process: "Crisis relates to situations featuring severe threat, uncertainty, and sense of urgency. A variety of phenomena may be approached from this perspective, such as natural and technological disasters, conflicts and riots, and terrorist actions."[2] Loughran attempts to understand the crisis from the perspective of the target group of people.[3] He defines it as a broad spectrum consisting of different affairs that are crises towards certain groups, but not towards others.

Crisis in the era of globalization is characterized by distinct features. First, crisis, with its high frequency, has become normal in people's lives. Second, the frequent exchanges between countries increase interdependence on each other, leading to the fact that crises are collective ones of a series of affairs, not isolated ones. Various reasons may trigger crises, and the post-crisis relative stability may result in new crises. Meanwhile, crises stand for a combination of threat and opportunity. "Whether they would admit it or not, authorities and decision-makers often do know that, apart from being a threat, crises may be an opportunity as well."[4] According to the ideas of functionalism, crises can effectively promote social coordination. As the energy underneath the earth's crust is occasionally released in the form of earthquakes, crises can serve as the "safety

---

[1] Hermann C. F., "International Crises: Insights from Behavioral Research," New York: Free Press, 1972, p. 13.

[2] Rosenthal U. and Pijnenburg B. eds., "Crisis Management and Decision Making: Simulation Oriented Scenarios," New York: Springer, 1991, p. 3.

[3] Loughran H., "Understanding Crisis Therapies: An Integrative Approach to Crisis Intervention and Post Traumatic Stress," London: Jessica Kingsley Publishers, 2011.

[4] Rosenthal U. and Pijnenburg B. eds., "Crisis Management and Decision Making: Simulation Oriented Scenarios," New York: Springer, 1991, p. 2.

valve" to ease political, economic and social discord and tensions.

Crisis management is broadly viewed as a process involving organizational leaders' actions and communication that attempt to reduce the likelihood of a crisis, work to minimize harm from a crisis, and endeavor to reestablish order following a crisis. [1][2][3] Specifically, crisis management means that the government and other social organizations take measures of monitoring, forewarning, pre-control and evaluation to prevent potential crises, deal with ongoing crises, mitigate damage, and even convert threats into opportunities. Hence, crisis management has the following features.

First, crisis management is aimed at interest protection. The fundamental objective of crisis management is to safeguard the broad interest of various organizations and individuals by maintaining social order, security and stability.

Second, the logical premise of crisis management lies in its preventability. The severe consequences caused by crises motivate people to realize the need and significance of preventing crises. When a threat has been deemed serious, the leader is obligated to mobilize people to try to prevent it. "We have distilled from our own research a set of practical steps that managers can take to better recognize emerging problems, set appropriate priorities, and mobilize an effective preventive response." [4]

Third, the external environment of crisis management is featured with openness and non-competitiveness. The outburst of crises endangers the interest of all parties concerned, requiring all organizations and individuals to interact and cooperate with each other. This is also true for international communities. All coun-

---

[1] Bundy J. and Pfarrer M. D., "A Burden of Responsibility: The Role of Social Approval at the Onset of A Crisis," Academy of Management Review, Vol. 40, 2015, pp. 345–369.

[2] Kahn W. A., Barton M. A., and Fellows S., "Organizational Crises and the Disturbance of Relational Systems," Academy of Management Review, Vol. 38, 2013, pp. 377–396.

[3] Pearson C. M. and Clair J. A., "Reframing Crisis Management," Academy of Management Review, Vol. 23, 1998, pp. 59–76.

[4] Watkins Michael D. and Bazerman Max H., "Predictable Surprises: the Disasters You Should Have Seen Coming," Harvard Economic Review, Vol. 81, 2003, pp. 72–80, p. 140.

tries concerned can hardly ensure self-preservation in the face of crisis. All governments, enterprises, non-governmental organizations and civilians should be involved in crisis management and weather the hard times.

Fourth, collective and systematic measures are taken in crisis management. The timeline of crisis includes embryonic, forewarning, outbursting, ongoing and fading-away stages. Furthermore, a crisis frequently triggers another one, featuring the complication effect. Therefore, crisis management requires comprehensive and systematic strategies to coordinate relations between different departments to guarantee a unified command of emergency management.

Fifth, crisis management can function both domestically and internationally. Traditionally, an international crisis is defined as a situation in which the occurrence area of events increases the effects of forces which make instabilities in the general system structure, activate the same type of factors in subsystems, and empower the probability of use of force and damage[1], or a "change of situation" that takes place in the actions between the rivals and affects the entire international political system.[2] Obviously, these definitions emphasize the disputes and conflicts between international actors. As a matter of fact, there is another kind of crisis in the global era that requires all countries to join hands and make concerted efforts to address, such as terrorism, climate change and economic slowdown.

In the realm of international politics, different approaches taken to address crises invite different circumstances for the parties concerned. One circumstance is that owing to the lack of prepared plans and effective measures, some countries can't stand the heavy blow dealt by crises, and the image and prestige of decision-makers are tarnished, which mires them in the crisis of legitimacy. The other circumstance is that at the initial stage of crisis, decision makers

---

[1] Young Oran R., "The Intermediaries: Third Parties in International Crises," Princeton: Princeton University Press, 1967, p. 10.

[2] McClelland Charles A., "The Anticipation of International Crises: Prospects for Theory and Research," International Studies Quarterly, Vol. 21, 1977, pp. 15-16.

not only withstand various pressures, but take active and effective strategies, which well control the momentum of the crisis, cementing and enhancing substantially their status and competitive advantages. Therefore, in light of national interest, domestically as well as internationally, it's necessary to explore how to reach a common position to tackle universal crises confronting international communities through crisis management.

## III. The Internal Connectivity between BRICS and Crisis Management

BRICS is an acronym created by then – chairman of Goldman Sachs Asset Management, Jim O'Neill, for an association of five major emerging national economies. ① Owing to a common experience that the five countries were all negatively affected by the world order dominated by the United States and its allies, they share a common vision for a new global order. By combining key countries in Asia, Africa, Europe and Latin America in a small but strategic organization, they will have a better chance of realizing that vision. ②

Actually, the growth of BRICS is not plain sailing. The five member countries have fundamental differences in politics and economy, which make them have different values and interests. ③ There is also great mistrust and tensions in the bilateral relations within the BRICS as they view each other as potential threats and competitors, which limits their cooperation. ④ This is particularly true

---

① O'Neill Jim, "Building Better Global Economic BRICs," Goldman Sachs Global Economics, 2001, https://www.goldmansachs.com/insights/archive/building-better.html.

② De Coning C., Mandrup, T. and Odgaard L. eds., "The BRICS and Coexistence: An Alternative Vision of World Order," New York: Routledge, 2015, p. 25.

③ Mottet Laetitia, "Cooperation and Competition among the BRICS Countries and Other Emerging Powers," French Centre for Research on Contemporary China (CEFC), 2013.

④ Glosny Michael, "China and the BRICs: A real (but limited) partnership in a unipolar world," Polity, Vol. 42, 2010, pp. 100 – 129.

for the regional competition between China and India in South Asia. [1]

A Community of shared Future for BRICS is a new idea repeatedly emphasized by the Chinese government, aimed at giving consideration to others' appeals while maximizing national interests. The core of the concept focuses on the coordination of one country's development and the joint development of BRICS as a whole. In this light, the theory of crisis management shares some similarities with the building of a Community of Shared Future for BRICS, namely basic goal, logical premise, external environment, implementation approaches and the scope of influence.

First, the basic goal of building a Community of Shared Future for BRICS is the welfare, such as peace, cooperation and development, of the people of the five countries, even the whole world, such as peace, cooperation and development. To begin with, the primary goal of a Community of Shared Future for BRICS is to maintain a peaceful environment that is in accordance with the basic needs of people from various countries. Hence, an equal partnership is effective in achieving this goal. The five countries need to pursue security, development and win – win benefits through cooperation in the process of building a Community of Shared Future. Meanwhile, common prosperity is a shared dream of the five countries, the pursuit of which should be guaranteed by considering others' appeals while ensuring national interests.

Second, the logical premise of building a Community of Shared Future for BRICS is that the various kinds of challenges and threats confronted by human beings are detectable, foreseeable and controllable. "As crisis prevention is a broader concept of crisis management and can be used as a type of control management, the three broad areas where crisis management can contribute to the prevention of any environment are to (1) systematically address the underlying causes of a potential crisis, (2) establish signal mechanisms to detect a foreseen

---

[1] Mottet Laetitia, "Cooperation and Competition among the BRICS Countries and Other Emerging Powers," French Centre for Research on Contemporary China (CEFC), 2013.

crisis, and (3) learn and understand the ongoing basic conditions of any crisis."[1] The Cuban Missile Crisis in 1962 indicated a new stage of international crisis management. Robert McNamara, the then United States Secretary of Defense, commented that the strategy thereafter may be replaced by crisis management.[2] With the acceleration of economic globalization from the 1990s, non-traditional security issues, such as epidemic diseases, ecological deterioration and terrorism, have been on the constant rise, urging scholars to address them from perspectives of crisis prevention and management.

Third, the building of a Community of Shared Future for BRICS demands an open and non-competitive external environment. In the face of complex global problems, any of the five countries cannot ensure an isolated development. The idea of a Community of Shared Future for BRICS exceeds the limits of nationalities, races and cultures, offering a new vision to explore the common interests and values. It requires all countries to make joint efforts to tackle global threats in the spirit of openness and non-exclusiveness.

Fourth, in terms of implementation, the building of a Community of Shared Future for BRICS needs to be processed in a comprehensive and systematic approach. Essentially, the building of a Community of Shared Future for BRICS is a grand design, concerning the interests of various groups at different levels. It is in search of fair and just international politics, reciprocal economic cooperation, green-development ecosystem, and all-round cultural exchange. Therefore, the implementation of plans has high degree of complexity and systematicness.

Fifth, the scope of influence of a Community of Shared Future for BRICS, as crisis management, is also concerned with domestic and international affairs. Domestically, people need to reach a consensus and join hands to deal with various social issues, such as unemployment and social security. Internationally, to

---

[1] Penuel K. B. Statler M. and Hagen R., "Encyclopedia of Crisis Management," Los Angeles: SAGE Publications, 2013, p. 375.

[2] Bell C., "The Conventions of Crisis: A Study of Diplomatic Management," London: Oxford University Press, 1971, p. 2.

address issues of common interest, BRICS should make joint efforts to bridge ideological gaps, strengthen mutual trust, and strive for win – win cooperation.

From what is discussed above, the theory of crisis management shares a logical consistency with the building of a Community of Shared Future for BRICS, which can be indicated from the following table:

**Table 3　A Comparative Analysis of the Intrinsic Logic between the Construction of a BRICS Community with a Shared Future and Crisis Management**

|  | Crisis management | Building CSF for BRICS |
| --- | --- | --- |
| Basic Goal | Interest protection | People's welfare in various countries |
| Logical premise | Controllability of crises | Detectability and controllability of various challenges threatening mankind |
| External environment | Open and non – competitive | Open and non – exclusive |
| Implementation approaches | Comprehensive and systematic | Comprehensive and systematic |
| Scope of influence | Domestic and international | Domestic and international |

Source of information: Prepared by the auther.

# Ⅳ. The Core Approach towards Building a Community of Shared Future for BRICS: to Strengthen the Cooperation of Crisis Management

Generally, crisis management can be divided into three stages: pre – crisis prevention, crisis management and post – crisis outcomes, and each stage should be viewed from internal and external perspectives. In the pre – crisis prevention stage, focus should be laid on organizational preparedness from the internal perspective and stakeholder relationships from the external perspective, to reduce the likelihood of a crisis. The crisis management stage concerns the actions taken by managers after a crisis, in which the internal perspective focuses on crisis leadership, and the external perspective focuses on stakeholder perceptions of the crisis. In the post – crisis outcomes stage, the internal perspective emphasizes the role of organizational learning following a crisis, while the external perspective highlights social evaluations as outcomes. ①

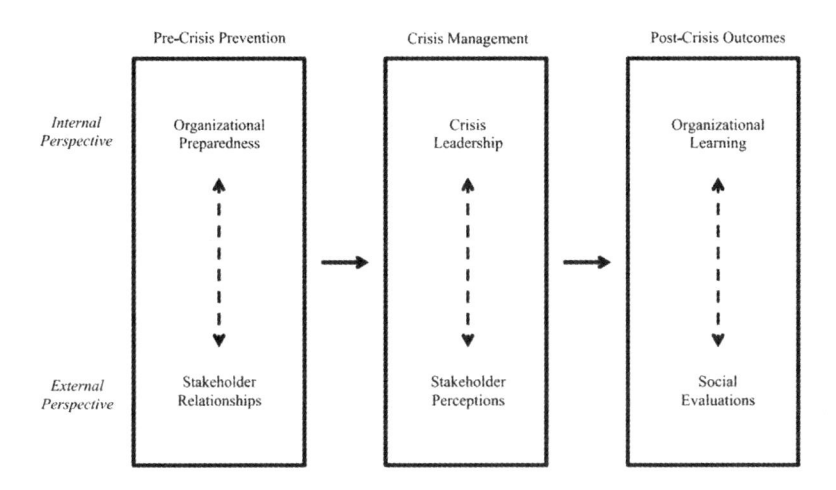

**Figure 1　Internal and External Perspectives of the Crisis Process**

Source of Information: Bundy, J., Pfarrer, M. D. Short, C. E. & W. Coombs, T., "Crises and Crisis Management: Integration, Interpretation, and Research Development," Journal of Management, Vol. 43, No. 6, 2017, pp. 1661 – 1692.

## Stage one: pre – crisis prevention

In terms of internal perspective, two topics should be covered in this stage: organizational reliability and the roles of organizational culture and structure in how an organization can prepare for a crisis. ② A highly reliable organization is

---

　① Bundy J, Pfarrer M. D., Short C. E and W. Coombs T., "Crises and Crisis Management: Integration, Interpretation, and Research Development," Journal of Management, Vol. 43, No. 6, 2017, pp. 1661 – 1692.

　② Bundy J, Pfarrer M. D., Short C. E and W. Coombs T., "Crises and Crisis Management: Integration, Interpretation, and Research Development," Journal of Management, Vol. 43, No. 6, 2017, pp. 1664 – 1667.

defined as one that has the capacity to manage unexpected events, resulting from a cognitive and behavioral process of collective managerial "mindfulness".[1] To put the definition of high-reliability organizations in detail, Bigley and Roberts[2] further focused on three aspects of the concept: mechanisms that allow for the alteration of formal structures, leadership support for improvisation, and methods that allow for enhanced sensemaking. Meanwhile, internal preparedness requires cultural and structural building. Greve, Palmer and Pozner[3] argued that an organization's culture can be more accepting of misconduct, often resulting from managerial aspirations or power contests. Similarly, Schnatterly[4] found that some governance practices—including the clarity of policies and communication—were more effective at preventing white-collar crime than other governance structures, such as increasing the percentage of outsiders on the board of directors.

Comparatively, pre-crisis prevention from the external perspective focuses on the role of stakeholder relationships. The key to doing it is to maintain positive relationships with stakeholders. A "total responsibility management" approach, proposed by Clair and Waddock[5], highlights the importance of recognizing an organization's responsibility to stakeholders in order to enhance crisis detection

---

[1] Weick K. E., Sutfcliffe K. M. and Obstfeld D. eds., "Organizing for High Reliability: Processes of Collective Mindfulness," In B. M. Staw, and L. L. Cummings eds., "Research in organizational behavior," Greenwich, CT: J AI Press. 1999, p. 37.

[2] Bigley G. A. and Roberts K. H., "The Incident Command System: High-Reliability Organizing for Complex and Volatile Task Environments," Academy of Management Journal, Vol. 44, 2001, pp. 1281-1299.

[3] Greve H., Palmer D. and Pozner J. E., "Organizations Gone Wild: The Causes, Processes, And Consequences of Organizational Misconduct," Academy of Management Annals, Vol. 4, 2010, pp. 53-107.

[4] Schnatterly K., "Increasing Firm Value Through Detection and Prevention of White-Collar Crime," Strategic Management Journal, Vol. 24, 2003, pp. 587-614.

[5] Clair J. A. and Waddock S. A., "'Total' Responsibility Management Approach to Crisis Management and Signal Detection in Organizations," In C. M. Pearson, C., Roux-Dufort and J. A. Clair eds., "International handbook of organizational crisis management," Thousand Oaks, CA: Sage, 2007, pp. 299-314.

and prevention. In the same sense①, Coombs noted that "stakeholders should be part of the prevention thinking and process," and that stakeholders can help in both identifying and mitigating the risks that may lead to a crisis.

In a similar logic, building a Community of Shared Future for BRICS also needs the coordination of internal preparedness and external stakeholder relationships. Internally, the five countries are expected to enhance the reliability of respective systems in political and economic performances and to achieve a higher standard of unity by pooling efforts of the people towards the same goal. Externally, building a Community of Shared Future for BRICS is in need of a holistic safety outlook, coinciding with the logic of "total responsibility management" approach put forward by Clair and Waddock. Each nation should refrain from isolationistic self – insurance, but take the initiative to embrace the global era and become participants and builders of global governance. Each nation is supposed to build a global safety net by means of communicating and cooperating with other nations in the world. As the five countries of BRICS are all regional powers, we should resist the temptation of pursuing security by undermining others', but rather give full respect to the interests of other nations, take into consideration others' security concerns, and put into practice obligations and responsibilities by substantial measures. Take ecological security as an example. It is a global issue beyond the capacity of any nation to address alone. Regional powers, with their respective regional influence, need to appeal to people of various countries not only to recognize its impact on the mode of human production and lifestyles, but also to initiate joint efforts and implement top – designed plans.

## Stage two: crisis management

When crises become unavoidable, crisis management enters into the second stage—crisis management. Traditionally, crisis management is characterized by a

---

① Coombs W. T., "Ongoing Crisis Communication: Planning, Managing, and Responding (4th ed.)," Thousand Oaks, CA: Sage, 2015, p. 107.

"classic engineering mandate"—to identify and fix the problems in inputs that lead to ineffective outputs.[1] While modern crisis management research does not specifically consist of the mandate, the international perspective continues to focus on a fix-the-problem approach, often by emphasizing the factors that influence within-organization crisis leadership, especially the relationship between crisis perceptions and crisis leadership.[2] Specifically, James and his colleagues[3] suggested that leaders who view crises as threats react more emotionally and are more limited in their efforts, but leaders who frame crises as opportunities are more open-minded and flexible. Furthermore, the personality of the crisis leader, such as charisma may influence internal cohesion in crisis management.[4][5][6]

In terms of external perspective in crisis management, quantities of research focus on how stakeholders perceive and react to crises and how organizations influence these perceptions. To fulfill this purpose, four tasks need to be accomplished. First, efforts should be made to build the positive image of organizations or nations, in the hope of eliminating wariness and distrust of stakeholders. A clear signal should be conveyed that the ultimate goal of active efforts is to unite multilateral powers, make concerted endeavors and bring the momentum and influence of a crisis under control, which is conducive to enhancing the sense of

---

[1] Kahn W. A., Barton M. A. and Fellows S., "Organizational Crises and the Disturbance of Relational Systems," Academy of Management Review, Vol. 38, 2013, p. 377.

[2] Bundy J., Pfarrer M. D., Short C. E. and W. Coombs T., "Crises and Crisis Management: Integration, Interpretation, and Research Development," Journal of Management, Vol. 43, No. 6, 2017, p. 1671.

[3] James E. H., Wooten L. P. and Dushek K., "Crisis Management: Informing A New Leadership Research Agenda," Academy of Management Annals, Vol. 5, 2011, p. 458.

[4] Howell J. M. and Shamir B., "The Role of Followers in the Charismatic Leadership Process: Relationships and Their Consequences," Academy of Management Review, Vol. 30, 2005, pp. 96–112.

[5] James E. H., Wooten L. P. and Dushek K., "Crisis Management: Informing A New Leadership Research Agenda," Academy of Management Annals, Vol. 5, 2011, pp. 455–493.

[6] Pillai R. and Meindl J. R., "Context and Charisma: A 'Meso' Level Examination of the Relationship of Organic Structure, Collectivism, and Crisis to Charismatic Leadership," Journal of Management, Vol. 24, 1998, pp. 643–671.

responsibility of various stakeholders. Second, sensible crisis reaction strategies should be adopted to promptly exchange information and coordinate actions with each other. For example, the information of crisis at different stages, such as disaster – affected areas, the number of affected people and the scale of disasters, needs to be shared with stakeholders whenever it is available, in order to minimize damages caused by the crisis. [1] Third, it is necessary to promote the cognitive level and identification capability of parties concerned, which is vital for the judgment and analysis of crises. Generally, organizations or nations with higher levels of identification capability can be sooner aware of the severity and direction of crisis development. [2] Last, credits are given to the role of media in crisis management. It comes as no news that media play a central part in how crises are viewed and interpreted. [3][4][5][6][7] For example, Graffin and his colleagues[8] demonstrated how the media functioned to make sense of a scandal.

The inspiration endowed by crisis management on building a Community of Shared Future for BRICS is to enhance leadership and cohesion from the internal

---

[1] Bundy J. and Pfarrer M. D., "A Burden of Responsibility: The Role of Social Approval at the Onset of a Crisis," Academy of Management Review, Vol. 40, 2015, pp. 345 – 369.

[2] Zavyalova A., Pfarrer M. D., Reger R. K. and Hubbard T. D., "Reputation as A Benefit and A Burden? How Stakeholders' Organizational Identification Affects the Role of Reputation Following a Negative Event," Academy of Management Journal, Vol. 59, 2016, pp. 253 – 276.

[3] Adut A. A., "Theory of Scandal: Victorians, Homosexuality, and the Fall of Oscar Wilde," American Journal of Sociology, Vol. 111, 2005, pp. 213 – 248.

[4] Greve H., Palmer D. and Pozner J. E., "Organizations Gone Wild: The Causes, Processes, and Consequences of Organizational Misconduct," Academy of Management Annals, Vol. 4, 2010, pp. 53 – 107.

[5] Hoffman A. and Ocasio W., "Not All Events Are Attended Equally: Toward A Middle – Range Theory of Industry Attention to External Events," Organization Science, Vol. 12, 2001, pp. 414 – 434.

[6] Rhee M. and Valdez M. E., "Contextual Factors Surrounding Reputation Damage with Potential Implications for Reputation Repair," Academy of Management Review, Vol. 34, 2009, pp. 146 – 168.

[7] Wiersema M. F. and Zhang Y., "Executive Turnover in the Stock Option Backdating Wave: The Impact of Social Context," Strategic Management Journal, Vol. 34, 2013, pp. 590 – 609.

[8] Graffin S. D., Bundy J., Porac J. F., Wade J. B. and Quinn D. P., "Falls from Grace and the Hazards of High Status: The 2009 British MP Expense Scandal and Its Impact on Parliamentary Elites," Administrative Science Quarterly, Vol. 58, 2013, pp. 313 – 345.

perspective, and polish image, optimize strategies, improve cognitive capability and emphasize the function of media from the external perspective. The grand plan of building a Community of Shared Future for BRICS cannot be done without powerful leadership that serves as the precondition to pool together the efforts and wisdom of the people domestically as well as internationally. As for external relationships, the five countries of BRICS need first to build a responsible and accountable image. For instance, in his statement made at the General Debate of the 70th Session of the UN General Assembly, Xi Jinping gave a speech entitled "Working Together to Forge a New Partnership of Win – win Cooperation and Create a Community of Shared Future for Mankind", in which he, for the first time, brought forward the triple identity of China: a participant of building world peace, a contributor to global development and a vindicator to uphold the international order. "China will continue to uphold the international order and system underpinned by the purposes and principles of the UN Charter. China will continue to stand together with other developing countries."[1] Second, each country of BRICS needs to employ such reasonable and active strategies as information sharing platforms, dialogue mechanism of different levels, and think – tank cooperation for effective communication mechanisms with others. Third, it is necessary to upgrade civilians' cognitive level toward crisis through people – to – people exchanges. Take trade protectionism triggered by the global financial crisis as an example. Since the economic recession in 2008, not a few countries' economic development stumbled into stagnation, with the rising unemployment rate, weakening consumption power and insufficient investment in the real economy. Some countries, in pursuit of short – term profit, shifted the crisis onto others by means of trade protectionism and non – trade barriers. This speculative approach is non – sustainable, which should be guided against by BRICS. Fourth, BRICS

---

[1] Xi Jinping. "Working Together to Forge a New Partnership of Win – win Cooperation and Create a Community of Shared Future for Mankind," Xinhua Net, September 29, 2015, http://www.xinhuanet.com//politics/2015 – 09/29/c_1116703645.htm.

should promote media cooperation among the member nations. Every day, a great number of vivid stories are happening among people with various cultural backgrounds. Media are expected to report and tell these stories with open – mindedness and inclusiveness, promote the dialogue and communication between different cultures, and eventually contribute to the progress of BRICS as well as the whole world.

## Stage three: post – crisis outcomes

The third stage of crisis management is post – crisis outcomes. From internal perspective, it needs to enhance the cognitive learning while the external perspective is primarily focusing on social evaluations to expand consensus.

In terms of organizing learning as a critical post – crisis outcomes, the prior experience can well reduce the crisis probability in the future. [1] Lampel[2] and colleagues described it as a deliberate and emergent process that can focus both on the event itself and also on developing organizational capabilities beyond the crisis event. In the same vein, it is important to move beyond the status quo to generate new competitive opportunities by learning from a crisis. [3]

From the external perspective, social evaluations include assessments of organizational reputation, legitimacy and trust. [4] The correlation between stakeholders' perceptions and an organization's response strategy has been repeatedly

---

[1] Madsen P. M., "These Lives Will Not Be Lost in Vain: Organizational Learning from Disaster in U. S. Coal mining," Organization Science, Vol. 20, 2009, pp. 861 – 875.

[2] Lampel J, Shamsie J. and Shapira Z, "Experiencing the Improbable: Rare Events and Organizational Learning," Organization Science, Vol. 20, 2009, pp. 835 – 845.

[3] James E. H, Wooten L. P. and Dushek K., "Crisis Management: Informing A New Leadership Research Agenda," Academy of Management Annals, Vol. 5, 2011, pp. 455 – 493.

[4] Bundy J., Pfarrer M. D., Short C. E. and W. Coombs T., "Crises and Crisis Management: Integration, Interpretation, and Research Development," Journal of Management, Vol. 43, No. 6, 2017, pp. 1661 – 1692.

argued by prior research. [1][2][3] For instance, in order to minimize stakeholders' negative reactions, an organization is suggested to provide a more accommodative response strategy when high crisis responsibility is perceived.

The post-crisis outcomes shed certain light on building a Community of Shared Future for BRICS. Take China-India relations as an example. In July 2017, the 9th BRICS Summit in Xiamen was affected by a longstanding border dispute between China and India, which gave rise to diplomatic tensions on both sides. Just days ahead of the summit, troops were pulled back by both countries from a face-off in the Himalayas. In the BRICS Leaders Xiamen Declaration, all five countries commit to build upon the outcomes and consensus of previous summits with unwavering conviction, so as to usher in the second golden decade of BRICS cooperation and solidarity. Similarly, BRICS Leaders Johannesburg Declaration, BRICS countries reaffirm the commitment to the principles of mutual respect, sovereign equality, democracy, inclusiveness and strengthened collaboration. To achieve this goal, efforts should be made to upgrade the learning process and optimize social evaluations. First, it is necessary to abandon institutional bias. The institutional design is rooted in each country's special history, culture and traditions, which means each country is justifiable to choose its own development path and institutional model. Second, it is important to transcend differences in ideology and values. In the present world, ideology should not be used as the pretext for confrontation or as the obstacle to political cooperation. Third, the BRICS countries, along with other developing economies, need to be further involved in globalization through structural transformation and innovation of the economy. The traditional international economic order needs to be updated

---

[1] Bundy J. and Pfarrer M. D., "A Burden of Responsibility: The Role of Social Approval at the Onset of a Crisis," Academy of Management Review, Vol. 40, 2015, pp. 345-369.

[2] Claeys A. S. and Cauberghe V., "What Makes Crisis Response Strategies Work? The Impact of Crisis Involvement and Message Framing," Journal of Business Research, Vol. 67, 2014, pp. 182-189.

[3] Coombs W. T., "Choosing the Right Words: The Development of Guidelines for the Selection of the 'Appropriate' Crisis-Response Strategies," Management Communication Quarterly, Vol. 8, 1995, pp. 447-476.

by increasing the weight of emerging economies to realize the diversification of governing subjects in the world economy. Fourth, a new concept of civilization should be upheld by the BRICS countries to strengthen communication and exchange between different civilizations. The steady progress and exchanges are commended in the fields of sports, youth, films, culture, education and tourism. For example, to enhance tourism cooperation, various countries can exchange knowledge, experience, and discuss best practices in the areas of travel trade, air connectivity, tourism infrastructure and tourism safety, etc.

## V. Conclusion

Since Chinese President Xi Jinping made a keynote speech at the United Nations (UN) Office in Geneva titled "Work Together to Build a Community with Shared Future for Mankind" in January 2017, the idea has gained wider international recognition for offering China's solutions to cope with global challenges. In the same vein, the building of a Community of Shared Future for BRICS is also guided by the spirit of pursuing an open, inclusive, clean and beautiful world that enjoys lasting peace, universal security, and common prosperity. According to the idea, BRICS countries should respect each other, consult issues as equals, and resolutely reject the Cold War mentality and power politics. Countries should take a new approach to developing state – to – state relations with communication, not confrontation, and with partnerships, not alliances.

The theory of crisis management sheds light on how to build a Community of Shared Future for BRICS. The potentiality of global crises, such as economic slowdown, climate change and terrorism, objectively offers opportunities to bond the people of all countries, requiring different stakeholders to abandon narrow – minded nationalism and fight side by side against the crises that have been threatening BRICS, even the whole world.

In light of the theory of crisis management, the entire process of crisis management can be divided into pre – crisis prevention, crisis management and post – crisis outcomes stages. Therefore, distinct efforts should be made at different stages. In the pre – crisis stage, efforts must be directed toward the coordination of between internal preparedness and external positions. In the crisis management stage, the internal ideology and actions should be synchronized by strong leadership and cohesion, and external endeavors need to focus on the support from other stakeholders. The post – crisis outcomes efforts include enhancing learning by reviewing of crisis internally and the building of positive social evaluations in the external environment to reach a consensus of higher level and greater range. In this light, the three stages of crisis management coincide with and offer referential significance for various missions of building a community of shared future for BRICS. In the pre – crisis prevention stage, internally, the five countries are expected to enhance the reliability of respective regimes in political and economic performances and to achieve a higher standard of unity by pooling efforts of the people towards the same goal. Externally, building a community of shared future for BRICS is in need of a holistic safety outlook, coinciding with the logic of "total responsibility management" approach put forward by Clair and Waddock. In the crisis management stage, the BRICS countries need to enhance leadership and cohesion from the internal perspective, polish image, optimize strategies, improve cognitive capability and emphasize the function of media from the external perspective. In the post – crisis outcomes stage, the BRICS is supposed to emphasize the learning process and upgrade the social evaluation of crises that have been jointly experienced.

Hopefully, guided by the principles of the theory of crisis management, the BRICS cooperation will be cemented and consolidated, thus providing a firm ground for the building of a community of shared future for BRICS.

# Development Status and Future Trend of Local Cooperation in BRICS Countries

Zheng Jiabao[*]

**Abstract**: In recent years, the international situation has been turbulent, geopolitical turmoil has continued, the global economic recession has intensified, and public health crises have occurred frequently, which puts forward higher requirements for the survival and development of emerging market countries represented by the BRICS countries. At first, the BRICS countries were initially doubted as a superficial "showpiece", gradually exploring multi – level and multi – field cooperation mechanisms, and striving to establish and maintain a more equitable and just functional mechanisms of the international order. The author believes that the BRICS cooperation has gone deep into local level and the local cooperation among member countries has gradually shown the trend of openness, pragmatism and diversification, but there are still many problems and challenges that need to be solved urgently. This study will review the achievements of the BRICS local cooperation and make predictions.

---

[*] Zheng Jiabao, Lecturer of College of Western Languages and Cultures, Sichuan International Studies University.

**Keywords**: BRICS countries; local Cooperation; institutional cooperation

In the context of deepening globalization, the world is in an era of intertwined development and change. With the global political, economic, cultural and religious conflicts, as well as the unbalanced regional development, the call for peace and development has become increasingly strong. How to find laws in the process of change and find peace in the process of conflict is the top priority of current foreign strategies of all countries. The BRICS mechanism was initially intended to respond to the international financial crisis, and has gradually become a functional cooperation mechanism to establish and maintain a more equitable and just international order. The local cooperation among BRICS countries has gradually shown the trend of openness, pragmatism and diversification. Development and challenges both coexist in the BRICS local cooperation, but the prospect is basically promising.

# I. Background of BRICS local cooperation

At the BRICS Business Summit held in September 2017, the leaders of the five countries agreed to develop a closer, broader and more comprehensive strategic partnership, consolidate the "triple helix – driven" cooperation framework of economic, trade, finance, political security and people – to – people and cultural exchanges, and establish the "BRICS Plus" cooperation concept. At the opening ceremony, Xi Jinping emphasized that the cooperation and development of the BRICS countries should be observed from two dimensions: the BRICS cooperation should be viewed not only in the historical process of world development and the evolution of the international pattern, but also in the historical process of the respective and common development of the five countries. On September 9, 2021, the 13th BRICS Summit, presided over by Prime Minister Modi of India, was held online, with the attendance of President Ramafosa of South Africa,

President Bolsonaro of Brazil and President Putin of Russia, adopted the New Delhi Declaration, and The Summit focused on the theme of "BRICS 15th Anniversary: Developing BRICS Cooperation, Promoting Continuity, Consolidation and Consensus", and adopted the New Delhi Declaration of the 13th BRICS Leaders' Summit, marking a new era of BRICS cooperation. ① In 2022, China assumed the presidency of the BRICS countries, and successfully hosted the 14th BRICS Leaders' Summit on June 23. The momentous event was attended by the leaders of the five countries, who had in – depth discussions on BRICS cooperation in various fields and major issues of common concern, reached several important consensuses, contributing to the establishment of high – quality partnerships and the creation of a new era of global development.

This is the second "Golden Decade" of BRICS cooperation. As the national strength of the five countries continues to increase, the BRICS cooperation has become deeper and more practical. The influence of cooperation has exceeded the scope of the five countries. The influence and attractiveness of the BRICS mechanism have continued to increase, becoming a constructive force to promote world economic growth, improve global governance, and promote democracy in international relations. The BRICS countries love and cherish peace, adhere to fairness and justice, actively promote the reform of the global governance system, and make a BRICS voice on international and regional hot issues. On the one hand, they have enhanced the international voice of emerging market countries and developing countries, and on the other hand, they have become an important platform for promoting South – South cooperation. ②

In the face of the new global political and economic landscape, the BRICS countries need to establish a robust cooperation mechanism, implement a top – down approach to cooperation, and deepen and expand their areas of collabora-

---

① Huang Maoxing Edited, "Development Report of BRICS New Industrial Revolution Partnership Innovation Base (2021)," Social Sciences Academic Press, 2022, p. 281.
② The Secretariat of the Preparatory Work for the 2022 BRICS Summit, "Introduction to BRICS Countries," February 21, 2022, http://brics2022.mfa.gov.cn/chn/gyjzgj/jzgjjj/.

tion. This will help them stabilize their position in the turbulent yet cooperative new environment and forge ahead together. Enhance cooperation in key areas within the "triple helix – driven" framework encompassing political security, economic trade and finance, and people – to – people and cultural exchanges.

## II. Status quo and characteristics of local cooperation in BRICS countries

In recent years, the comprehensive national strength and international influence of the five BRICS countries have become increasingly strong, the influence of the five countries' joint action has grown day by day, the BRICS cooperation mechanism has been continuously enhanced. Despite the ongoing international geopolitical turmoil, the lasting impact of the epidemic and economic recession, and the resurgence of anti – globalization and nationalism, the BRICS member states continue to maintain an open and inclusive attitude amidst the challenging international situation, actively promoting practical cooperation and engaging in mutual assistance and collaboration across various fields, and gradually form an open, pragmatic and diversified local cooperation mechanism.

The BRICS countries have already formed a multi – level and multi field cooperation framework. The local cooperation has achieved significant results in multiple areas, including politics, economy, finance, trade, society, humanities and other fields. The promotion of local cooperation among member countries has further strengthened the BRICS cooperation mechanism and helped promote the reform of the global governance system.

This paper will present several representative examples to illustrate the significant achievements in local cooperation made by different countries during the latter half of the second "Golden Decade" of BRICS cooperation, in order to evaluate and predict the effectiveness of the local cooperation mechanism among BRICS countries.

## 2.1 Promote infrastructure construction

At present, most emerging economies represented by BRICS countries have old and insufficient infrastructure. For example, India, more than half of its territory, has not yet been connected by roads, and its railway system is seriously inadequate; Although Russia has a certain infrastructure of highway and railway facilities, the facilities are generally outdated, and cannot meet the demands of new economic development; South Africa's power facilities need to be upgraded urgently, and most of the country's roads are in poor condition; Brazil's transportation infrastructure is very imperfect; Although China has made remarkable achievements in infrastructure construction, there is also an issue of uneven regional distribution with facilities in some backward and remote areas far from those in densely populated areas. [1]

The demand for infrastructure investment in emerging economies is enormous, and the government budget is the main source of funds. However, most emerging countries' governments and relevant international financial organizations can only provide limited funds. As an active defender and promoter of BRICS and "The Belt and Road" Initiative, China has invested a lot of money in assisting member countries to develop infrastructure, sharing development achievements, and this investment serves as a means to share development achievements and achieve mutual assistance and win – win results.

On April 9, 2021, the BRICSDisaster Management Working Group Summit was held online, inviting representatives of the five BRICS countries to exchange views on issues such as multi – disaster early warning systems, voluntary services, disaster management, disaster resilience infrastructure. Representatives of all countries generously shared their own experiences and insights, and expressed

---

[1] China Development Bank, University of International Business and Economics, "BRICS Sustainable Development Strategy Report – Innovating BRICS Meat Financing Mechanism, Promoting Practical Co-operation and Mutual Benefit," China Social Sciences Press, 2019, p. 44.

a strong desire to further strengthen practical exchanges and cooperation in relevant fields, continuously improve the disaster management capacity and infrastructure construction for disaster prevention of all countries.

### 2.2 Promote social and cultural exchanges

The BRICS countries have rich historical and cultural backgrounds. People – to – people and cultural exchanges are an importantpillar of BRICS cooperation. They play a fundamental role in BRICS cooperation and also hold great potential for its further growth. The BRICS countries have signed a series of cooperative agreements in the area of people – to – people and cultural exchanges, continuously enhancing cooperation in areas such as parliaments, political parties, youth, think tanks, and local governments, with the establishment of the BRICS University Alliance and the BRICS Network University which further promoted the people – to – people and cultural exchanges and cooperation of the BRICS countries to a new stage. [1]

In June 2015, the first BRICS Culture Ministers' Summit was held in Moscow, Russia. In July, at the seventh BRICS leaders' Summit, the signing of the BRICS Intergovernmental Cultural Cooperation Agreement laid a solid foundation for cultural exchanges and cooperation among the BRICS countries.

On July 25, 2017, the BRICS Youth Forum opened in Beijing. During the three – day Summit, 50 youth representatives from the five BRICS countries held a heated discussion on the theme of "Building Partnerships and Promoting Youth Development", including young civil servants, young scholars, young entrepreneurs, young artists, young media workers and college students, and Finally, the Action Plan of 2017 BRICS Youth Forum was formed. [2] In 2017, the BRICS countries reached a series of documents, including the Action Plan for the Imple-

---

[1] Huang Maoxing Edited, "Development Report of BRICS New Industrial Revolution Partnership Innovation Base (2021)," Social Sciences Academic Press, 2022, pp. 160 – 161.

[2] Huang Maoxing Edited, "Development Report of BRICS New Industrial Revolution Partnership Innovation Base (2021)," Social Sciences Academic Press, 2022, p. 266.

mentation of the (BRICS Intergovernmental Cultural Cooperation Agreement) (2017 -2021), the Action Plan for BRICS Countries to Strengthen Media Cooperation, the Action Plan for BRICS Youth Forum, the Plan for BRICS Countries to Cooperate in Filming 2017 -2021, and established library alliances, museum alliances, the Art Museum Alliance and the Youth and Children's Drama Alliance, with the result of expanding cooperation in the field of people - to - people and cultural exchange and cooperation. In July of the same year, the Beijing Education Declaration jointly signed by the Ministers of Education of the BRICS countries proposed to support the members of the "BRICS Network University" to carry out cooperation in education, scientific research and innovation related fields.

In June 2018, at the BRICS Think Tank International Seminar and the 21st Wanshou Forum, participants reached broad consensus on issues such as institutional innovation of BRICS people - to - people and cultural exchanges.

In November 2019, the global premiere of the first BRICS joint documentary "Children and Glory" was held simultaneously at the BRICS people - to - people Exchange Forum. [1]

On December 3, 2020, the opening ceremony of the BRICS Seminar on Governance and Administration of State Affairs and the people - to - people and Cultural Exchange Forum was held online. Huang Kunming, member of the Standing Committee of the Political Bureau of the CPC Central Committee and head of the Propaganda Department of the CPC Central Committee, attended and delivered a keynote speech, officially launching the second global call for submissions for joint BRICS production and broadcast documentaries. This event provided an important opportunity for BRICS countries to exchange experiences in governance and administration of state affairs. It also offered a platform to deepen people - to - people and cultural exchanges and cooperation, promote the deepe-

---

[1] Huang Maoxing Edited, "Development Report of BRICS New Industrial Revolution Partnership Innovation Base (2021)," Social Sciences Academic Press, 2022, pp. 160 - 161.

ning and implementation of BRICS partnerships, and build a community with a shared future for mankind. ①

On June 10, 2021, the International Seminar of BRICS Think Tanks 2021 with the theme of "Jointly Building an Innovation Base and Building a BRICS Cooperation Model" was held in Xiamen. This summit was co-sponsored by the Chinese Council for BRICS Think Tank Cooperation and the Xiamen Municipal People's Government. Think tank experts, scholars and industry representatives from member countries gathered in Xiamen to discuss the construction of the BRICS innovation base, and seek practical cooperation among BRICS countries. On August 25, 2021, the 13th BRICS Intellectual Property Office Directors' Summit was held online. Through this video conference, the directors of the member countries' intellectual property offices jointly listened to the progress of the projects led by the bureaus around the "BRICS Intellectual Property Office Cooperation Roadmap" and discussed the next work plan. Focusing on the application of digital technology and other emerging technologies, they shared their successful practical experience and actively discussed the areas of possible cooperation in the future. ② In September 2021, the New Delhi Good Words released at the 13th BRICS Summit pointed out that digital solutions should be used to ensure inclusive and equitable quality education, strengthen cooperation between education and training leaders, and launch initiatives to cooperate in the development, distribution and access to public digital content.

## 2.3 Promote cooperation in talent cultivation

2.3.1 Confucius Institutes and Luban Workshop Project: As the main carrier of talent training cooperation among the BRICS countries, Confucius Institutes have blossomed everywhere in the BRICS countries, making outstanding con-

---

① Huang Maoxing Edited, "Development Report of BRICS New Industrial Revolution Partnership Innovation Base (2021)," Social Sciences Academic Press, 2022, p.278.

② Huang Maoxing Edited, "Development Report of BRICS New Industrial Revolution Partnership Innovation Base (2021)," Social Sciences Academic Press, 2022, p.280.

tributions to the dissemination of Chinese culture and the promotion of cultural and educational exchanges between China and foreign countries. Among them, Russia has the largest number of Confucius Institutes. Luban Workshop, as a pioneer in the internationalization of China's vocational education, has established a well-known brand for people-to-people and cultural exchanges between China and foreign countries. It has outstanding performance in vocational education in BRICS countries, especially India and South Africa. It shares China's excellent vocational education experience and advanced production technology, and helps BRICS member countries learn from China's experience, cultivate more excellent professional and technical talents who can meet the requirements of the times.

2.3.2 BRICS Law School Alliance: In October 2015, the BRICS Law School Alliance Agreement signed by St. Paul Catholic University, Ural National Law University, Moscow National Law University, Amity University, Indian Law Research Institute, East China University of Political Science and Law and Cape Town University announced the establishment of the BRICS Law School Alliance. The Alliance aims to implement bilateral and multilateral legal cooperation between universities of member countries, carry out cooperative education and training programs, and jointly cultivate a group of jurists and lawyers who have a global vision, are familiar with international rules, have the ability to participate in international legal affairs, and can provide talent support for governments, lawyers and multinational enterprises of BRICS member countries. [1]

2.3.3 BRICS National Standardization Research Center: In September 2017, the Zhejiang Provincial Government and the National Standards Commission signed a plan to receive the BRICS National Standardization (Zhejiang) Research Center to promote the "going global" of Chinese standards. On December 22, 2018, in the context of the new industrial revolution partnership, the BRICS standardization international exchange and talent team building and the

---

[1] Huang Maoxing Edited, "Development Report of BRICS New Industrial Revolution Partnership Innovation Base (2021)," Social Sciences Academic Press, 2022, p.63.

second seminar on "Zhijiang Standard" was held in Yiwu. Experts from BRICS countries jointly discussed international standardization cooperation, talent team building, talent education and other issues. In May 2019, the BRICS National Standardization Center passed the acceptance inspection, formed a batch of research achievements in home appliances, textiles, leather and other fields, built a BRICS national standardization information sharing and service platform, and established a number of related research alliances to promote BRICS standardization exchanges and cooperation.

2.3.4 BRICS Skills Development and Technological Innovation Competition: In 2017, China, as the rotating presidency of the BRICS, successfully held the first BRICS Skills Development and Technological Innovation Competition from June to August, covering CNC competition, 3D printing and intelligent manufacturing competition, maker competition, intelligent manufacturing challenge, welding competition and other events, attracting more than 4,500 participants. In 2018, the second competition held 23 events, with nearly 50,000 participants, and the competitions took place in China, South Africa, and Russia. The third and fourth competitions were also successfully held. In 2021, nearly 100,000 people participated in relevant competitions and conferences. The BRICS Competition has become an important event for talent exchange between member countries and friendly countries, and has built an international platform for talent cooperation. ①

2.3.5 BRICS University Alliance and BRICS Network University: Under the framework of "The Belt and Road" Initiative, these two mechanisms have been established in the field of multilateral cooperation in higher education in BRICS countries, as the carrier of cooperation in cultural education and talent cultivation among BRICS countries. Among them, BRICS network universities refer to high-level new network university entities distributed in five countries. In

---

① Huang Maoxing Edited, "Development Report of BRICS New Industrial Revolution Partnership Innovation Base (2021)," Social Sciences Academic Press, 2022, pp. 65–66.

2022, the annual Summit of BRICS online universities will be held in Beijing in a combination of online and offline. So far, 55 universities from BRICS countries have been admitted as members. ① By jointly promoting the basic cooperation based on the research of the advantageous disciplines of the alliance universities, we will use the information network platform to promote long – term cooperation integrating information technology and teaching, and promote the in – depth cooperation of the alliance universities based on the establishment of a joint college. These cooperation modes are called "point cooperation", "line cooperation" and "area cooperation", which reflect the diversified cooperation channels and innovative cooperation spirit of the organization. ②

## Ⅲ. Problems and challenges faced by BRICS local cooperation

In the early days of the establishment of BRICS cooperation, the outside world was generally worried about its sustainability, and believed that the BRICS could become a small group of emerging powers for self – entertainment, but rather as a superficial and ineffective organization. "The impact of the BRICS countries on development cooperation has traditionally been divided into two dimensions: North South cooperation and South cooperation, both of which are simultaneous and mixed. The BRICS member countries have diverse agendas, making cooperation between countries more effective."③ "Another factor that will shape the future of the BRICS countries is the relationship between India and

---

① "People's Daily: The annual Summit of BRICS online universities in 2022 will be held at Beijing Normal University on April 28," 2022, http: //edu. people. com. cn/n1/2022/0428/c1006 – 32410988. html.

② Huang Maoxing Edited, "Development Report of BRICS New Industrial Revolution Partnership Innovation Base (2021)," Social Sciences Academic Press, 2022, pp. 65 – 66.

③ Ricxhard Carey and Xiaoyun Li, "The BRICS in International Development: The New Landscape," IDS Evidence Report 189, 2016, p. 12.

China. Recently, the two countries have diverged on some issues, such as terrorism, border issues and India's growing alignment with the United States and Japan."① Such pessimistic views on the operation mechanism and development prospects of the BRICS countries are not uncommon. Their views focus on concerns and doubts about the stability of their organizations, the pragmatic degree of cooperation, geopolitical conflicts among member countries, and the collective nature of their actions.

In terms of local cooperation, although BRICS countries have achieved certain results, there are still many urgent problems to be addressed, and they face multiple challenges from inside and outside:

### 3.1 Lack of long-term mechanism

At present, BRICS cooperation is still mainly in the form of forum, lacking a stable and formal long-term mechanism and a powerful permanent platform to deepen cooperation. For example, there are only high-level Summit mechanisms such as the Summit of leaders at the national level, but no permanent body has been set up to supervise the implementation of conference resolutions; Local governments or social institutions at all levels in member countries lack an effective platform for communication, which makes it difficult to mobilize resources and play a synergistic role. ②

### 3.2 Economic growth in various countries slowed down

In recent years, the international economy has been in a continuous downturn. By the end of 2019, the COVID-19 epidemic has swept the world. The border issue between China and India has triggered conflicts. The Russia-Ukraine war has triggered an energy game. The global economic situation has wors-

---

① Rajiv Bhatia, "Whither BRICS?" Eurasia Review, 2017, https://www.eurasiareview.com/02052016-whither-brics-analysis/.

② Wei Jianguo, Li Feng, "Research on BRICS Cooperation Mechanism," Social Sciences Academic Press, 2018, p. 162.

ened. A new round of financial crisis may come. BRICS member countries bear the brunt. As the major emerging economies in the world, they are not the most pressure resistant economies. Industrial reform, energy trade, employment and infrastructure have all been hit hard, and economic growth has slowed significantly. As a result, the local finance of member countries is generally under great pressure, and they have to reduce their cooperation in order to smooth out the crisis.

## 3.3 Unstable cooperation foundation

The degree of regional economic integration fundamentally determines the level of regional cooperation, and the BRICS countries have limited geographical and economic proximity. In addition to being restricted by geographical location, the economic development of member countries is mainly extensional, lacking the power of sustainable development. The member countries are at a similar stage of development and have a high degree of dependence on foreign countries. According to statistics, South Africa's total imports and exports of goods and services in 2020 reached US $169.2 billion, while Russia, India and China reached US $683.8 billion, US $684.7 billion and US $5,095.1 billion respectively. [1] An economy heavily reliant on exports and trade protectionism can easily lead to competition and conflicts of interest.

The member countries have different historical backgrounds and development trends. Although they areall emerging market countries, their economic strength gap is obvious. The development potential of China and India is generally better than that of Russia, South Africa, and Brazil. Additionally, there is an imbalance in the development of financial systems among these countries, which makes it difficult to optimize the allocation of financial resources, and restricts

---

[1] National Bureau of Statistics of China, etc. , "BRICS Joint Statistical Manual 2021," China Statistics Press, 2022, p. 168.

the deepening of financial cooperation among BRICS countries. ①

### 3.4 Severe external challenges

Amidst the global and regional economic slowdown and the looming financial crisis, BRICS countries are also facing severe challenges from the outside. All countries in the world are competing to attract foreign investment, guide the return of manufacturing and employment opportunities, weaken the original international competitiveness of BRICS countries, and restrict their development of international cooperation.

A new round of technological and industrial revolution has enabled developed countries to gain greater technological leadership, and emerging markets such as BRICS countries do not have an overall advantage. Even cooperation is difficult to resist the technological impact of developed economies, and there is a possibility of falling behind again. Under the new technological conditions, the original production factor endowments and price advantages such as raw materials and labor may no longer have economic significance, the global division of labor and trade system are facing restructuring, and the economic status and development potential of BRICS countries are facing huge instability. ②

## Ⅳ. Trends of BRICS local cooperation③

After more than ten years of development, the cooperation mechanism of the BRICS countries is undergoing an important transformation, that is, from a "dialogue forum focusing on economic governance andprinciples" to a "comprehen-

---

① Wei Jianguo, Li Feng, "Research on BRICS Cooperation Mechanism," Social Sciences Academic Press, 2018, p. 164.

② Wei Jianguo, Li Feng, "Research on BRICS Cooperation Mechanism," Social Sciences Academic Press, 2018, p. 163.

③ Huang Maoxing Edited, "Development Report of BRICS New Industrial Revolution Partnership Innovation Base (2021)," Social Sciences Academic Press, 2022, p. 168.

sive coordination mechanism focusing on both political and economic governance and combining pragmatism and principles". The cooperation among BRICS member countries is increasingly focused on practicality rather than theory, hoping to bring tangible benefits to governments and people of all countries. The governments of BRICS countries all encourage 'project – based' cooperation, which has led to the implementation of numerous practical local cooperative projects, making BRICS countries an institution that provides opportunities for exchange and development for the governments and citizens of member countries. With the help of "grounded" projects, resources and ideas will be implemented into the social foundation.

The current international political situation is grim, the economic crisis is imminent, and nationalism and "right wing" ideology are returning. As a new international organization, BRICS cooperation among member countries may also be influenced, leading to some level of contraction and conservatism. As the largest economy in the BRICS countries, China has made remarkable achievements in politics, economy, military, culture, health and other fields, and its overall competitiveness ranks first among the BRICS countries. Although China does not face some of the serious problems that other member countries do, it cannot isolate itself in the globalized world and pursue unilateral self – interest. China can assist other countries through the BRICS cooperation mechanism and international organizations, promoting common development, mutual benefit, and the further deepening of cooperation among member countries. BRICS countries have great cooperation potential and development space in key areas such as trade and investment, science and technology, finance, environment, energy, agriculture, information and communication technology, and people – to – people and cultural exchanges. Cooperation in key areas will enhance the voice of BRICS countries in the international community and sing the "BRICS voice" in the global economic recovery.

The author believes that in the new stage of BRICS cooperation, local cooperation among countries will continue to advance in the following key areas:

## 4.1 Further deepen local economic, trade and financial cooperation

Economic and trade cooperation has always been an important driving force for BRICS cooperation. Promoting comprehensive economic, trade, and financial cooperation among BRICS countries plays a crucial role in deepening the strategic partnership within BRICS with significant strategic value. The BRICS economic and trade cooperation system has facilitated the formation of significant and beneficial trade partnerships among member countries. Although global trade has been greatly impacted by the ongoing COVID – 19 pandemic since 2020, under the guidance and promotion of the BRICS economic and trade cooperation mechanism, BRICS countries have strengthened practical economic and trade cooperation, which not only ensures the supply of essential materials during the epidemic but also paves the way for expanding trade in various sectors in the future. It will lay a foundation for the economic recovery of BRICS countries and the safe and efficient operation of the global industrial supply chain. The achievements of several cooperation agreement frameworks have effectively promoted trade and investment cooperation among member countries, such as the BRICS Multilateral Trade System Cooperation Statement, the Framework for Professional Services Cooperation, and the BRICS Economic Partnership Strategy 2025.

The New Development Bank serves as the flagship project of BRICS financial cooperation. At the sixth BRICS leaders' Summit, representatives of all countries unanimously decided to establish the New Development Bank, which was inaugurated in 2015. It provides a cooperative platform to support financing, mitigate financial risks, encourage bilateral and multilateral financial cooperation, facilitate infrastructure construction, promote sustainable development projects, and expand cooperation opportunities for BRICS countries as well as other emerging and developing economies.

## 4.2 Further strengthen sustainable cooperation in energy and environment

After the first industrial revolution, fossil energy has become an important driving force for the development of social production and life. With the widespread use of fossil energy, the environmental and resource challenges associated with fossil energy have attracted global attention. Currently, the BRICS countries consist of nations that play a significant role in both energy demand and supply. The demand for resources and energy will continue to increase with future economic and social development. Energy and environmentalproblems will become issues that cannot be ignored in the process of achieving sustainable development and high - quality development in the BRICS countries, Therefore, in the future, the focus of energy and environmental cooperation between BRICS countries and other emerging markets and developing countries will revolve around clean energy transitions, environmental pollution prevention and control, and green finance.

During the 11th and 12th BRICS Leaders' Summits, the Articles of Association for the BRICS Energy Research Cooperation Platform, the Roadmap of BRICS Energy Cooperation, and the Joint Statement of the 6th BRICS Environment Ministers' Summit were passed. BRICS leaders expressed their commitment to further strengthening energy and environmental cooperation in the future, highlighting the importance of consolidating existing achievements, promoting the construction of energy research platforms and environment - friendly technology cooperation platforms, strengthening and expanding the scope of joint energy research, implementing joint energy projects, building energy research platform, establishing environment - friendly technology platform architecture model and other work. They reaffirmed confidence and determination to further strengthen the strategic partnership in energy and environmental protection in BRICS countries.

## 4.3 Promote the joint construction of health care

Since the outbreak of the epidemic, BRICS countries have carried out in - depth cooperation in health areas, which will further promote the establishment of a BRICS health community. This cooperation enables member states to participate in anti - oandemic efforts, consolidate achievements in epidemic containment, and jointly adress COVID-19's negative impacts, and other global challenges.

During the COVID-19 epidemic, China and South Africa held several video conferences to exchange their experiences in combating the epidemic, focusing on nine themes, such as virus detection, epidemic prevention strategies, and vaccine research and development. On April 28, 2020, at the BRICS Special Foreign Ministers' Summit on Coping with the COVID-19 Epidemic, representatives of all countries carried out in-depth discussions around the theme of fighting the epidemic and deepening BRICS cooperation, and discussed topics such as adhering to close epidemic information sharing and experience exchange, conducting drug and vaccine research and development cooperation, and firmly supporting the leadership role of international organizations such as the World Health Organization in the international fight against the epidemic, and reach consensus; By May, China had dispatched 21 medical expert groups to 19 countries, including Cambodia, providing valuable assistance, guidance, and advice on epidemic prevention and control. Anti-epidemic cooperation between other BRICS countries and other countries is mainly in the form of vaccine research and development cooperation.

BRICS countries can promote the integration of emergency medical and health cooperation and embedded medical and health cooperation among member countries. At the same time, they can set short-term goals and medium-to-long-term goals for medical and health cooperation. The short-term cooperation goals can assist in emergency coordination, consultation and cooperation in response to sudden epidemics. While medium-to-long-term goals can help enhance vaccine R&D collaboration among BRICS countries, international institutions and external partners. Additionally, initiatives such as traditional medicine cooperation and health personnel training can improve medical and health capabilities and reduced the potential risks of the epidemic for the international community.

## 4.4 Further promote people – to – people and cultural exchanges and co-operation

As one of the three pillars of BRICS cooperation, people – to – people and cultural exchanges have always played a positive role in promoting the cooperation among the "BRICS five" countries. Extensive exchanges and cooperation in education, culture, sports, science and technology and other people – to – people and cultural fields have played an important role in enhancing mutual understanding and friendship among the people of the five BRICS countries while bolstering public support for collaboration. The culture and civilization of the BRICS countries under different national conditions and social backgrounds have their own characteristics and advantages and are highly complementary, which lays a solid foundation for mutual learning and reference between the BRICS countries. Given the differences, the political, economic, and social systems among BRICS countries, fostering people – to – people and cultural exchanges is essential to building public concensus, strengthening mutual trust, and advancing cooperation.

Since the establishment of the BRICS cooperation mechanism, BRICS cooperation has mainly focused on the economic field, whereas progress in the people – to – people and cultural exchanges and cooperation has lagged. Challenges of people – to – people exchange mechanism include an underdeveloped framework, weak inter – mechanism and limited enforceability of aggreements. In addition, the potential for cultural exchange and cooperation among the BRICS countries is untapped. How to realize the complementary advantages of their respective cultures and civilizations is still an important topic for BRICS cooperation.

As BRICS cooperation moves towards a new stage, all member countries should play the role of government guidance and coordination to fully mobilize and integrate various resources, build a platform for people – to – people and cultural exchanges and cooperation, and leverage the synergy between government and non – governmental mechanisms. Given the limited resources, the BRICS mechanism for people – to – people and cultural exchanges and cooperation should be based on the practical needs of the five countries and urgent needs of the people by allocating resources to facilitate people – to – people and cultural exchanges and cooperation that effectively enhance mutual understanding and trust among member countries, giving priority to mechanism building in key areas and creating exemplary results, as well as leveraging the professional advantages and synergies of think tank cooperation carrying out basic and strategic research on the construction and development of the mechanism.

## *Os BRICS NA OMC*: *Políticas Comerciais Comparadas de Brasil, Rússia, Índia, China e África do Sul*: Book Review

Pei Yinqi[*], Xie Xiaoli[**], Zhou Xinyu[***]

**Abstract**: International trade among the BRICS nations (Brazil, Russia, India, China, and South Africa) has become a central focus in today's global economic and trade discourse. Simultaneously, against the backdrop of a constantly shifting global economic landscape, these BRICS members, as active participants in the World Trade Organization (WTO), continue to exhibit striking economic vitality. They are expanding their sphere of policy influence within international institutions and the global trade arena. In recent years, the BRICS countries have intensified their trade collaboration, both among themselves and with other developing nations. However, due to the varying economic conditions of these five nations, divergences in interests persist in certain domains. Therefore,

---

[*] Pei Yinqi, Student of Portuguese Language Program, College of Western Languages and Cultures, Sichuan International Studies University.

[**] Xie Xiaoli, Student of Portuguese Language Program, College of Western Languages and Cultures, Sichuan International Studies University.

[***] Zhou Xinyu, Teacher of Portuguese Language Program, College of Western Languages and Cultures, Sichuan International Studies University; PhD student of University of Lisbon, Portugal.

conducting a thorough examination of "Comparative Trade Policies among the BRICS Countries within the WTO" holds significant practical significance. This analysis aims to uncover more effective pathways for achieving extensive collaboration across diverse domains, taking into account the unique national contexts. Through this comprehensive analysis, it is evident that such cooperation can provide robust support for the BRICS nations and other developing countries, empowering them to play more substantial roles on the international trade stage.

**Keywords**: BRICS; WTO; Comparative trade policies; Multilateral trading system; Dispute settlement mechanism; Interest divergence and cooperation

# Ⅰ. Introduction

The current global political and economic landscape is fraught with significant uncertainty. As the BRICS nations assert themselves on the world stage, boasting substantial domestic markets and burgeoning economies, scholarly interest has grown in dissecting the evolving relationships among these BRICS countries within prominent international political and economic forums. Among these, the World Trade Organization (WTO) holds a pivotal position, offering ample opportunities to scrutinize the roles played by BRICS member states as international stakeholders. In this context, the Brazilian Institute for Applied Economic Research (IPEA) and the Directorate of International Economic Relations (DINTE) launched the Global Trade Governance Project and published a book that provides a comparative analysis of the trade policies of BRICS countries. The book is titled as "*OS BRICS NA OMC: Políticas Comerciais Comparadas de Brasil, Rússia, Índia, China e África do Sul*" (Comparative Trade Policies of Brazil, Russia, India, China, and South Africa). [1]The book's purpose is to con-

---

① "*OS BRICS NA OMC: Políticas Comerciais Comparadas de Brasil, Rússia, Índia, China e África do sul*" is a book published in 2012 in Brasília as part of the Global Trade Governance project initiated by the Institute for Applied Economic Research (IPEA) and the Bureau of International Economic Relations (DINTE). This book offers a comparative analysis of trade policies among the BRICS countries. It was organized by Vera Thorstensen and Ivan Tiago Machado Oliveira, with contributions from researchers affiliated with IPEA and the Center for Global Trade and Investment at the São Paulo School of Economics, Getulio Vargas Foundation (CCGI – FGV).

duct a comprehensive comparative analysis of the trade policies of each BRICS member within the framework of the WTO. By delving into the positions of BRICS countries in international trade, as well as their engagement in the multilateral trade system (including their diplomatic and legal underpinnings, dispute resolution mechanisms, and their political and negotiation strategies, such as participation in the Doha Round negotiations), the book illuminates the central role played by BRICS countries within the context of the multilateral trade system.

Each chapter of the book furnishes an overview of the deployment of key trade instruments, introduces the trade policies of each BRICS country, highlight their similarities and disparities, and elucidates their respective roles within the WTO. This meticulous analysis offers substantiated evidence of areas where BRICS member states converge and diverge in their interests, thereby providing valuable insights into potential avenues for cooperation among them within the complex realm of multilateral trade. The overarching aim is to underscore that, notwithstanding pronounced differences in commerce and politics, there exists room for strategic alignment among BRICS countries to advance their shared interests. This book serves as an invaluable resource for gaining a profound understanding of the intricate trade dynamics among BRICS countries and their active involvement within the WTO, a critical facet for evaluating the prospects of cooperation and discord within their collective economic agenda.

The book is systematically divided into five sections, each addressing specific facets: the distinctive characteristics of BRICS countries' performance within the WTO, key milestones in the political development and interaction among BRICS countries, a comprehensive analysis of the international trade situations of BRICS countries, investigation of major trade policy issues of BRICS countries, the roles assumed by BRICS countries within the WTO's dispute resolution mechanism, and the active participation of BRICS countries in the Doha Round negotiations.

## II. Summary of the Main Points

The book provides a concise and lucid summary of key observations regarding the activities of BRICS member countries.[1] It underscores that political collaboration among these nations has been steadily gaining momentum, translating into concrete actions across various spheres. BRICS nations share a collective interest in staying attuned to new developments on the international stage. In their pursuit to fortify their influence in global governance, they predominantly engage by actively participating in decision – making forums within international organizations, thus expressing their viewpoints while seeking resolutions to urgent global challenges.

Within the context of the World Trade Organization (WTO), BRICS countries encounter substantial and multifaceted challenges in aligning their policy directions. This cooperative endeavor hinges on the varying priorities within their economic policies and their distinct stages of economic growth. Consequently, conducting a comprehensive comparative analysis of the trade policies of each BRICS member assumes significance. Through a comprehensive analysis of primary policy instruments and the discernment of points of convergence and divergence, we can pinpoint sectors within BRICS nations where cooperation is poised to flourish and identify areas necessitating greater effort to foster such collaboration.

The book underscores the exceptional case of collaboration among BRICS member countries within the context of the Doha Round negotiations, which commenced in 2001. This undertaking has solidified their political presence on the global stage as an emerging bloc of nations. Over the protracted negotiations of the Doha Round, the WTO has served as an effective platform for harmonizing the positions of various stakeholders, particularly in the realm of agriculture. This

---

[1] Vera Thorstensen and Ivan Tiago Machado Oliveira, "OS BRICS NA OMC: Políticas Comerciais Comparadas de Brasil, Rússia, Índia, China e África do Sul," Brasília: Ipea, 2012, p. 23.

successful practice underscores that a convergence of diverse interests can facilitate alignment among BRICS nations within the international trade agenda. However, it also underscores the existence of certain areas characterized by divergent interests, which render such cooperation more challenging. It is in these specific domains that BRICS countries must exert greater diligence to solidify their central roles on the international stage.

## III. Summary of the Main Content

### 1. Analysis of the Distinctive Performance of BRICS Countries in WTO Activities

The book points out that BRICS countries have consistently demonstrated their unique characteristics within the World Trade Organization (WTO) activities. Through analysis, it is possible to identify the priorities in their international trade policies and determine the interests they uphold on the international stage. [1]

The book mentions that international trade among BRICS countries represents different priorities within their growth models. For China, international trade has been a core element of its economic policy built on a capitalist foundation for the past three decades. China initially prioritized the liberalization of imports and exports for both state-owned and foreign enterprises until signaling in early 2011 a greater focus on domestic market growth. In contrast, for Brazil, India, and South Africa, international trade has been a less significant factor, with their priorities centered around expanding domestic markets through increasing demand and controlling inflation. India and South Africa maintained economic closedness until the 1990s when they began opening up to international trade. India prioritized export of services, but even today, it maintains high lev-

---

[1] Vera Thorstensen and Ivan Tiago Machado Oliveira, "OS BRICS NA OMC: Políticas Comerciais Comparadas de Brasil, Rússia, Índia, China e África do Sul," Brasília, Ipea, 2012, p. 24.

els of protectionism in various sectors, particularly agriculture. Brazil followed an inward development model but opened up its economy since the late 1980s. For Russia, which is in a transition phase from a planned economy to a market economy, trade has become the quickest way to reduce dependence on activities related to energy products such as oil and natural gas. As a result, Russia expressed interest in joining the World Trade Organization (WTO) with the goal of diversifying its international trade and promoting economic development.

Additionally, the BRICS countries exhibit varying degrees of priority in their participation in the World Trade Organization (WTO). Brazil, India, and South Africa are among the twenty – three contracting parties to the General Agreement on Tariffs and Trade (GATT), which took effect in 1948. These countries participated in the initial discussions and all negotiation rounds concerning the establishment of GATT, and they played leadership roles in the context of developing countries. China is also a contracting party to GATT, formally joining the WTO in November 2001.

Following the dissolution of the Soviet Union in 1993, Russia applied for GATT contracting party status. After nearly two decades of negotiations, Russia completed its process of joining the WTO in December 2011.

Before China's accession to the WTO, the country underwent comprehensive economic adjustments, representing a significant political decision by the Chinese government to reintegrate China into the global trade arena, thereby transforming trade into a driving force for its development. China's accession satisfied the interests of both itself and WTO member countries.

The accession of China and Russia to the WTO, formerly planned economies, has increasingly drawn scholars' attention to the economic and political reasons behind their decisions to join the organization. They argue that the lengthy and intricate process of joining the WTO has economic and political rationales, and the cost – benefit balance of such decisions is deemed reasonable.

## 2. Refined Analysis on the International Trade Dynamics of BRICS Nations

Since 2010, there have been significant shifts in the paradigms of international trade. According to the data provided by the World Trade Organization, 2009 was a landmark year when China, with its export values soaring to $1.2 trillion, ascended to the status of the global pacesetter in merchandise exports, eclipsing both Germany and the United States. However, in the sphere of imports, the United States retained its premier stature in international trade. Between 2000 and 2010, China realized a 6.4 – fold augmentation in exports and a 6.2 – fold increase in imports. Russia, another pivotal entity in global exportation, attained the 12th rank in 2010. Following its accession to the World Trade Organization in December 2011, it was projected to experience substantial enhancement in its international trade operations. By 2010, compared to the figures from 2000, Russia had observed a 3.8 – fold elevation in export values and a 5.3 – fold rise in imports. India has consistently manifested considerable advancements in its international trade activities. In the span of a decade, India's exports have proliferated by 5.2 times, and imports have surged by 6.2 times. Brazil, compared to the year 2000, marked a 3.7 – fold increase in export values and a 3.2 – fold increase in import values by 2010. South Africa experienced a growth of 2.7 times in import volumes and 3.1 times in import volumes over the same period. [1]

In the context of global trade engagement, from 2000 to 2010, China experienced a significant elevation in its rank, moving from fifth place, with a 5% share in total exports, to second place, with a 13.3% share in total exports. Russia ascended from the 11th to the 7th position, contributing 3.4% to the total exports. India, with a 0.9% share in total exports, rose from the 20th position to the 14th, holding 1.8% of total exports. Brazil improved its standing from the 19th position, with 1.1% of the total share, to the 16th, with 1.7%

---

[1] Vera Thorstensen and Ivan Tiago Machado Oliveira, "OS BRICS NA OMC: Políticas Comerciais Comparadas de Brasil, Rússia, Índia, China e África do Sul," Brasília: Ipea, 2012, p. 29.

of the total share. Meanwhile, South Africa progressed from the 27th position, accounting for 0.6% of the total, to the 24th position, comprising 0.7% of the total.[①]

In the realm of services, data from the World Trade Organization highlights substantial progress between 2000 and 2010. Within this decade, China manifested an increase of 5.6 – fold, India of 6.1 – fold, Russia of 4.4 – fold, Brazil of 3.3 – fold, and South Africa of 2.8 – fold in the services sector.[②]

In terms of contribution to global service exports, analytical insights reveal that China and India have sustained consistent augmentation in this area. Conversely, Russia's growth has been relatively moderate, Brazil has preserved equilibrium in its contribution, and South Africa has experienced a diminishing in its relative prominence in this sector.

When evaluating the openness of each country, Brazil exhibits the lowest trade – to – Gross Domestic Product (GDP) ratio amongst the BRICS members. Between 2008 and 2010, international trade constituted 24% of Brazil's GDP, contrasted with 52% for Russia, 48% for India, 55% for China, and 61% for South Africa.[③] Brazil's economic alignment is more parallel with developed economies, like the United States, France, and Germany, rather than with the most dynamically evolving emerging countries.

## 3. Exploration of Principal Trade Policy Matters in BRICS Nations

(1) Overview of Tariff Structures in BRICS Countries

This book, through detailed analysis and succinct comparative studies of the tariff policies among BRICS nations, infers a shared characteristic in their tariff

---

① Vera Thorstensen and Ivan Tiago Machado Oliveira, "OS BRICS NA OMC: Políticas Comerciais Comparadas de Brasil, Rússia, Índia, China e África do Sul," Brasília: Ipea, 2012, p. 30.

② Vera Thorstensen and Ivan Tiago Machado Oliveira, "OS BRICS NA OMC: Políticas Comerciais Comparadas de Brasil, Rússia, Índia, China e África do Sul," Brasília: Ipea, 2012, p. 30.

③ Vera Thorstensen and Ivan Tiago Machado Oliveira, "OS BRICS NA OMC: Políticas Comerciais Comparadas de Brasil, Rússia, Índia, China e África do Sul," Brasília: Ipea, 2012, p. 450.

strategies, namely, economic liberalization. Historically, every country within the coalition had embraced protectionist strategies, concentrating on fortifying domestic markets to stimulate industrialization. Within this coalition, China stands out as the sole nation to devise an economic progression strategy with an emphasis on overseas markets. Brazil and South Africa, due to their alignment with their respective regional blocs—the Southern Common Market and the Southern African Customs Union—have limited autonomy in policy alterations, subordinating their tariff strategies to these blocs. Among them, India manifests the least integration in tariff structures. Brazil is singular within BRICS, maintaining an average agricultural tariff lower than that for non – agricultural commodities. In a generalized view, other members, notably India, uphold relatively elevated agricultural tariffs. The book particularly emphasizes that, commencing from the financial crisis of October 2008, BRICS countries have been orchestrating cohesive stances to avert the intensification of global protectionism. In this context, the crisis has precipitated diverse influences on the tariff strategies of the BRICS members: India, China, and South Africa have endeavored to strike a balance between liberalization and constriction, Brazil has embraced a series of expansive policies, while Russia has opted to fortify its protectionist measures. [1]

(2) Overview of Agriculture in BRICS Countries

The analysis of main agricultural indicators in this book elucidates that the national conditions and objectives of BRICS member nations are clear and possess distinct characteristics. Brazil is agriculturally self – reliant and a significant exporter of capital – intensive agricultural products. Given its competitive advantages, the country employs its tariff policies judiciously, adopting average tariffs. Brazil's potential role as a chief exporter of agricultural goods has led it to seek enhanced access to the markets of developed nations during negotiations, aiming to minimize agricultural subsidies and other barriers imposed on its prod-

---

[1] Vera Thorstensen and Ivan Tiago Machado Oliveira, "OS BRICS NA OMC: Políticas Comerciais Comparadas de Brasil, Rússia, Índia, China e África do Sul," Brasília: Ipea, 2012, p. 88.

ucts. China, while capable of agricultural self-sufficiency, primarily imports agricultural products due to its lower agricultural productivity and relies heavily on government interventions to ensure food security and maintain stability amongst its rural populace. India is fundamentally an agrarian nation, with a significant portion of its population residing in rural areas and relying on agriculture. The country oscillates between subsistence agriculture and export-oriented production, aspiring to safeguard small-scale farming through high tariffs and subsidies provided via minimum support prices and concessional credit rates. For India, gaining broader access to European and American markets while maintaining unified tariffs seems to be the preferable route. South Africa periodically grapples with infrastructural deficiencies and land allocation issues. The government's primary focus is on involving small to medium-scale farmers in export-oriented agriculture through land reforms, infrastructure advancements, and the stimulation of private investments. Even with constrained potential in agricultural production, South Africa harbors a profound interest in exporting its products and is also advocating for the liberalization of international agricultural trade. Russia is distinguished as a potent agricultural economy, with its export focus primarily centered on grains.

According to the statements from the World Trade Organization, in the period following the 2008 financial crisis, the BRICS nations not only augmented their agricultural subsidies but also softened their stances and limitations in the Doha Round discussions. This was to counteract the burgeoning protectionist tendencies of the developed nations. There are also other shared characteristics among BRICS nations, such as implementing governmental aid measures under Special and Differential Treatment and dispensing substantial subsidies.

Within the negotiations of the Doha Round, nations with a significant export profile like Brazil embraced more liberalized positions in the dialogue, while nations like India and China displayed a preference for maintaining their tariff structures. The alignment of interests is likely to foster cooperation amongst the BRICS in agricultural sectors, bolstering the coalition's position in multilateral deliberations.

(3) Technical, Sanitary and Phytosanitary Barriers

In the wake of diminishing import tariffs, technical standards and sanitary and phytosanitary controls have progressively become significant impediments to import regulation in recent years. Although the World Trade Organization monitors their application, the intricate evaluations required for human, animal, and plant health by importing countries, alongside continuous appeals, make this kind of trade protection particularly challenging to regulate.

Since 2010, BRICS countries have been harmonizing technical and quality standards, expanding the realm of mutual recognition agreements, and synchronizing domestic laws with international practices. Recently, China has achieved modernization in its sanitary inspection regimes, standardization, and technical norms. Nonetheless, there remains a considerable journey towards achieving legislative harmony with international standards and modifying corporate manufacturing techniques. In this context, India is substantially more advanced than China. The widespread technical and sanitary examinations of domestic production can mitigate the barriers products encounter in European and American markets. Brazil demonstrates superior administrative proficiency in executing technical and sanitary oversight, although it has only recently indicated a readiness to enhance inspections to ensure adherence to obligatory norms. Brazil and China, in comparison to India and South Africa, have more comprehensive frameworks for oversight of measures and are more proactive in their participation in WTO committees, with objectives including shielding their benefits from the potential protectionist actions of other members.

There exists the potential for widespread collaboration amongst the member nations of the BRICS, as each acknowledges the crucial role of technical, sanitary, and phytosanitary barriers in export endeavors. As every member is at a pivotal phase of development in this area, the amalgamation of interests empowers them to express their individual positions effectively on multilateral platforms dealing with such concerns.

(4) Trade Defense Measures in BRICS Countries

For years, the principal instruments of international trade policy have been tariffs and tariff quotas, recognized as the sole protective elements allowed by the World Trade Organization under the General Agreement on Tariffs and Trade. However, with the advancement of multiple rounds of negotiations, tariffs are being diminished, and in some cases, supplanted by less transparent non-tariff barriers like technical, sanitary, and phytosanitary barriers. Certain financial mechanisms, such as exchange rates and export ratios, and even barriers related to labor or the environment, are being deployed even in the absence of backing from multilateral agreements. To address unfair trade or import surges, additional trade policy tools including anti-dumping, countermeasures against subsidies, and safeguard measures are employed as means of trade defense for commodities.

Many countries prefer to use anti-dumping measures as a method of trade defense, and each of the BRICS nations also has its distinct characteristics. It is specifically highlighted in the book that China, among all BRICS and WTO member nations, is the principal subject of anti-dumping actions due to its ultra-competitive exports, low labor costs, and assertive currency devaluation strategies. India is the country within the BRICS that makes the most extensive use of trade defense mechanisms. Furthermore, compared to the United States and the European Union, more anti-dumping actions have been employed by WTO member countries against China. [1]

This book delivers a thorough analysis of the application of trade defense instruments by the member countries of BRICS within the World Trade Organization's trade defense framework, concluding as follows: Every member of the WTO has been actively utilizing trade defense mechanisms. Over the years, China, being a principal exporter, has faced anti-dumping measures not just

---

[1] Vera Thorstensen and Ivan Tiago Machado Oliveira, "OS BRICS NA OMC: Políticas Comerciais Comparadas de Brasil, Rússia, Índia, China e África do Sul," Brasília: Ipea, 2012, p.139.

from developed nations but also from those developing. According to data-driven analysis, Brazil has exhibited a lack of efficacy in protecting its national interests. The book posits that Brazil needs to assume a more assertive role in trade defense sectors and should refrain from, and cannot afford, politicizing the deployment of trade defense strategies. Trade defense should not serve as a pawn in the arena of political negotiation and maneuvering. ①

(5) Overview of the Service Industry in BRICS Countries

The service sector has gained significant traction in the economies of the BRICS nations. Notably, this sector now contributes to over half of the GDP in countries such as Brazil, India, South Africa, and Russia. Meanwhile, its influence in China is on a steady rise. In nations like Brazil, South Africa, and Russia, an upswing in the service sector has mirrored a downtrend in the industrial segment's contribution to GDP. However, for India and China, the growth spurts in both industrial and service sectors seem to have overshadowed the agricultural sector's productivity.

Acknowledging the paramount importance of service trade in the global economic landscape, the book delves into the commitments that BRICS nations have made under the World Trade Organization's umbrella thus far. It also shines a spotlight on potential shifts in service trade regulations within the ambit of the WTO's legal framework.

A clear trend towards service trade liberalization is evident among the BRICS countries. Both China and Russia, during their respective WTO accessions in 2001 and 2011, negotiated fervently, making pledges towards service liberalization. They committed to enhancing market access and refining national treatment across multiple sectors. However, the landscape varies across these nations. For instance, in India and China, foreign participation and joint ventures face considerable constraints in numerous sectors. Surprisingly, Brazil places the most

---

① Vera Thorstensen and Ivan Tiago Machado Oliveira, "OS BRICS NA OMC: Políticas Comerciais Comparadas de Brasil, Rússia, Índia, China e África do Sul," Brasília: Ipea, 2012, p. 164.

stringent limitations on its domestic service providers, even more so than its BRICS counterparts. South Africa, despite its restrictions in pivotal sectors like telecommunications, remains more open in terms of market access than nations like Brazil and India.

Given the service sector's potential, it provides a conducive platform for political dialogue among the BRICS nations, with aspirations for enriched negotiations in the larger multilateral system in the future.

(6) Intellectual Property Management

While economic growth fuels scientific advancements, technological progress—often indicated by patents—equally drives economic expansion. With the knowledge economy's evolution and an emphasis on global intellectual property rights, the BRICS nations are progressively employing intellectual property strategies to bolster their technological, economic, and cultural development, thereby augmenting their global competitiveness. An increased inflow of foreign capital has prompted these countries to focus more keenly on intellectual property protection, especially in areas like patents, branding, and industrial designs.

Each BRICS member has meticulously adapted its domestic policies to suit its unique national circumstances:

China has enhanced its intellectual property safeguards to lure foreign investments and foster technology transfers.

India has progressively fortified its protection mechanisms, predominantly in the sectors of chemicals and bioproducts.

Brazil's legal framework permits the suspension of intellectual property rights during national emergencies, allowing them to prioritize over market demands.

Russia has overhauled its customs regulations and the licensing process for drug circulation.

Contrasting with other BRICS peers, South Africa boasts a relatively uniform intellectual property legislative framework with minimal amendments.

Highlighting the dynamic shifts in the BRICS alliance, there is a notable evolution in patent registrations. In 1990, the combined patent registration of Brazil, India, China, and South Africa constituted less than 2% of the US's yearly total. By 2010, China's submissions to the World Intellectual Property Organization (WIPO) neared half of the US's figures. Meanwhile, Brazil, India, and South Africa still languished below the 1% threshold of the US total. Russia, once at 21% of the US's patent registrations in the early 1990s, saw a decline to 12% by 2010.[1] This shift could influence the BRICS nations' perspectives on multilateral intellectual property regulations.

Given their accelerated growth trajectories, it's imperative for BRICS countries to bolster their patent procedures, foster innovation, and prioritize the management and safeguarding of patented technologies. Despite their accomplishments, the journey in the intellectual property realm remains vast and challenging for the BRICS nations.

(7) Investment

In the evolving landscape of global economic integration, the enhancement of trade and investment serves as a catalyst for strengthening connections between domestic and international corporations. This, in turn, spurs international commerce, economic interactions, and fosters diplomatic relations. Indeed, investment has emerged as a cornerstone of cooperation among the BRICS nations.

During the 2000s, BRICS economies witnessed meteoric growth rates, becoming magnets for significant investments. These funds were adeptly channeled into bolstering production capacities and promoting international commerce. To harness greater market potential and foster economic growth, each BRICS member state has, with varying intensities, devised and executed policies geared towards incentivizing capital influxes.

A unifying thread weaving through the BRICS consortium is the collective endeavor to entice investments, all the while assimilating cutting-edge technologies and fostering domestic synergies during their respective economic growth

---

[1] Vera Thorstensen and Ivan Tiago Machado Oliveira, "OS BRICS NA OMC: Políticas Comerciais Comparadas de Brasil, Rússia, Índia, China e África do Sul," Brasília: Ipea, 2012, p. 212.

trajectories. However, there is a mosaic of approaches when it comes to the operationalization of these policies, influenced by their distinct strategic blueprints in industry and service – sector development.

China predominantly channels its investments into infrastructure and agriculture, emphasizing technological sophistication. Interestingly, it generally earmarks these investments for its less developed regions.

India, on the other hand, places a premium on fortifying its information technology domain.

Russia is driven by an ambition to usher investments into its energy sector, aiming for a diversified energy portfolio.

Brazil's investment pulse beats strongly for oil and gas exploration, with infrastructural endeavors like airports and ports also garnering attention.

South Africa's investment landscape is painted with endeavors in mineral extraction and tourism, drawing a lion's share of its investments from the developed world.

In essence, while united in their aspirations, each BRICS nation distinctly showcases its unique investment forte and strategy.

(8) Plurilateral Trade Agreements

The BRICS nations' engagement with the plurilateral agreements of the World Trade Organization (WTO) aptly showcases the diverse interests each member brings to the global arena. Their distinct trajectories of economic development further underscore the challenges in finding a unified stance on international economic negotiation platforms. Notably, the singular point of convergence among the BRICS countries is the perception of government procurement and information technology as vital tools for development and employment generation. [1]

Taking the Information Technology Agreement (ITA) as a case in point, the BRICS nations exhibit significant disparities in their progress and interests.

---

[1] Vera Thorstensen and Ivan Tiago Machado Oliveira, "OS BRICS NA OMC: Políticas Comerciais Comparadas de Brasil, Rússia, Índia, China e África do Sul," Brasília: Ipea, 2012, p. 462.

Notably, some BRICS members haven't even acceded to the ITA, rendering intra-BRICS consultations on this front non-existent.

In the realm of the Government Procurement Agreement (GPA), the perspectives of BRICS members diverge considerably:

Brazil firmly believes that multilateral agreements should take precedence over plurilateral ones.

South Africa, if it were to consider joining plurilateral accords, faces the intricate challenge of honoring its historical obligations towards its black populace, making adherence to the national treatment principle complex.

India has displayed a keen interest in the GPA but remains in the contemplative phase.

Russia and China, given the unique contours of their economies, would inevitably encounter misaligned interests if they were to align with the GPA.

In summation, while the BRICS alliance symbolizes a coming together of emerging economies, the inherent asymmetry in their interests often restricts the bandwidth for cohesive collaboration.

(9) New Topics

As the tapestry of international trade becomes ever more intricate, the World Trade Organization (WTO) finds itself grappling with the imperative to evolve in response to contemporary global challenges. This is particularly evident when considering the hurdles emanating from new multilateral negotiations, especially the emergence of "new topics" on the international trade negotiation agenda.

While the BRICS nations have predominantly exhibited reticence towards the WTO's initiation of these fresh topics, their apprehension stems from the belief that new regulations might disproportionately benefit already thriving economies. Yet, the emergence of these subjects in alternative international forums, combined with the evolution of national regulations echoing similar themes, indicates that BRICS' resistance isn't rooted in fundamental opposition. They are, in fact, scouting avenues for meaningful engagement.

Prominently, environmental concerns and trade facilitation emerge as the flagbearers of these "new topics." Of these, trade facilitation shines as a beacon of consensus, where alignment among member nations appears most promising.[①] However, the heart of the discourse is still firmly anchored in addressing developmental disparities.

This represents a seminal shift in the tenor of WTO's multilateral negotiations. Led by several BRICS nations, developing countries are recalibrating their negotiation strategies, championing coordination, and redefining their tactical approaches. Furthermore, these evolving dialogues on new topics present BRICS countries with the exciting prospect of forging novel alliances, driven by mutual objectives.

## Ⅳ. The Role of BRICS in the WTO Dispute Settlement Mechanism

As illuminated in the book's descriptions regarding BRICS nations' involvement in the WTO Dispute Settlement Mechanism, several conclusions can be drawn:

The BRICS nations have been witnessing an ascending trajectory of influence within WTO disputes, congruent with their burgeoning economies and burgeoning national stature. Their escalated involvement in the dispute resolution mechanism has critically defended the legitimate rights of developing countries. Consequently, as their economic clout has swelled, so has their voice within the WTO.

Bar South Africa, the rest of the BRICS nations have marked their footprint with proactive and effective defense of both sectoral and systemic interests. Significantly, Brazil, China, and India have deftly navigated the WTO dispute resolution system to champion their interests, providing clarity to disputed nuances.

---

① "Ver discurso do diretor – geral da OMC," Pascal Lamy, em 24 de junho de 2011. Disponível em: http://www.wto.org/english/news_e/sppl_e/sppl197_e.htm.

Brazil, in particular, has anchored the WTO dispute resolution system as a linchpin of its foreign trade policy, cultivating a harmonized partnership between the government, private enterprises, and third – party consultants. India and China echo similar strategies, although there's room to better synergize with the manufacturing sector and bolster capacity across both public and private spheres. [1]

For South Africa, a pivot from its current passive demeanor is imperative, necessitating a more assertive interventionist role. [2]

On the whole, BRICS nations exhibit a predilection for consensus – driven dispute resolutions, pledging allegiance to the verdicts of the dispute resolution body should litigation prove fruitless.

A spike in cases presented before the WTO Dispute Settlement Body underscores an amplifying trust in this mechanism by member nations, indirectly refining its procedures.

Brazil and India stand out, harnessing the WTO mechanism adeptly to broker mutually beneficial outcomes. Their landmark cases have carved out precedents, bolstering the mechanism's reliability and consistency.

Although China, a relatively nascent member, initially displayed reticence, it predominantly sought observer status in WTO disputes to glean insights and refine its advocacy capabilities.

By embracing the WTO dispute resolution mechanism, BRICS nations negotiate and ameliorate trade differences with global counterparts, fortifying their negotiating positions and unlocking prime opportunities. They've consistently counteracted actions by developed nations like the US and the EU that defy WTO norms, solidifying their stance as pivotal global players.

With the interwoven fabric of the global economy growing tighter and the as-

---

[1] Vera Thorstensen and Ivan Tiago Machado Oliveira, "OS BRICS NA OMC: Políticas Comerciais Comparadas de Brasil, Rússia, Índia, China e África do Sul," Brasília: Ipea, 2012, p. 466.

[2] Vera Thorstensen and Ivan Tiago Machado Oliveira, "OS BRICS NA OMC: Políticas Comerciais Comparadas de Brasil, Rússia, Índia, China e África do Sul," Brasília: Ipea, 2012, pp. 390 – 391.

cent of BRICS nations, the international community's expectations of BRICS have surged, resonating with a clarion call for them to shoulder more global responsibilities. Their pivotal role in the WTO dispute settlement mechanism is undeniable.

Statistically, developed countries, chiefly the US (33%) and the EU (32%)[①], pose the primary challenges to BRICS in global trade. Yet, BRICS nations lean towards diplomatic overtures and reconciliation to thwart potential legal confrontations.

Amongst the conglomerate, China faces the brunt of challenges, with Brazil, India, and South Africa trailing. The disparity in case numbers mirrors each country's resource bounty and their gravitational pull in global trade. Their expanding trade footprint underlines a convoluted trade dispute scenario, symptomatic of the burgeoning tide of global trade protectionism.[②]

In summation, while the intensity and scope of BRICS nations' engagement within the WTO dispute settlement mechanism might vary, their unwavering goal is the apolitical resolution of trade spats and the cultivation of common ground amongst nations. By astutely leveraging the WTO dispute mechanism, they dismantle trade obstructions, fortify their trade positions, shield their interests, and deepen their economic affiliations globally.

# V. Participation of BRICS Countries in the Doha Round Negotiations

The book delineates how BRICS nations have been proactive leaders during

---

① Vera Thorstensen and Ivan Tiago Machado Oliveira, "OS BRICS NA OMC: Políticas Comerciais Comparadas de Brasil, Rússia, Índia, China e África do Sul," Brasília: Ipea, 2012, p. 382.
② Vera Thorstensen and Ivan Tiago Machado Oliveira, "OS BRICS NA OMC: Políticas Comerciais Comparadas de Brasil, Rússia, Índia, China e África do Sul," Brasília: Ipea, 2012, p. 387.

multiple negotiation rounds, vigorously putting forth proposals[1]. Their triumphant strategies during the Doha Round redefined the dynamics of WTO negotiations, amplifying the voice of the BRICS on global platforms while championing the interests of developing nations. [2]

In the realm of agricultural negotiations, there was a unanimous nod to extend special and differential treatment to developing nations, affording them preferential terms. While Brazil proactively engaged across a spectrum of topics, both India and China, where family farming predominates, opted for more guarded positions. Regardless of their disparate economic landscapes, the BRICS collaborated with developed countries via the G20 Agriculture, advocating for tariff reductions and curtailing both export and domestic subsidies. They consistently showcased a balanced and constructive approach, adeptly navigating the complex maze of member country interests to foster collective growth.

As for non-agricultural market access, the BRICS played a pivotal role in sculpting mechanisms to counter non-tariff barriers. China demonstrated an aggressive stance, while Brazil, India, and South Africa, grouped within Nama-11, exercised prudence. On tariff slashes, the trio of China, Brazil, and India championed formulas mandating deeper cuts by developed nations. The Swiss formula, with distinct coefficients for developed and developing nations, was endorsed, granting enhanced tariff reduction flexibility. Through the Nama-11 coalition, they also steered dialogues aimed at eradicating non-tariff obstructions, forging an innovative blueprint to tackle such trade impediments. Nonetheless, the Doha Round wasn't devoid of contention, with friction especially palpable between developed and developing nations over tariffs on commodities like cars, automotive components, textiles, and chemicals.

In anti-dumping talks, the BRICS nations provided clarity on vague terms

---

[1] Vera Thorstensen and Ivan Tiago Machado Oliveira, "OS BRICS NA OMC: Políticas Comerciais Comparadas de Brasil, Rússia, Índia, China e África do Sul," Brasília: Ipea, 2012, p. 401.

[2] Vera Thorstensen and Ivan Tiago Machado Oliveira, "OS BRICS NA OMC: Políticas Comerciais Comparadas de Brasil, Rússia, Índia, China e África do Sul," Brasília: Ipea, 2012, p. 402.

within the "Anti – Dumping Agreement". Brazil lobbied for more rigorous criteria, China voiced concerns over the non – market economy stipulations and resisted the incorporation of anti – evasion rules, whereas India and South Africa's engagements were comparatively subdued. Notably, India vocally rejected the zeroing methodology, endorsing the de minimis principle.

On the compensatory measures front, Brazil emerged as a torchbearer, advocating for a lighter proof burden on developing nations challenging subsidy practices by their developed counterparts. The nation also championed the causes of high – value exports, substantial injury, and the nuances of export subsidy definitions for developing nations.

In the services sector, the BRICS upheld the tenets of the General Agreement on Trade in Services (GATS). They championed economic progression by brokering commitments that facilitated easier market entry for services and streamlined licensing for local providers. Both China and India were instrumental in collaborative proposals with a mix of developed and developing nations, championing further market liberalization.

Lastly, the intellectual property discussions centered around the TRIPS Agreement and the Convention on Biological Diversity. With external pressures at play, like China's absence during the Uruguay Round and the sway of the balance of payments crisis over Brazil and India, the BRICS encountered formidable challenges, predominantly from developed nations spearheaded by the U. S. The Doha Round witnessed a chasm between the developed and developing worlds concerning the interpretation of IP rights.

To encapsulate, BRICS nations have unwaveringly championed the multilateral trading ethos, staunchly defending the aspirations of developing countries. Their recognition of the value of multilateral dialogues, ability to bridge vast disparities, articulate their sovereign interests, and identify shared objectives have galvanized synergistic collaborations. Their historical finesse in orchestrating diverse interests during the Doha Round stands testament to their success.

## VI. Insights

The increasing turbulence in the global landscape cannot be overlooked. Amidst escalating global challenges, the ascent of emerging markets and developing nations, epitomized by the BRICS, is reshaping the balance. They are vital torchbearers, pushing the international order towards a more balanced and judicious orientation. This underscores the BRICS countries as staunch proponents of the multilateral trading system, dedicated to preserving the mutual interests and developmental aspirations of emerging markets and developing nations. Hence, in a world where both political and economic terrains are fraught with volatility, a thorough examination of the BRICS nations' role in the WTO, their global trade dynamics, and a deep dive into salient trade policy themes becomes imperative. Such an exploration can pave the way for harmonizing disparities and cultivating expansive collaborative growth among BRICS constituents.

This book offers a meticulous and encompassing exploration of the BRICS nations' footprint within the WTO framework. It delves into their pivotal political engagements, dissects their international trade paradigms, probes the central trade policy narratives, examines their involvement in the WTO's dispute adjudication apparatus, and sheds light on their participation in the Doha Round discussions. Such insights are indispensable for scholars seeking a comprehensive grasp of the BRICS trade matrix and their influence within the WTO. This knowledge is a linchpin in unraveling avenues for enriched multilateral trade synergy and aligning collective BRICS aspirations.

Drawing from the revelations within this book, it is apparent that the BRICS nations, given their distinct developmental trajectories, navigate the international trade waters with varied strategies. While there exist points of contention and areas needing enhancement, it doesn't render mutual trade collaboration and economic exchanges untenable. As standard – bearers for emerging markets and the developing world, the BRICS consortium shares numerous converging interests and will undoubtedly carve out more profound developmental paths ahead. This is an irrefutable trajectory of contemporary times. Capitalizing on the BRICS synergy, amplifying economic policy dialogues, and fostering tangible cooperation is paramount. Such efforts will bolster the representation of developing nations within the multilateral trading arena, ensuring their interests remain at the forefront.